The Spirit of Sonship

An Apostolic Grace

REVISED EDITION

JOHN KINGSLEY ALLEY

PEACE PUBLISHING

The Spirit Of Sonship, An Apostolic Grace - Revised Edition
Copyright © 2008, 2009, 2015 by John Kingsley Alley.

Published by:
Peace Publishing,
Rockhampton, Queensland, Australia.

Distributed in Australia by:
Peace Apostolic Ministries
PO Box 10187
Frenchville Qld 4701
Phone: 07 4926 9911
Fax: 07 4926 9944
Email: books@peace.org.au
Web: www.peace.org.au

First Edition: Hardcover - June 2008
ISBN 978-1-920780-00-5

Second Edition: Paperback - April 2009 & Revised August 2015
ISBN 978-1-920780-01-2

Dedication

to the
Lord Jesus Christ,
*"whom I serve, as my forefathers did,
with a clear conscience"*

(1 Timothy 1:3)

The Prayer of Jesus
*"... that all of them may be one, Father,
just as you are in me and I am in you.
May they also be in us
so that the world may believe
that you have sent me.*

*I have given them the glory that you gave me,
that they may be one as we are one:
I in them and you in me.*

*May they be brought to complete unity
to let the world know that you sent me
and have loved them
even as you have loved me."*

(John 17:21-23)

 Foreword

By Charles W. Clayton

John Kingsley Alley is, above all else, a man of God with a peaceful spirit, full of grace, wisdom and integrity. He is the apostle of *Peace Apostolic Ministries* in Rockhampton, Australia.

C. Peter Wagner declared John Alley's first book *The Apostolic Revelation* to be "the premier biblical theology of the apostolic movement today."

John has the call of God upon his life to declare and model the apostolic heart and authority of Father God across the land of Australia and wherever else the Spirit may open doors. His walk with the Lord brings inspiration and challenge to everyone who meets him. His gentle authority brings correction, alignment and affirmation to the Body of Christ in such a way there is no tearing, division or condescension, but rather the edification and building up of the saints.

John is an apostle whom God has entrusted with this revelation because his heart is as that of Father Abraham, as in Genesis 18:17-19. *"And the Lord said, shall I hide from Abraham that thing which I do; Seeing that Abraham shall surely become a great and mighty nation, and all the nations of the earth shall be blessed in him? For I know him, that he will command his children and his household after him, and they shall keep the way of the Lord, to do righteousness and justice; that the Lord may bring upon Abraham that which he hath spoken of him"*. And Apostle John's family is a beautiful expression of Christ and His Church, loving and serving the Lord.

John Alley is not only an Apostle in his own right; but he is a son as well. He recognizes the urgent need to pursue a *spiritual father* in order to receive a greater impartation of his inheritance through *relationship*.

Father God is a *generational* God, imparting from one generation to the next His blessings. This is not head knowledge in John's life; but heart knowledge through his own experience of a father-son relationship in the ministry. John has been a son to me now for twelve years. During this time I have observed how he has taken this revelation and allowed it to work, first in his own life; then, after being broken and molded, he has modeled the message before others; in the process, he has become a father to many.

I highly recommend this book, because the author's life has exemplified what is recorded in these pages. This book is more than ink on paper – it is a written impartation of a man's life, his family and his heart. This book will be a great opportunity for the Body of Christ, not only to *learn*, but to *experience*, the Goodness of God.

Chuck Clayton,
Apostolic Resource Ministries,
Versailles, Indiana, USA.

Introduction

By Rev. Dr. John McElroy

The book you are about to read will impact your life and the way you view other people, particularly within the family of Christ. The first time I heard John Alley speak on the 'spirit of sonship' was at a conference where we were both guest speakers. As I listened, it was like being taken to an altitude of 30,000 feet where you get a bird's eye view stretching in all directions. Like the disciples on the road to Emmaus, my heart began to burn with a desire to become a true spiritual father.

Like many pastors, I had learned most of what I knew about ministry by trial and error. While there were pastors and colleagues I looked up to, I never really had a consistent spiritual father to speak into my life. As the pressures of ministry increased and our church grew, I found myself more focussed on programmes than relationships.

God used John to make me face some important questions: What was my purpose in the ministry? Did I evidence more of an orphan spirit than a spirit of sonship? Was I leaving a legacy to younger leaders? What kind of a father was I to my kids? Why wasn't I enjoying life and ministry more?

Teaching on 'the spirit of sonship' challenged my thinking and put me on a new compass heading toward building a 'culture of honour' within our local church. I gradually discovered that relational Christianity, and sonship, were actually part of a wider body of truth called 'apostolic revelation'. I also began to see that the restoration of the five-fold ministries of Ephesians 4 were foundational to bringing churches into alignment with God's highest purposes.

Much has been written in the past two decades on the restoration of 'apostolic grace' to the church. I enjoyed John's first book, The Apostolic Revelation, published in 2002. It provided for me a much needed clarification on the ministry of apostles, their significance, and the grace they carry in shaping a new wineskin that will enable the Church to fulfil its purpose and mission.

As director of a network of churches, in consultation with John and other apostles, I was able to see how our group actually reflected 'apostolic' principles and structure. I am thankful for the many apostolic 'pioneers' like John, who have modelled and taught of what it means to be 'apostolic'.

One of John's most endearing qualities is the genuine care he shows for others. Not only does he radiate the love of Christ, but he teaches with Christ's authority. The fruit of John's ministry is seen in the diverse array of men and women around the world who call him 'spiritual father' and 'apostle'. He is a 'family' man in every sense of the word.

One of the most gripping aspects of 'apostolic grace' is seeing the fulfilment of Malachi 4:5-6 in our generation. Malachi wrote of a time when the hearts of the fathers would be turned to the children and the children to the fathers. As you read this book, you will see how God is returning the church to its relational foundations of honour, trust, humility, love and sonship.

The grace of sonship is not an option, it is a mandate. Races are won or lost at the handing off of the baton. True spiritual sons and daughters are the product of godly spiritual fathers and mothers who have faithfully built themselves, and their wisdom, and character into the younger generation. When these spiritual sons and daughters are released into leadership, they perpetuate empowering intergenerational relationships and model a high degree of emotional maturity.

The Apostle Paul wrote in Romans 8:19, *"The creation waits in eager expectation for the sons of God to be revealed."* For the past nineteen centuries, many godly and learned Christians have pondered the meaning of this verse and whether they would live to see its fulfilment. As you read, you will gain a sense that you live in a generation where God's grace is increasing to bring this word to pass.

Finally, remember this book is not about theory, Everything John writes is amply illustrated by testimonies and real life lessons. You are about to glean from a man who's been on an incredible journey of revelation and discovery. I know of no other book published on this subject that is so biblical, inspiring, and practical.

John McElroy,
Director, Southern Cross Association of Churches,
Perth, Australia.

ACKNOWLEDGEMENTS

I wish to acknowledge that I am surrounded and blessed by wonderful believers, men and women, and young people, Christian leaders, pastors, apostles and prophets, and prayer warriors and faithful workers, and great Christian families, from across Australia and many nations.

I love these people, and they have loved me. These teachings I did not develop in a vacuum, but in walking with good people who prayed and believed. I am very grateful to God for His people. He promised me many years ago, *"I will send you help from Zion,"* and I see clearly now that He has indeed.

I am especially grateful to the people of Peace Christian Church, and my leadership team. We who *"were not a people, have become a people."* So many have stood firm with me over many years, and prayed, and believed, and sacrificed, and supported – and trusted. I thank you sincerely. I told you that I loved you, and I promised I would lead you to Christ, and so we have walked together.

In particular, I thank my wife Hazel. We met at 17, both knowing the call of God, and married later, committed to the same ideals. Hazel has worked harder than anyone, shared with me the good fight of faith and the brunt of the warfare and the work. She has been unstinting in sacrifice, faithful in love, and her discernment is second to none. God blessed me in Hazel more than I knew when He put us together.

A big thank you to my ministry and office staff, who have always immediately responded to my requests and the needs of the ministry with such a whole heart, and who serve Jesus Christ with me. Their love has proven true.

Contents

AUTHOR'S PREFACE TO THE REVISED EDITION

It has been over seven years since I wrote this book, and since we need to print once again, and in more nations and languages, it is a good time to revise what had been written. The alterations are few, but helpful, and include the fact that the name of our church has been altered to simply, Peace Christian Church.

And there is one area of Bible doctrine which has advanced in me through a greater understanding of the Holy Scriptures. I refer to our view of the future, that is, the doctrine of 'Last Things,' or Eschatology. That is not the particular subject of this book, but as in all things, our assumptions colour much else that we address. So I have reviewed the manuscript for any place where the text needed to be adjusted in favour of a better understanding, and corrected any inadvertent misapplication of Scripture in that connection. Notable here was my previous understanding of Malachi 4:5-6, compared to the more correct application of that passage which can be found in Chapter Five under the heading of "The Spirit and Power of Elijah," on pages 88-92. (For those interested in what I teach about Eschatology, there is available free on our website more than 20 hours of teaching, both audio and video, which I have produced over the last two years, and for which I have received strong affirmation from the Body of Christ across many nations, Western, Asian, and African.)

Furthermore, three years after this book was first published, my spiritual father, Chuck Clayton, who wrote a foreword for this book, and of whom I have spoken at some length, passed away, to my great sorrow. I decided to not alter the text of the book, but have added at the end an important Postscript, similar to the speech I gave in Restoration Christian Church, Sellersburg, Indiana, on Sunday 4th December, 2011, just a couple of days after his passing into the presence of the Lord.

There has been much blessing reported as a result of this book, and I am thankful for the grace of God that so attends the teaching of this important subject.

OPENING REMARKS

BY THE AUTHOR

I received a note from a young man in my congregation. He was one of the most prophetically gifted people I have known, and from time to time would contribute the outline of some very compelling vision he had received, along with its meaning. These were invariably accurate, powerful really, and with an unusual degree of grace upon them. On this occasion he wrote:

"Dear John,

Last Sunday as soon as you began to pray I was aware of an angel that entered the room. He was much taller than I and was holding something on his arm on which he appeared to be writing. As you continued to pray he walked up and down each aisle, intently watching every person in the room as he went.

Suddenly I was aware he was standing right next to me, and something wasn't right. I asked the Lord why I felt this way, and He said that it didn't matter that I thought the message was true, and it did not matter that for many months now I had been hearing that we needed to listen more, what He was looking for was whether I had made the decision for 'listening' to become part of my life rather than just acknowledging it was something I should do.

After you had finished praying, he was still earnestly looking around the room, looking for people who might still make the decision to act on what they had just heard."

This, of course, immediately brings to mind the passage in Malachi 3:16-18, about the scroll of remembrance that is written in the presence of the

Lord concerning those who listen to what He says and who act upon it out of holy reverence.

Not everyone (in a meeting, say) responds the same way to the word of God being preached. Not everyone acts as if God is speaking – but God is speaking! And each one is responsible for their heart attitude and their response to God in such a meeting.

Likewise with the message of this book. It is the word of God, it is being preached in many formats, and here it is in the printed word. Each one of us, including you the reader, is responsible before God for the attitudes we take to His word.

I believe this to be a very serious matter indeed, and the subject before us to be as important to every believer, and as mission-critical to the whole church, as any subject that could be raised.

I would have liked to have written concerning these things at a more thoughtful and leisurely pace. Instead, I have found myself surrounded with such opportunity and progress in the kingdom, and such need for preaching and prayer for the advancement of our people, and such opposition from dark forces in the spirit realm, as well as everyday distractions, that in the end, and even though I have preached these themes often enough, I have had to write them in a great hurry.

It seems there is an urgent need for this book – and the need of the body of Christ, and of the work of the Holy Spirit, and of the advance of the faith in the world, must not be kept waiting for a more leisurely production. I have already taken too long to commit the matter to print.

I remember reading Frederick Booth-Tucker in the preface to his expansive biography *The Life of Catherine Booth – The Mother of The Salvation Army* (published 1892). He remarked concerning *'the life of interruption'* that was the experience of the Salvationist pioneer:

> *"...seclusion, privacy, and the quietude supposed to be necessary for literary enterprise – the words have been obliterated from his dictionary, the very ideas have almost faded from his mind.... he writes as best he may amid the whizz and crash of flying shot and shell, the rush and excitement of a never-ending battle, in which peace and truce are words unknown, and rest, in the ordinary sense of the word, is relegated to heaven."*

Booth-Tucker was the pioneer of The Salvation Army in India in the 1880-90's, and the son-in-law of General William Booth. Those old soldiers knew what it was to war for the gospel and the Kingdom of God.

And so, in the midst of the modern gospel war and the shot and shell of spiritual life, leadership and ministry today, I hope that I have managed to produce herein a reasonable explanation of that message of Christ which must again be made clear and brought to God's people.

The central thesis of this book is: That the values and heart attitudes of what we may call the *spirit of sonship* is the very nature and essence of authentic apostolic New Testament Christianity.

When I say authentic, I mean the genuine article, not just a similar one. And when I say apostolic, I refer to the true and original apostolic *faith* as brought forth by the early apostles and prophets of Christ to whom Paul refers in Ephesians 3:2-12; the *faith* as it was lived and understood by many in its early form under apostolic leadership in the churches of the first century. This, we need to see, is the true and biblical faith of our apostolic fathers. And we will see that this apostolic and relational *nature* of the church and the faith is indeed the essential word of truth embedded in all the Scriptures.

Gender Vocabulary: The biblical language concerning our subject is almost exclusively 'father' and 'son'. Concerning God and Christ, this must never be changed, but in the church there has to be some understanding, for scripturally, all believers, men and women, boys and girls, are *sons* of God. Furthermore, we are considered firstborn sons (Hebrews 12:23), since we are in Christ. If we were not counted as firstborn sons, we could not share a joint inheritance with Christ, it would instead be a partial inheritance. But we are joint-heirs, and each of us, with Him, inherits all the Father has.

Furthermore, the apostle John refers to all believers as being either infants, children, young men, or fathers. In a book such as this, it would become very ponderous, and you would soon tire of reading, if in every place that required personal pronouns I recorded he/she, or him/her, and if, instead of simply saying 'sons' it was always 'sons and daughters', or where required, 'fathers and mothers'. I have felt under no obligation to do so, and have simply taken the liberty of speaking simply using the Bible terminology. I would like to ask the reader, based on your Bible knowledge, to simply put yourself in the picture on every page, so as to aid simplicity and directness of communication.

Questions Concerning Matthew 23:9 – *"And do not call anyone on earth 'father,' for you have one Father, and he is in heaven."* I am often asked what was meant by Jesus in this statement, since it appears to conflict with other passages in the New Testament, and the apostles made what seems to be a freer use of the term. It is therefore an important question to answer, and I have addressed the issue in Chapter Six.

Personal Testimonies: To illustrate Christian relationships, I have included throughout this book personal testimonies, written by people I know well and love; but these are testimonies that often involve me, because I happen to be in meaningful and accountable relationships with those sharing.

I wrote asking if they would write a short testimony concerning how they have found the experience of being a son to a father in the ministry, and what they thought were the benefits of sonship, etc., but I didn't get exactly what I asked for. Nevertheless, to add colour and flavour, I have printed these in the hope they will be seen as a testimony of the grace of God that flows through genuine relationships of love.

It was not my intention to draw the attention of readers to myself personally – the purpose of my testimony and others is not to put the focus upon us or our people unduly, but I think there is no more effective way of aiding the communication of these truths of the faith and the values that we have learned from Christ, except by including the sharing of these valid witnesses.

Therefore I ask your understanding – please read our stories, experiences, feelings, and insights as simply the best illustrations I felt I was able to provide, of the truths the church now needs to hear.

It is not that these stories should motivate people to follow me – I endeavour not to do anything that causes people to follow me personally. I go everywhere as a messenger, simply seeking to give people the truth they need, and in the hope that they will employ and live by this truth wherever they are. I do not go out seeking followers, and I hate the thought that there would be in me or any of our people the kind of spirit that seeks a personal following. I hate this in others, and I have seen it too often.

Naturally, along the way the Lord brings us into wonderful and dynamic heart relationships with good people all over the world, and these we love, and they love us. If God gives me such relationships of the heart, I rejoice; but I do not go out motivated by the desire to obtain meetings for their own sake, nor to obtain offerings, nor to develop a personal following. I would be just as happy to stay at home and prune my mango trees, but I am compelled to go, by love and by the Word of God. So the mango trees remain largely neglected.

Apostle Chuck Clayton tells me that he heard the Lord say: *"The reason we have not seen the fruit that we are looking for is that the fathers have not demonstrated their love to such a place that the sons are willing to lay down their own agendas."* I am hoping that the spirit or grace of this book will help fathers in the ministry, as much as sons.

My wife Hazel remembers a personal visit we received from the senior pastor of one of Australia's larger churches. As he was leaving, he made strong expressions of gratitude for our input into his life, and how much a difference this had made to him, and how much understanding had come to him as a result of it. It is actually incredible to us that people feel like this, and we wonder, why is there such impact, because we are just ordinary people, and don't do anything spectacular when people visit us. We just talk and pray. But in listening to the Lord, Hazel heard Him say that the reason our lives have this powerful effect on people is because we do not just *teach* relationships and preach it as doctrine; rather, this is the way we *live*; and when people come to visit, relationships have the priority. We just spend our time with them. It is not a meeting just for business; relationships are what our agenda is. Therefore it has this powerful outcome.

There are many people that would agree precisely with what we say about relationships, but they never change their agenda, they never change their lifestyle, they don't change the inner values by which they live, and they do not minister differently. I have seen some very bad examples over the years of people being so busy in ministry, there was virtually no relationship at all. I have been a visiting speaker to some churches, where you are received publicly, you preach and pray, but when the meeting is over, it's just, 'Well, thank you, good-bye.' You blessed them, you brought the word of God, but time, relationships, the knitting of the hearts, means absolutely nothing – all that is left after the visit is a vacuum.

I believe there has to be a whole new approach to grace, through *relationships*. The subject is huge; the whole of the Scriptures and all of salvation history must now be seen in the light of *sonship* and all its implications.

In this book, I offer something of a biblical theology of Christian relationships, and of the apostolic life of the body of Christ.

Concerning the life and ministry of Peace Christian Church in Rockhampton, and my apostolic team, if we have nothing else to offer the body of Christ, we do have this: We love each other.

John Alley,
Rockhampton,
Qld, Australia.

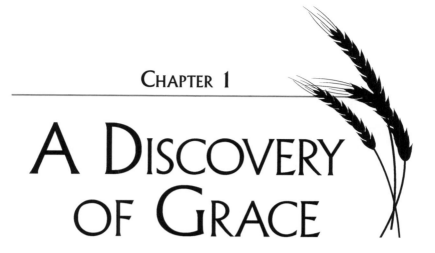

CHAPTER 1

A DISCOVERY OF GRACE

"They asked each other, 'Were not our hearts burning within us while he talked with us... and opened the scriptures to us?"

(Luke 24:32)

Every little boy and girl needs a dad. Every teenager growing up, every young husband, and every young wife and mother, needs a father too. We all need the love, the encouragement, the instruction, and from time to time the correction, of a father.

It is a great tragedy in this world when little boys and girls, as well as young men and women, do not have a dad. A father occupies a huge place in the hearts and minds of us all, which is most noticeable when he is missing. From a father we get most of our sense of identity, our sense of approval, and a great sense of security. God has designed it to be like this. None of us are meant to walk alone. We require not only the companionship of siblings and friends, and the love, succour, and comfort of a mother, we need also the strength, the protection, the peace, and the sense of richness and belonging that comes from having a father.

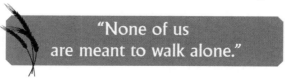

"None of us are meant to walk alone."

It is precisely the same spiritually as it is naturally. It is meant to be the same in the life of the church, the family of God, as it should be in the family at home. Every one of us, without exception, genuinely needs to walk with a father, no matter what our position in life.

It is not as if God in his wisdom does not supply these things. It is man, especially independent, legalistic, self-sufficient man, that sometimes avoids these things as far as his spiritual life or the leadership of the church is concerned.

Some amongst us have not had good experiences with earthly fathers. This has often provided the deepest of hurts, sometimes leaving a lifelong struggle. Very often, the emotions remaining from an experience of absent fathers, silent fathers, abusive fathers, or the like, produces serious spiritual problems. People like this often find it hard to trust or develop intimate relationships. In particular, it is difficult for some to trust those in authority, or draw near to God. Bad experiences of earthly fathers often make it difficult for people to know God as He wants to be known.

But Christ provides a wonderful healing and deliverance for every human trauma. There are solutions to these spiritual problems, and they need to be sought and applied. Otherwise, the believer struggling with this heart condition does not draw near to God, and does not walk in healthy and transparent relationships with church leadership because they are hindered from trusting by their past experiences. The solution is not to reject fathering, but to find and build relationships of trust with the fathers you need.

God always chooses to provide fathers. And at this time when fatherless families are an epidemic and fatherlessness has become a great curse in large parts of society, it is time that we embrace with faith the great promise God has made in Malachi 4:5-6, that *"he will turn the hearts of the fathers to their children, and the hearts of the children to their fathers."* Yes, the promise was specifically fulfilled in the ministry of John the Baptist and the coming of Jesus Christ into the world, but it's application and power did not end there. And since *"no matter how many promises God has made, they are 'Yes' in Christ,"* (2 Cor 1:20) we must conclude that God intends the power of this great promise for all under the gospel, and take hold of this revealing of God's heart and purpose with faith and intentionality. The church must be a model of fathering love, to be lived out in the first instance by all church leaders.

Wherever I go and share the things of God with other Christian leaders, there are many interesting subjects we may discuss. I find there is no shortage of important things to teach, for there are many needs to be met through good Bible teaching. But when I speak of fathering and sonship, and the need for spiritual leaders to walk with spiritual fathers, a noticeable change takes place. The hearts of pastors become tender, their thoughts wistful – sometimes the room goes very quiet.

There is a deeply felt need in the heart of us all, but which is not always understood. This is an emotive need for love and relationships, and especially to find the affection of spiritual fathers amongst the leaders of the church. Fathering is the greater need of people in the body of Christ everywhere, and especially it would seem for the pastors themselves.

My personal story of discovering the love, affection, strength, and heartfelt blessing that comes from walking with a spiritual father I will begin to tell here, and continue later in the book.

It has often been taught that we should love one another – this is, after all, the great commandment. We are often told how important it is to walk in proper relationships with other believers. But we are not so often told just *how* to love one another, nor instructed as to the pattern of the relationships we need. What *kinds* of relationships are required? What is the *biblical pattern* for relationships in the faith? And how does one genuinely love other believers as Christ loved us? Answers to these questions and more are explored in this book.

It is essential that we have such answers and understand them. They must become the central values of our belief systems, so that we may live out of them. Loving one another, and walking together in healthy relationships, is the heart of what Christianity actually is. Without these values, and the corresponding lifestyle, we may find that we have fallen seriously short of what is called for in the gospel and in our response to Jesus Christ our Saviour. For Jesus Himself warned, *"Not everyone who says to me, 'Lord, Lord', will enter the kingdom of heaven, but only he who does the will of my father who is in heaven."* (Matt 7:21)

It is not how well we understand biblical theory, but whether we live it that counts. It is not how hard we work in ministry, not even how much we might labour for the winning of souls. Heart motive is everything. Paul said, *"If I give all I possess to the poor and surrender my body to the flames, but have not love, I gain nothing."* (1 Cor 13:3) Without the surrender of the heart, without the giving of ourselves to others in a way in which we genuinely love, and seek to honour and serve them, we have denied the faith.

There is an old saying, "You can lead a horse to water, but you cannot make him drink". This we find is a spiritual truth. Some who claim the deepest convictions in biblical doctrine have experienced its realities the least. I know someone who holds strongly to the doctrine that for true salvation there must be genuine repentance in the heart. But recently I asked the pastor who cares for him, "Has he repented?" And the pastor said, "No." It's not that he is not a professing Christian. He is, and very active in the church in his own way. But he has never dealt with his hurts, offences, fears, and inner lies enough to overcome, and so there has been no great yielding, no real surrender to the truth he 'believes'. With his mind he knows it is the truth, but as you know the heart is desperately wicked, and he seems to be still very full of himself. Without realising it, he does not yet walk in the true grace of Jesus Christ.

I can only recommend to you these wonderful truths of Jesus Christ. You yourself must surrender to them, and cry out to God for that grace which transforms heart and mind. The power of this grace enables us to see and walk in things that are beyond and foreign to our normal human and fleshly limitations. When grace comes, the light of His glory shines in our inner being. You are from that moment gloriously in the truth, and wiser than your teachers with respect to that which has now been given you.

Sonship is, of course, an eternal spiritual position into which we have been placed in relationship to God through Christ. But the *'spirit of sonship'* to which I refer is also a holy *attitude,* and a set of values, out of which we are meant to live in walking with Christ and with His people. Not only is it our attitude to Him, but also our heart attitude to others, and especially to the leaders He has given us. Furthermore, it is our attitude to our leaders that shows whether *'sonship'* is really in us, for as the apostle John said, *"And he has given us this command: Whoever loves God must also love his brother."* (1 John 4: 21)

And don't say He has not given you leaders. In making covenant with David, He made reference to a context for His promises, *"...ever since the time I appointed leaders over my people..."* (2 Sam 7:11). And the Scriptures of the new covenant are even clearer for our sake. Hebrews 13:7 instructs, *"Remember your leaders, who spoke the word of God to you. Consider the outcome of their way of life and imitate their faith."* Later in the same chapter this is clarified further with, *"Obey your leaders and submit to their authority. They keep watch over you as men who must give an account. Obey them so that their work will be a joy, not a burden, for that would be of no advantage to you."* (Hebrews 13: 17)

The passage in 1 Thessalonians 5: 12-13a is especially rich with meaning: *"Now we ask you, brothers, to respect those who work hard among you, who are over you in the Lord and who admonish you. Hold them in the highest regard in love because of their work."* We will return to these passages later and find out what the Lord means here by *'respect'*.

We should especially note that these sonship attitudes and values to which we are called were firstly Christ's. We are told to be *"like-minded, having the same love, being one in spirit and purpose"* and that in this *"your attitude should be the same as that of Christ Jesus."* (Phil 2:2,5)

There is a personal story behind my understanding and teaching of the 'spirit of sonship' as a set of Christian values. In telling the story, you will notice I often use the words 'us' and 'we'. This feels more natural to me, for I and my leadership team and our people learned these things together, and to this day we walk closely together. Although I certainly obtained many spiritual victories alone in prayer, many of my experiences have been shared experiences too. On many occasions others have been with me, and we have prayed together, heard God together, made choices and decisions together, and said "yes" to God, willing to pay the price together. We have spent a lot of time together, and regularly have scheduled meetings for no other reason than to be together – because without relationship, we would not be what we are meant to be as Christ's people. And through difficult times, my ministry leadership team and our people have stood unshifting, believing together.

I have always involved those around me in my calling, in the belief that what I am called to in Christ, they are called to also. Am I called to be an apostle to the nations? Then they also are called to go to the nations in apostolic ministry; and whatever grace I have been given, they too shall carry. And they do!

In growing and learning as a people, we experienced deep sorrows and the pain of struggle together, as well as the great joys of success, progress, and many miracles in answer to prayer. The progress did not come without the years of struggle and pain. We had to go through a period of vociferous opposition and vilification, even hatred, from people who, whilst using the name of Christ, made themselves such enemies of the gospel that their actions and words could only be understood, even now after many years, as demonically driven. There was no rational reason for their behaviour, except that, just as Joseph was told to take Mary and the baby Jesus and flee to Egypt because there were those who sought to take the life of the child, Satan also tried to kill the expression of Christ that was being born in us. The restoration of apostolic grace, and in particular the re-establishing of apostolic life in the church, is a huge threat to the kingdom of darkness.

Not only was there a serious testing period of opposition and vilification, it was followed by a longer and more difficult period of powerlessness and 'insignificance'. I had not expected this. The story of most churches I had heard was that after the troublemakers leave, blessing and growth occurs and even financial strength improves. I was looking forward to that, but found instead a long period of great quiet. We had more success and had even baptised many people during the trouble, but in the period that followed there seemed to be no such successes. I did not understand for quite some time that this also was an essential process as part of our preparation for our calling.

Everyone faces opposition, and whilst opposition questions one's identity, when it is dealt with by prayer and faith, and the resolve to obey God, it strengthens our character and clarifies our identity, while at the same time challenging our motives and cleansing the soul in various ways. God uses opposition for His own purposes, not least to train, strengthen, and purify us. Anyone called to leadership, especially to fivefold ministry, and in particular to the role of the true prophet, and even more so to the authority of the genuine apostle, will be called upon to face opposition. It is the way of Christ, it is a means of grace, and without it, I'm afraid, leadership will be very shallow.

So I also had to persevere during this season of powerlessness, and for me this was a much more difficult period – one for which I had not understood any precedent. During this the Lord stripped away every outward form of success. I heard Him say, and I shared it with our people the following Sunday, "I've taken away from you everything that normally makes people think they're successful, so that you can concentrate on being successful in the one thing that really counts – intimacy with God, and intimacy with each other."

This was the year 2000. We had just handed back our huge, multimillion-dollar property to the denomination, for the Lord had spoken to quite a large number of our people earlier that year telling us to resign as a church from the denomination. When I sought the Lord about this, I heard Him say clearly that for us to do what we were called to do in the world, we would have to operate from outside the denominational system.

We walked away in freedom, owning little but owing nothing. Now we had no property, and therefore no program. Unexpectedly, the Lord saw to it that finance also was now limited. In the light of the Lord's words to us, I said to our people, "There is nothing for you to do from one Sunday to the next, except to walk with God and walk with each other. We have no program. There is no building, therefore no cleaning and no gardens. We have no rooms, so there is no Sunday school. There is nowhere to meet during the week except in houses. You are free to walk with God, to pray and do His will, and we will all meet together again every Sunday."

Even for Sunday services we had no permanent place where we could meet – the facilities in the city were not available for permanent bookings at the time. Each week I would advise our people by letter where we would be the following Sunday. Sometimes we met in the Botanical Gardens. Our fellowship was rich, the teaching and ministry was a blessing, but no new people were joining us, and there were few baptisms or other signs of progress, even though the Spirit of God was really with us. It was difficult, for even though we had a good ministry, and the Lord was very close, we could not seem to succeed at anything.

I realise now that 'powerlessness' is a more difficult training period because it tests you to the very core of your spiritual identity. You are not now facing the opposition of other people questioning your identity; instead, you begin to question yourself. Am I who I thought I was? Am I really called to the ministry? Are we really God's people? Have we really heard the Lord? Are we really in the will of God? And all the while, in the eyes of others (meaning other churches or Christians) you look like a failure. Yet throughout God is very much with you. Personally, I regard the season of powerlessness and insignificance as the most crucial of preparatory seasons in the life of the apostle. And who knows what issues of the heart, whether of pride, or trusting in self, or some other fleshly weakness, have been dealt with in the long process of this desert experience.

I read somewhere that the early Church fathers did not trust a man who had not been broken by failure. Perhaps that is a helpful illustration to amplify this truth: there is a need for God to address something in each of us that must be broken. This is especially true of those called to leadership. At the time, I was very much aware that, whatever these difficult times might be doing for me, it was also doing an important work in the hearts of our people.

My understanding of having a 'relationship' in the ministry with a senior leader or an apostle did not go beyond getting to know someone and learning from them, accepting their wisdom and seniority, so as to let them speak into your life. Really, this was very basic indeed, but that's where I began.

In fact, my understanding was more primitive than that. I had been raised in denominational, evangelical Christianity, where working for, maintaining, and advancing in the *system* was everything. To build a church meant one had to build the organisation. Accountability and covering was supplied by the denominational structures – therefore if you worked with them you had accountability. There was no such thing as personal relationships of the heart with leaders over you, no spiritual fathering, and apostolic covering was unheard of.

The religious values we were taught required loyalty to the religious system (i.e. the denomination), not to an individual leader. We were here to serve the denomination in the belief that it was the church. We were not especially taught how to follow, honour, or serve individual leaders, even though they were the anointed ministers of Christ. Our allegiance was to an institution, but never to a man. We were taught to not trust any man, but were obliged to trust a committee or a democratic vote. It was all very religious, but not Christian.

I nevertheless had great relationships, I thought, with church members, staff, the ministry team, denominational leaders (whom I did love and serve, for to do so had always been in my heart), and I had growing numbers of young apostles and others in South-East Asia who were looking to me as a spiritual father. But I myself did not have a spiritual father, did not know I needed one, and would have found it very difficult to relate to one. I was stable, mature, emotionally and spiritually secure, loved by many people, finding success in life, and thought I had all the relationships and accountability that I needed and was required.

But then the Lord intervened. I met apostle Chuck Clayton in Brisbane in 1994, where he was speaking at a conference called the *School of the Prophets*. He was a unique kind of man, full of authority, a highly experienced spiritual leader, a no-nonsense kind of person whom I would find it hard at first to get to know. I was asked to take him to lunch.

Afterwards, I felt I wanted the benefit of Chuck's ministry in the church at home, so I invited him to come. Thus began a series of visits, including

my regular visits to his house. The Lord told me to visit him, and spend
time with him. He said Chuck had learned important lessons through
making mistakes, mistakes that He did not want me to make. I was to
learn from him.

I found it difficult at first to relate to Chuck – it was easier to feel at
home with any of the other people I met around him in America. But he
was the one with whom I was meant to pursue relationship. I had many
dreams directing me to receive his ministry, yet I still did not understand
the deeply personal nature of the relationship the Lord was calling for. I
was just glad that our church was receiving the occasional ministry of an
apostle, and we had the blessing of his prayers and his input. We gladly
received his visits, and I greatly enjoyed visiting him, but I was not giving
much of myself away. It was all very cautious, but we had established the
first stage: receiving the ministry and the blessing of an apostle.

In 1999 it became evident to me that my relationship with apostle Chuck
had to go much further. Apostolic covering did not derive from a casual
relationship in which we received blessing and input from time to time.
There had to be a real commitment, and it needed to be public and official.
I had asked the Lord why we had seemed to lack certain protections and
graces, and His immediate response was *"You have to make the apostolic
covering official"*. This meant my personal commitment to relationship
with Chuck had to be firmly established. We needed to openly acknowledge
in our church his authority to speak into our lives, to represent Christ to me,
and to bring a new level of leadership and accountability through personal
relationship with an apostle.

I telephoned and made that heart commitment. He would be an apostle
to me, and I would be accountable to him, and honour him, for the Lord's
sake, and for the sake of our people. The following Sunday I stood and
prayed for our church. I asked the Lord if He would place upon us the
apostolic covering of Christ. In this prayer I acknowledged to the Lord that
I received from Him the ministry of Chuck Clayton as the one who would
be an apostle to us in Christ. As I offered that prayer, an evident change in
the spiritual atmosphere over our church occurred; in that moment people
in the congregation received physical healings. Something very important,
a crucial protection and an apostolic grace, had come into place.

Things began to move very quickly after that, and the best was yet to
come. We were not aware there was a master plan; we were simply seeking
the face of God day by day, walking in the grace we had, and doing the
things that were before us in the ministry. But early the following year the

Lord led us to leave the denomination to explore the fullness of apostolic community, and to build the apostolic ministry to which we were called.

I had always thought that we would never leave the denomination. It had not been my intention to do so, nor had I anticipated any reason why we should. But unexpectedly, within the space of about two weeks, many of our people came forward, one after another, to share that they had received a dream, a vision, or a prophetic word to say that we were to leave the denomination. People all around me were certain this was what we were to do, and it did have that inner witness of the Spirit. In discussion at the church council, the leadership team was agreed – they unanimously believed this was the word of the Lord to us.

I knew in my heart it was the truth, and felt we should act in accordance with this wide consensus, but I was uncomfortable about leading the church into something concerning which I personally had not received any instructions from the Lord. Burdened about this, I rose one night around 2a.m. and sat in my unlit office at home talking to the Lord, asking questions and listening; there He told me a series of things I needed to know.

Once we left the denomination, we began to find new freedoms, and within seven months achieved a major breakthrough in the spirit realm. From that time we began to see many changes. Problems were solved, needs were met, insight came – breakthrough progress occurred in finance, property, relationships with other churches, and other spiritual victories. We still had to fight the fight of faith, and work through testing experiences, but we were making progress toward a goal.

We always had daily prayer meetings. One morning in early 2001, David Hood, my senior associate in the *Peace* apostolic team, came into the meeting and said that he believed the Holy Spirit was speaking concerning 'inheritance'. He kept hearing this word, and felt we were to pray for our inheritance. I began praying a simple prayer, "Father, give me my inheritance". It felt right and good to pray this. A sense of blessing and the witness of the Holy Spirit was on it, so we daily continued to seek the Lord for our inheritance.

What began to unfold from that time was an increasing revelation to our hearts of *sonship*. Why? Because *inheritance* is given to *sons*. If we were to walk in the riches of our inheritance, we would have to live, think, and believe as sons.

> **"If we are to walk in the riches of our inheritance, we will have to live, think, and believe as sons."**

Soon afterwards the Lord also began to talk to us about revival. We had often prayed for revival, but had always prayed for revival as if it were some future event to be hoped for, rather than something that one is expecting today, or this week, or this year. I had personally prayed for revival for over 25 years.

Late one night, the Lord strongly impressed upon me that revival was really on, that it was coming, but that it was to be believed for as something for 'now,' not later. Then after some weeks, He said, *"The revival that is coming is not the same as previous revivals. Do not be so fixated on looking for the kind of revival that you have read about in Church history that you miss what I am about to do. I am about to do something that has never been done before."*

Early in 2002 one of our ministry leaders, Michael Appleton, who has served me faithfully as a son ever since 1992, felt led to spend a week in prayer. He felt he should devote himself to prayer for 24 hours a day for seven days. This was a big task. By the second or third day I was expecting him to look terrible, but he looked wonderful, bright, and cheerful. He prayed through that whole week, and I spent the seventh night with him in prayer.

At about 5:20 a.m. a word came from the Lord. I had been praying, and when I finished Michael said, "John, while you were praying, I felt the Lord draw my attention to the photo of apostle Chuck and Karen Clayton at the other end of the room." We had many photos on the wall, and theirs was one of them. Michael continued, "I feel strongly that the Lord is saying that this man is meant to have a very significant impact upon us, and a much greater place in our lives than we understand!"

I could not see how it would be possible that he could have a greater impact, or be more important to us than he had been. He lived in the USA, a long way from Queensland, and we simply could not see him very often. In fact we had not had much personal contact with him over the previous 2 years, except for the occasional phone call. And honestly, I was not aware of anything more that he had that we needed or could help us.

In the meantime, we had scheduled a church family camp, to be held on the first weekend of autumn. Over previous months as the Lord had impressed the idea of a coming revival upon us, He had promised autumn and spring rains.

I felt the Lord did not want us to prepare any messages for these camp meetings. There were to be five meetings, but no preparation. I also felt we were to "under prepare" the worship. So I said to our senior worship leader that she was to prepare less worship than she thought we would need – to choose a few songs only, not many.

Then I explained to my senior associate, David Hood, *"David, I will be at the family camp, and will sit in the front row every meeting. But I am preparing no messages, and no one else is to prepare any messages either. My intention is to sit there and be silent, saying nothing in any meeting, unless the Spirit of God gives me things to say. I want you to take charge of those meetings – you guide them through, you lead them in whatever way you want, but I want you to make no preparation for worship or preaching."* Of course David did not know what to do. He is an organised man, self-disciplined, and this put him squarely outside his comfort zone.

We turned up for the first meeting on Friday night, and found David had made inspired arrangements. He had all the chairs in a circle – to have sufficient chairs for about 120 people coming required three rows around in a big circle. He included in the circle a place where the musicians could sing and play if required. He decided that we would not commence the meeting in the usual way, therefore the band members sat down with everybody else. There would be no songs unless the Spirit of God called for a song.

To commence, David welcomed everyone and said, *"Many of us have come to camp with expectations of the Lord. I would like to ask as many people as possible to come and take the microphone and share their expectations. What have you come to camp expecting? What do you expect of the Lord?"* and he placed the microphone on the table and sat down.

Someone immediately arose and shared their excited expectations. They were thrilled, they said. They had so much anticipation of the wonderful things God was going to do in this camp. Another arose, and expressed the most amazing expectations of all the fabulous things that God was going to do amongst us that weekend. And then a third arose, also filled with strong and vibrant expectations of the Lord, and great anticipation of what blessings there would be.

As that third person laid the microphone back on the table, and began to step away, a stunning event took place. She was instantly frozen in place like a statue. Her arms and legs were positioned as if walking away from the table, but she could not move. And she remained frozen, in a trance, for the next two and a half hours.

The meeting continued around her, as one after another shared their expectations of the Lord that weekend. But as the night progressed, the nature of the sharing changed. People began to share their lives. They shared their hopes and dreams. They shared the dealings of God, and they shared their desires. It was a wonderful experience of personal intimacy, of the opening of hearts. This was a greater expression than we had ever experienced of the personal sharing of our lives.

After the first hour, David felt we should sing. The musicians helped us, and entering into the first song, heaven seemed to be present. The second song also held such passion, such sweetness. But as we began to sing the third song, the anointing lifted completely, so we stopped the song. We were not meant to sing any more. We went back to sharing, and for another hour and a quarter hearts were continually being opened toward the Lord and their brethren.

Then it came time to close the meeting, but all the while I had been looking at our sister still frozen in the trance, and pondering the meaning of it. I had seen many manifestations of the Spirit in the course of my life, and I was convinced this was not just a manifestation of the Spirit. This was something more; it was a sign! A sign is a miraculous intervention, something put in front of you by the Lord, which carries a message and points to a truth. I was convinced God had given us a sign! But what did it mean?

As David was closing the meeting, I signaled to him that I wanted to speak. I told everyone that it was possible for us to simply pray and release our sister from her immobile state, but we ought not go to supper without pondering the meaning of what God was saying through her. I said, "I believe if we will listen, the Lord will tell us what this sign means." Immediately somebody said, "I think I know what it means." Then there was another, and another. Many people had a sense of what God was saying. So opened another round of sharing, and out of this came deep insight into the heart and word of God for us at that time. Finally, one of our number stated the precise truth the sign pointed to. In that moment, the Spirit of God released her, and she began to walk, and talk, and laugh as usual.

The Lord had not finished with us. We had another four amazing meetings. More signs, many more hours of sharing, and we finished that weekend a totally changed people. God had been amongst us, yet we had not done any of the things we normally do to make a meeting 'successful'.

From that time, we have always had our chairs facing each other as much as possible when we meet, and have occasionally conducted Sunday services also in this style, in which we fill up the whole meeting with sharing. It is of course risky to just put the microphone on the table, and let anyone who wants speak for as long as they like in an open-ended meeting. And in all honesty, not all the sharing was totally selfless, and not all the people were clean. They were just normal Christian people, with weaknesses and faults. But we trusted the Lord, and He faithfully moved among us and somehow worked deeply in us, bringing miracles out of those meetings.

What was the central theme that came out spontaneously in that camp weekend? It was *sonship*! The Lord spoke of what it meant for us to be sons to a Father in heaven. We pondered the parable of the prodigal son, and we weighed up Galatians chapters 3 and 4.

The story of the prodigal son illustrates a great issue. The prodigal said to himself that he would return to his father and say, *"I am no longer worthy to be called your son; make me like one of your hired men."* (Luke 15:19) This is a problem many believers have. Whilst they come to God to confess their sins and get right with the Father, even though the Father welcomes them unconditionally and seeks to bring them into His house, they still often continue to hold within their own heart this belief, *"I am no longer worthy to be called your son; make me like one of your hired men."* Thus many believers, whilst knowing they have been received by God and adopted into his family, in their own minds live in the servant's quarters, not in the Father's house as a son, believing they are not worthy.

All believers have to overcome the issues associated with this struggle. All of us must come to understand what it means to live and think and act like a son, rather than a servant. Of course a son also serves – he serves his father, he works in the harvest field along with the other labourers – but in his heart he serves, not because he is a slave or hired labourer, but because he is... *a son.*

In Galatians 4 Paul says that Abraham had two sons, one born in the natural way by the bondwoman, but the other, the son of the promise, born of the free woman. In the church there are also these two kinds of people: those still in bondage, and those who, as sons of the promise, walk in the experience of liberty through faith. The Bible is very clear: *"the slave woman's son will never share in the inheritance with the free woman's son."* (Galatians 4:30)

At that camp, the Spirit of God brought our people to tenderness of heart. At one point late on the Saturday night David came to me and said,

"John, I really think the Lord is saying that many of our people need to be born again, again." I gave that call, and that night many people, weeping before the Lord, came to a fresh understanding of their position in Christ, and their place in the Father's family.

We thought this alone was the big lesson, but more was to come. Within a few days apostle Chuck phoned. He mentioned that he had been preaching sonship for the last six or seven months in the US, and was receiving such an amazing response from people that he felt he had never had so much fun in all his life. I immediately appealed to him to visit us as soon as possible to preach his sonship messages, to add to what we had experienced at the camp. I wanted to take advantage of whatever grace or truth he had.

He came less than three months later to our annual Australian Apostolic Summit, in June, 2002. I was expecting he would preach more of what we heard at the camp. But this was not the aspect of sonship that Chuck had been given by the Lord. Instead he had a clear revelation concerning how the *spirit* of sonship is to be in each of us with respect to those who lead us in the church. One of our pastors, Tony Ponicke, who had himself had some breakthrough at the time of the camp, was given an astounding spiritual breakthrough when the Holy Spirit fell upon him under Chuck's teaching. His story of deliverance through the message of *sonship* is told later in this book.

For any believer to fully experience the grace that God has given us in Christ, we need understanding not only of our relationship with God our Father in heaven, but also of the relationship He brings us into with all His people. In the faith, in the ministry, there are always God-appointed leaders; many of these become fathers in the faith, and indeed this is the goal of spiritual maturity. We must have the heart of a son toward them if we are to walk fully in the grace of God, and become ourselves mature. There are many biblical examples of this grace of 'sonship' as we shall see. What we call *sonship* is the biblical model for healthy relationships, healthy discipleship, and satisfying and meaningful church life.

> "What we call sonship is the biblical model for healthy relationships, healthy discipleship, and satisfying and meaningful church life."

David Hood shared with me one day a personal insight. He said, "John, I believe that the spreading message of sonship and the relational blessings so many are discovering, is the revival that the Lord promised." These words felt like profound truth.

I remembered that the Lord had told us that the coming revival was not like anything we had seen before, and warned us not to be so fixated on traditional revival that we missed what He was about to do. I also remembered that in the year 2001, after David had heard that word "inheritance", and we began to seek the Father concerning this, that He had led us into an understanding of *sonship* and had given us a clear apostolic message on sonship to proclaim. Furthermore, He had said that revival was for *now*. We found that even the first instalment of experiencing the grace of sonship (at the 'autumn rain' family camp) had affected us so much that it began to totally transform our lives and the life of the church.

Wherever we have taught the 'spirit of sonship' message, many pastors and believers have come alive with this truth. This is not just a 'truth' to be believed; it is an experience of God and a relationship with people in which to walk.

At the time of our 2002 Apostolic Summit, something really changed. Something wonderful shifted into place in the relationship between apostle Chuck and me. In fact the shift took place between all of us – between his wife Karen and my wife Hazel, and between our people and apostle Chuck as well; but principally, it was in my heart toward him that God gave great light and grace.

From 1994 until 1999 I had looked on 'apostolic covering' as simply knowing an apostle and receiving his ministry. From 1999 until 2002 we saw the apostolic covering as a permanent, but voluntary and non-controlling relationship, in which we were committed in love to an apostle, and he was committed to us. In this relationship, we would be accountable, give financial support, and receive and honour him as one over us in the Lord. He would seek to bless, instruct, be available, and help guard our lives in Christ.

But from June 2002, I began to see Chuck as a father, and I became in my heart a son. This was where the Holy Spirit had always been taking me in Christ.

I often tell people that for me there were three stages in discovering the power of fathering and sonship. We moved from where at first relationship with an apostle was simply a convenient arrangement, to where it became a true apostolic covering through commitment, to where finally it became a deep, heartfelt, and emotive relationship between people who love each other, and who are there for each other. Emotive? Yes! I do not believe that relationships, if true and holy, should ever be without heartfelt depth of feeling, and I will show this to be true from Scripture.

From the time this change took place, where I found I had the heart of a son toward a father in the ministry, it seems as if the heavens were opened. This happened because a mature son is entitled to receive inheritance. Stepping into an experience of relational sonship in the ministry, as I did, I found I had stepped into great blessing.

Every senior leader of a ministry needs apostolic covering. Each needs to be in relationship with, and accountable to, an apostle of Christ. And each needs to find the grace whereby these relationships become meaningful as genuine 'father and son' relationships. Every believer in the church needs the blessing of that sense of security that follows when their leadership walks in such relationships. In turn, the whole church can and will experience the greater security, and sense of acceptance and belonging that Christ provides to His people through this expression of family life in the ministry.

David Hood, Associate Senior Minister
Peace Christian Church,
Rockhampton, Queensland, Australia.

I am at this time 55 years of age, have been married to Judy for 34 years, and we have five children. I have been involved with *Peace Apostolic Community* since January 1991. I am John Alley's senior associate minister, a position I have held since January 1995. I was raised in a Christian home, and I give thanks to God for Christian parents and the Christian heritage I have. I was saved when 7 years old and attended an evangelical church with my parents and siblings. We were raised to respect, honour, and obey those over us, and to be committed to our denomination and the things we were involved in.

My father was a perfectionist who expected us to be good at what we did. Encouragement was rarely given, but was substituted with an expectation of improvement. A statement that I remember well my father saying was, 'Nothing is too good for the King of Kings'! At the time I reasoned that this was true, and I worked to do everything perfectly. Of course this is not possible, and the statement doomed me to a life of striving.

This background moulded in me a belief that a person's value was directly related to how well they did things, and how committed and reliable they were. In 1987, when I was serving as a leader in a church, I was encountered by the Lord and subsequently baptised with the Holy Spirit. This was a significant time of change in my life as the Lord dealt with me and set me on a journey of discovery that was to turn my belief system on its head. I was confronted by my lack of knowledge of God, His word, His will and His ways; I felt quite undone and yet so impacted by the Holy Spirit that I had a passion for the Lord and His will that I had never known before.

It was this encounter with God that led me in 1988 to move out of secular employment and to enter full time ministry as an assistant minister. This was a time of much challenge and growth. After nearly two years in this position I attended a 9 week intensive training school followed by a 3 week mission trip to the Philippines. It was after this time of adjustment, learning, and soul searching that the Lord led us to *Peace* in 1991. We had determined that we wanted our children to grow up in an atmosphere of faith, and where the Lord was free to have His way.

The fellowship of *Peace* was experiencing a move of God that I would call renewal. They were good days; the church grew and we personally and corporately experienced many blessings from the Lord. During the early 90s' I served as a 'deacon' and then as an 'elder' at *Peace,* before circumstances and the Lord opened the door for me to become John's senior associate minister.

The Lord had been speaking to John for several years about the restoration of apostles and he had been teaching our fellowship everything the Lord had shown him. There seemed to be a ready acceptance in our fellowship that John was an apostle and had a calling to travel and take this message to the nations. I supported John in everything and did all the things that a good and faithful servant should do. The way I had been raised made me a very good associate; faithful, reliable, committed, and obedient.

Although we had experienced many wonderful times with God and His people, we were about to enter a very difficult period of time with many trying and painful events. All through the years the Lord continued to reveal His heart and ways to us. At some point as I pondered more deeply what it meant for John to be an apostle, I realised that God was not just restoring apostles, for if there were apostles there needed to be an apostolic church! This understanding was not received in an inert atmosphere but in the furnace of trials and disharmony; in the cauldron of opposition and accusation; in a time of soul searching and uncertainty.

Searching the scriptures led me to understand more deeply the example of Christ as a son to a father, and the attitude He had to His father. It is obvious in looking back that the Lord had His hand upon us, guiding us to a place we were quite unaware of. We came through the trials weaker, but richer; wiser, but humbler; smaller, but in unity. God had laid us low to strip from us the things that would hinder the work He had for us to do. Competition and striving was mostly gone. Although in the past we had been known as 'family,' we were now being family. This was a critical transition, for in an organisation there are leaders (bosses) and workers (servants), but in a family there are fathers (and mothers) and children. Other people in a house who are not family are servants and orphans. John Alley is the spiritual father of the house at *Peace*, and he is my spiritual father.

The Lord ushered us toward this understanding through revelation by His Spirit, and by His messengers (Chuck Clayton, John's spiritual father). It is important to understand that each of us moves to sonship through personal revelation of what God has done, what He has said, what Christ showed us, and facing what we have believed. There is a sense in which everyone moves from being an orphan, to being a servant, to becoming a son. This is true spiritually but also applies to us physically and emotionally. For me, sonship is completely different from being a servant or worker.

It is interesting and yet should have been obvious to me, or anyone reading scripture, that God uses the vocabulary of father to son, and of son to a father. I discovered that my understanding of being a Christian was about what I did (servant) instead of who I was (son). The primary consideration is of identity, who am I and how did I become this? My identity had been based on how much I did, and how well I did it. God said of Jesus, "This is my son, whom I love; with Him I am well pleased" – yet at this point Jesus had not commenced His ministry and had not done anything. There are many passages in John's Gospel that speak of the Son's relationship with the Father and His dependence on Him to the extent that He could do nothing without Him. This is true also of us as God's children, and as sons to a spiritual father.

Over the past four years I have had to renew my mind so as to be a spiritual son and not a servant. It is one thing to learn a theory, but quite another to be. The complication and necessity of still doing something well, and with an excellence separate from identity, is a learning process. Most of our struggles are in the area of our own beliefs. Our beliefs need to be bible based.

A critical element that a true son understands is inheritance. A servant performs tasks out of a 'have to' mentality, with no sense of this benefiting them in any way. A son knows that whatever they do for their father also benefits them, as they have an inheritance in whatever is their father's. The scripture has much to say of this, and I have come to a deeper understanding of the reality of this in my daily life.

True sonship positions me for many important things. Personally, I have in John someone who watches over my life to protect me from wrong attitudes and from error. He genuinely wants me to grow in every area of my life and ministry. He provides opportunity for me where I would have had no opportunity. A father's blessing helps release to us God's power to succeed in every aspect of life; family, relationships, finances, health and ministry; everything will benefit.

Being a son provides blessing, protection, counsel, and more rapid advancement as John instructs and advises me. One never ceases to be a son, but the nature of the relationship changes! I have been John's senior associate for 12 years but for the majority of this time I was a good servant, not a son. Outwardly things probably don't look any different from before, but inwardly there is a world of difference. I have learned that having a good father does not make us a son. Sonship is determined by our decision to be a son; we can also choose to be a servant or to believe that we are orphans (i.e. we don't belong).

A son has a permanent place; I am not worried about someone else taking my place because it is not possible. A son can abdicate his place, but it cannot be taken. Sonship provides great security as we are sons for as long as we are willing to be.

Sonship is not about being controlled or manipulated; fear and insecurity are not part of it. Honour, love, and Godly submission are all essential elements of true sonship. An interesting point to make is that we must be a son before we can be a father. If we choose not to be a son to a father, we may well become a boss to someone but we will never be their father!

I thank God for John and for his input into my life over the past 16 years. I am thankful for the journey that we have been on that has led us thus far; I am truly blessed. I believe that as we continue in these relationships, our lives will become even more entwined and enriched.

David Hood.

CHAPTER 2

GOD AS FATHER & SON

"In the past
God spoke to our forefathers through the prophets
at many times and in various ways,
but in these last days he has spoken to us by his Son,
whom he appointed heir of all things,
and through whom he made the universe.

The Son is the radiance of God's glory
and the exact representation of his being,
sustaining all things by his powerful word.

After he had provided purification for sins,
he sat down at the right hand of the Majesty in heaven.

So he became as much superior to the angels
as the name he has inherited is superior to theirs."

(Hebrews 1:1-4)

The greatest and most astounding revelations of God were reserved for exactly the right time and place in history – the time referred to in the text above when God spoke to us by His son. The apostle Paul said of this: *"But when the time had fully come, God sent his Son..."* (Gal 4:4a) The word translated 'sent' is *'exapostello'* (to send forth on a mission) – an apostle, the apostle of the Father, had come into the world.

We will later examine more closely the relationship between sonship and apostleship. For now, we must consider God as Father and Son. This is the primary revelation that the Son of God brought.

Many prophets were entrusted with all kinds of revelations concerning God's nature – His holiness, love, justice, mercy, faithfulness, wrath and judgments, for example. In fact, over many centuries there was a constant unfolding of revelation concerning His names, the meaning of those names, His nature, His purpose, His love, and His ways. Nevertheless, it was reserved for one particular person to bring the most astounding revelation of all.

That amazing revelation is that God is God in father and son; that God is a father-son God. But it is not just that God is a father who has a son, but also that God is a son who has a father.

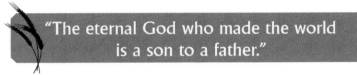

"The eternal God who made the world is a son to a father."

This is astounding. The eternal God who made the world, the One who called all things into being and upholds them by the power of His word, is a son to a father. And this is the very nature of His being.

This Father and Son are just like each other, as in that old saying, "like father, like son".

Many people who struggle spiritually have greatly mistaken notions of what God is like. They think that Jesus, as saviour, is loving, kind, merciful, forgiving, tender, gentle, and humble, while at the same time they think that God the Father is tough, judgemental, hard to get to know, law-keeping, and rigid in dealing with sinners. But please understand: the reason Jesus is gracious, loving, and merciful, etc is because that's exactly what His father is like. Jesus specifically said, *"I tell you the truth, the Son can do nothing by himself; he can do only what he sees his Father doing, because whatever the Father does the Son also does. For the Father loves the Son and shows him all he does."* (John 5:19-20)

If the revelation that 'God is God in Father and Son' had not come to us from the Son of God Himself, but had come from some other prophet, say Amos or Jeremiah, we might not have been inclined to believe it. But this revelation was the most important and critical of all, something we must truly know and understand if we would walk with God. Therefore, it had to be brought by Christ Himself.

There are, no doubt, many mysteries in the Godhead pertaining to the life of an eternal God. As it is, the Bible does not say much at all about the relationship between God the Father and the Holy Spirit, nor much about the relationship between the Holy Spirit and God the Son. But the Bible has a tremendous amount to say about the relationship between God the Father and God the Son. This is so because this relationship is such a vital one, and the revelation of it such a critical one, for our sakes.

Understand then that God is by *nature* a Father-Son God. And being self-determining, God has chosen for Himself the kind of God He will be. (Exodus 3:14) Being holy and perfect, and having been perfect and holy from eternity past, God is unchanging. He chooses to be Father and Son, and has always been Father and Son. This is the perfection of holiness.

Does this mean that one is superior and the other inferior? No, the Father and the Son are co-equal in power and glory; they are each eternally equal.

Note that whilst one is Father and the other Son, neither has lived a 'moment' longer than the other, even though the Son is the begotten of the Father. One of the early church fathers called Jesus the unbegotten begotten. He had no beginning. Both are of identical "age," equally of eternity. Father and Son can each be referred to by the biblical term, "the Ancient of Days". But they eternally choose to walk together as Father and Son, and this means that one takes the 'office' or role of father, and the other takes the 'office' or role of son, in relation to each other.

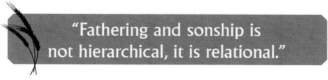

"Fathering and sonship is not hierarchical, it is relational."

Fathering and sonship is not hierarchical, it is relational. It is not a superior/ inferior relationship, but a relationship of equals to serve each other in particular ways. Father and Son are of one spirit, therefore equals. Even in human terms, you can't be a father and call someone a son without this being, at the least, a calling of that person to become what you are, to stand where you stand, and to become one with you. This is why the Pharisees were so shocked about Jesus, because by declaring Himself to be the Son of God, they knew He was claiming to be equal with God. (John 5:17-18)

How does this relationship work?

It is important for us to understand how this relationship works between God the Father and God the Son, because this will give us the biblical insights we need concerning the way in which we must walk in Godly relationships also. If we do not take this in, we will not have really listened even though *"he has spoken to us by his Son."* It is not only from Jesus' words we must find life, but also from the example of His way of life – otherwise we are not His followers.

Firstly, how does God the Father feel about His Son? The Father loves the son deeply and passionately; He cherishes Him above all. (John 3:35) As far as the Father is concerned, there is no one like His Son. He is the apple of His eye. He watches over Him, and holds Him in loving and tender embrace. Nothing is too good for His Son. We are told the Father entrusts all things to His Son, including all judgement. (John 5:19-23) When it was necessary to choose a saviour for lost mankind, and there was no man righteous, God the Father chose to send His own Son, to embrace both human nature and a physical body, to redeem man from his sin. He sent His Son into the world to be the saviour of the world, and in this the Father has made a determination. All things will be consummated in His Son. As far as the Father is concerned, the Son is so important, so central to all that the Father is, that unless a man receives the Son, he cannot come to the Father. (John 14:6) *"Whoever believes in the Son has eternal life, but whoever rejects the Son will not see life, for God's wrath remains on him."* (John 3: 36)

How does the Son feel about the Father? The Son of God loves and reveres His Father, honouring Him in all things and above all things, and chooses to only and ever live for His Father. He came into the world in obedience to His Father, and lived His whole life upon earth in that same, submitted obedience. He was totally surrendered to the will of the Father. He said, *"For I have come down from heaven not to do my will but to do the will of him who sent me."* (John 6:38) For the Son, the Father is the centre of all things. He said, *"...but the world must learn that I love the Father and that I do exactly what my Father has commanded me."* (John 14:31) He had earlier remarked, *"By myself I can do nothing; ...for I seek not to please myself but him who sent me."* (John 5:30)

In teaching His followers, Jesus constantly pointed them to the Father. He said, *"Be perfect, therefore, as your heavenly father is perfect."* (Matt 5:48) He would spend many hours in prayer, and long nights in lonely vigil, seeking His Father. And He longed for the day when He would return to His Father in glory. *"Father, the time has come. Glorify your Son, that your Son may glorify you."* (John 17:1)

At the end of the age, all things shall find their consummation in Christ, the Son of God. But when God the Father has made all things subject to Christ, then Christ shall submit all things, including Himself, to His Father. (1 Cor 15:24-28)

The ONENESS of God and of the Believers

Thus the Father and the Son are completely devoted to one another. There is no independence, no personal agenda, no private action. Each is totally and completely one with the other.

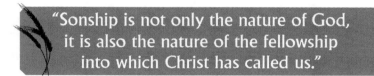

"Sonship is not only the nature of God, it is also the nature of the fellowship into which Christ has called us."

Now this is not only the nature of God, it is also the nature of the fellowship into which Christ has called us. You and I, as believers in our Lord Jesus Christ, are not called to independence, or unilateral action, but we are called to find oneness, not only with Christ but with each other too. The Lord Jesus, in His high priestly prayer recorded in John 17, prayed for us, *"...that all of them may be one, Father, just as you are in me and I am in you. May they also be in us..."* (John 17:21). And John the apostle, urging upon the church the need to remember the essential place of love, shows the amazing significance of our oneness: *"We proclaim to you what we have seen and heard, so that you also may have fellowship with us. And our fellowship is with the Father and with his Son, Jesus Christ."* (1 John 1:3)

This greatly clarifies something we must understand; the intimacy and unity of fellowship that is shared by the Father and the Son is the *same* fellowship into which you and I are called. When the Son of God described us as being called to *"complete unity"* (John 17:23), He was describing the kind of unity and relationship that exists between God the Father and the Son. We are called to share the father-son nature of God. Just how this might be, in practical terms, I will take up later. For now, there are other matters we must consider about the nature of God as Father and Son.

No Independence in the Son

There never was any independence in the Son of God. On earth with fallen humanity we see all kinds of sons – rebellious sons, independent sons, lazy sons, disrespectful sons, foolish sons, as well as healthy, fine, upright, loving, caring, hard-working, respectful sons. But true sonship is defined by the life of Christ, the Son of the living God.

In answer to those who were accusing Jesus, He gave them this reply: *"I tell you the truth, the Son can do nothing by himself; he can do only what he sees his Father doing, because whatever the Father does the Son also does. For the Father loves the Son and shows him all he does."* (John 5:19-20a)

The Father-Son 'Relationship' of God

One day I was reading the book of Hebrews chapter 1, and came to the place where it says, *'But about the Son he says, "Your throne, O God, will last for ever and ever, and righteousness will be the sceptre of your kingdom. You have loved righteousness and hated wickedness;"'* As I looked in particular at those words *"you have loved righteousness and hated wickedness",* I heard the Lord speak.

In a moment I will share what He said, but I want you to notice the context here; God the Father is speaking about God the Son, with the Father calling His own Son, *"God."* Wonderful, isn't it? We are looking at holy things here.

God is a self-determining God; He chooses for Himself the kind of God He will be. God is perfect, God is holy, God is unchanging, and God is a three-persons-in-one God. Do you know why God chooses to be three-persons? Because if God was only one person, He could not be perfect, and could not be holy. Even if God was two persons, He could not be holy. For God to be a *holy* God, a *perfect* God, He must be three – or more.

Here is how to understand what I just said. You know that the Bible says, *"God is love."* (1 John 4:16) It is not possible for God to be perfect or holy if God is not also love. In eternity, God must fellowship or this statement is meaningless and love is powerless. If God were to be love but have no fellowship, then God would be powerless to express His nature. And so it is not possible for God to be holy, or to be love, unless he lives in perfect communion with others – without division and without independence, there must be a perfect union.

The holiness of God is directly related to the relationships of God, i.e. the way God walks in relationship within Himself. This is *Holy Communion,* this is the *fellowship* of God, without which we cannot have a holy God, and without which there is nothing for us to be invited into by way of salvation or the marriage supper of the Lamb.

Now we will understand more clearly the meaning of what I heard the

Lord say whilst reading Hebrews 1:9, *"You have loved righteousness and hated wickedness."* He said, **"With the Son of God, there never was any independence."** Then immediately He spoke again, **"If the Son of God had been independent of the Father, even for a moment, God could not be holy."**

I was startled by this thought for a moment, but as I pondered it, I realised – this was a profound truth. For God to be holy, He must have unity within Himself. There can be no holiness without oneness.

There never was a time when the Son said to the Father, "I need some time off. It's been hectic around here lately. I need some time to myself. I'd like to go and think about who I am for a while; I'll be back later." Neither has there ever been any unilateral action by the Son. He never said to His Father, "It's a mess down there. I know how to fix humanity. You stay here; I'm going down to take care of it – I'll be back later."

Then, after a little while, I again heard the Lord speak: **"If the Son of God had been independent of the Father, even for a moment, you could not be saved"**.

This was a further truth. If the Son of God had not lived in submission as a son to a father, as one with the Father, you could not be saved. Be very clear about this: your eternal salvation totally depends upon a certain *son* walking with a certain *father* forever. Unless this Father and Son continue to walk in unity and holiness, there can be no eternity and no glory. There can be no redemption and no salvation of souls. Your eternal security is totally dependent upon a father-son relationship, which is at the heart of all eternal existence and which upholds all creation.

How central to all things is this father-son relationship! This is what godliness is all about! All things are dependent upon it! Without an understanding of the *spirit of sonship*, we will not understand God's ways at all, nor the nature of our salvation nor the true essence of the church and Christian life.

Here we have a holy community in which three persons walk with one another in perfect harmony. God has to be a father who loves a son, honours a son, cherishes a son, trusts a son, entrusts all judgement to a son, and further, must trust a son to represent Him in all things, or God cannot be holy, or perfect. And for God to be holy, He must also be a son who honours a father. It is not possible for us to have a holy God if He is not a son who has a dad. He must care about His father, must serve His father, love His father, honour Him, obey Him, submit to Him, walk with Him – and unless these things are present, God cannot be holy.

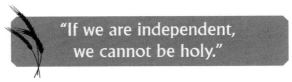

"If we are independent, we cannot be holy."

So let us realise concerning ourselves, if we are 'independent,' we are not holy. If a church is independent, it is not holy. (By this I do not mean independent of denominationalism; I mean independent of proper relationships in the body of Christ, independent of apostolic leadership and the like. But it is also possible to have these outward things in place and still have an independent spirit.) If a prophet is of an independent spirit, he or she cannot be holy. If an apostle is independent, we do not have a holy apostle – we have an impostor.

For God does not prepare and send just apostles or prophets – He raises and sends holy apostles and holy prophets. We have no choice but to seek to walk in the relationships which He ordains for us, or we do not really know what it means to be a holy people or to walk in apostolic grace. We have to be made like the son of God in every way.

The 'Spirit of Sonship'

This 'spirit of sonship' embodies certain attitudes, certain values, and certain actions. Principally, this is an attitude or grace we hold in our hearts toward other people, as well as being an attitude of heart toward God.

Yes, in Christ we are brought into dynamic relationship with God the Father and with His Son Jesus Christ, and so we are indeed a son to the living and holy one, but we must also learn what it means to live out the values of sonship in the church. We must learn just how to relate to other people, with the spirit of sonship in us all the while.

I have heard the Lord say, "Father and son relationship in the ministry *is* the new wineskin of the church." In other words, the true 'wineskin' for an apostolic people is established through relationships – but in particular, accountable relationships.

In another chapter I will explain that there are also boundaries, i.e. there are some safeguards for us in terms of how to understand these relationships. There are certain positions you should not adopt, certain things you should not think, there are some very common-sense and practical limits to what we understand by all this.

But we also need to know what it means to have a big heart toward other people as a son. Our love is not to be limited. We have the model of the Lord Jesus, who walked with His Father so perfectly.

> "If the Son of God had been independent
> of the Father, even for a moment,
> you could not be saved."

Let's go back for a moment to what I heard the Lord say – "If the Son of God had been independent of the Father, even for a moment, you could not be saved." If that relationship breaks down, everything is lost. The strength of the chair you are sitting on is only held together by the word of the Son of God, for the Bible tells us that all things hold together by the power of His word.

At the heart of the universe is a father-son relationship. Everything that has been made has been made through that father-son relationship, including your salvation in the cross and the shed blood of Christ. That shed blood only has power for you because a certain son had a certain relationship with a certain father, and they walk in it forever. If that relationship did not exist, you could not be saved.

At the heart of the cosmos is this father-son relationship, and everything comes forth from that. Your eternal security, your welfare, the fact that your name is written in heaven, the fact that you can believe your sins have been forgiven, and that you will live forever with Christ, is dependent on one thing and one thing only – that a certain son walks with a certain father, and walks with Him forever. We ought to thank God for such a father and son.

Testimony

Martin Goodall, Senior Pastor
Southern Life Christian Church,
Noarlunga, Adelaide, South Australia.

How I Feel About Being Fathered

It is only now that I have a formalised relationship with John that I can look back and see God's hand leading me to this point. I have come to realise that the best and most productive times in ministry were whenever I was in relationship with a man of God who treated me like a son.

Realising that I needed to be a spiritual son to someone has changed my life. It has caused me to change my beliefs about church and God. I had been trained to build a church and had been reasonably successful; the only problem was that often I was left feeling that something was not right.

I had come to God looking for love and found it in Him. However the further on I went the more I realised that on the whole the church did not know how to love, and my ability was somewhat limited. I realised that much of my identity and purpose in life was built on the size of my church, and not on John 13:35.

I had always sought someone to submit to for most of my Christian life. Even as a leader I always sought to have relationship with someone I could submit to. Unfortunately this was not always possible. For one reason or another I could never easily get to talk with those I was supposed to submit to. This all changed when I came into relationship with John.

This form of relationship opened my heart to love more as I was loved by someone over me. This has allowed me to love those whom I pastor and freed them to love me to a level I had never experienced before.

Becoming a son has also changed my perspective on how I pastor people. No longer do I view myself as their leader and try to help them with their problems so that they can help me build the church. Now I father them and seek the best for them just like I have with my children. This has then released them to truly be what God meant them to be. As an outcome from this, I have now received far more respect and love from people than ever before.

Martin Goodall.

CHAPTER 3

JESUS THE APOSTLE OF THE FATHER

"Therefore, holy brothers...
fix your thoughts on Jesus,
the apostle and high priest whom we confess."

(Hebrews 3:1)

There is a very important reason why Holy Scripture tells us, *"...fix your thoughts on Jesus, the apostle..."* or, as another translation of the text reads, *"Consider Jesus, the apostle...".* This is because it is in His life, His relationships, and His submission to the father, that we find the ultimate and pure definition of what it really means to *be* an apostle. By understanding this we also come to understand the nature of apostolic Christianity.

Jesus as High Priest

First we must consider what it means for Jesus to be *High Priest.* A *new* priesthood, and therefore a *new high priest,* was required for the new covenant God had long promised His people, and God the Father appointed His Son to become that high priest. A priest offers sacrifices – in this case, Jesus would become both the high priest offering the sacrifice, and the sacrifice being offered.

Prior to commencing His public ministry, Jesus came to the Jordan River to be baptised by John. The Jordan represented both *death* and *change.*

Jesus was being baptised to signify the fact, amongst other things, that there was to be a *change of the priesthood*, and He was being baptised in *anticipation of His death.*

It was for this very purpose of becoming high priest and dying a sacrificial death that Christ had been sent into the world. But before He could be made High Priest, He had to be made something else. To qualify to be High Priest, He had to be *an apostle*! And this is what the word means – sent for a purpose, sent with a commission. To come into the world and be our great high priest, Christ was appointed and sent as *the apostle of the Father!*

Jesus as Apostle

What does it mean for Jesus to be such an apostle, since this precedes His ability to become High Priest? We get our best definition of what apostleship is by considering Jesus.

When Jesus came into the world, He did not come on His own mission, but His Father's. He did not come of His own accord, but came to do the will of another. In doing so, He was in complete submission to another person, one who had authority over Him. The result of that submission was He fully carried the authority of this other person. These things in particular are what define a true apostle.

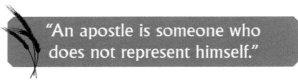

"An apostle is someone who does not represent himself."

For the church, an apostle is someone who does not represent himself, but is completely submitted to the will of Christ and comes to us representing Christ. Not only is he submitted to and fully represents the One who sent him, but in coming he carries the authority of the One who sent him. He is the personal representative of Christ, humbly walking in the authority of Christ. This defines the true apostle.

Now we understand the importance of the following statement made by the Lord Jesus: *"For I have come down from heaven not to do my will but to do the will of him who sent me."* (John 6:38)

The Scriptures tell us He *"made himself nothing."* (Phil 2:7) This is speaking directly about Christ's submission to the will of another so that He might be an apostle. If someone truly is an apostle, they will indeed be emptied of self. A servant attitude in them toward others will be natural and unfeigned.

We often speak of Jesus *"laying aside his glory"*. What does this mean?

Amongst other mysteries, it does mean that He laid aside His eternal power, His eternal knowledge, and His eternal ability to be present everywhere as God. These eternal qualities of God are called omnipotence, omniscience, and omnipresence. These powers were Christ's as God, but He laid them aside. The only thing He did not lay aside was His identity – He remained who He was, the Son of God. In obedience to the Father He became a human baby, in a created body. Now He was dependent on a mother to feed and care for Him, and His parents to protect and provide for Him, under the watchful eye and sovereign providence of His Father.

The gospel says, *"And Jesus grew in wisdom..."* (Luke 2:52). As the Son of Man, he did not perform miracles or give amazing discourses and produce wise answers to difficult questions because of His own ability, but rather because He was full of the Holy Spirit. This is the same way in which you and I are to live and serve as sons of God. Notice that He performed no miracles, nor was He active in any public ministry prior to being baptised by John, when the Holy Spirit came upon him supernaturally.

Jesus said, *"All authority in heaven and earth has been given to me..."*. Notice the word *'given'*. The authority that Jesus exercised was not His own, because He had laid aside His glory. The authority and power that Jesus exercised on earth was that which was given to Him by God as His *apostle*. It was a conferred authority, a delegated authority – not His own. The reason the authority and power of God could rest upon the Christ was because of His submission – the submission of *a son to a father*.

So an apostle has a *delegated* authority, which is given to him because he has laid aside whatever authority he thought was his own. Thus, true apostolic authority is always *received*. It always rests properly upon those in submission to authority. This is the only true form of apostolic authority in the church, i.e. that which results from submission to another.

Any true apostle, prophet, or five-fold minister of Christ, must be able to say, like Christ, *"I have not come to do my (own) will, but the will of him who sent me"*. The true apostle does not live for himself, but for another. The true apostle does not represent himself when he speaks, but another. This true apostle fully and completely represents the Lord Jesus Christ, for he has faced and experienced the death of self which brings him to the place of being a submitted, yielded, humble, and dead man – dead-to-self in Christ, so that others may live. And it is the grace of God that works these things in His servants, both men and women – it is not the work of our own ability or desires.

The church, if it is to enjoy walking in apostolic grace, must also live by this principle of authority through submission, and life through dying to self.

Jesus, in commissioning His apostles, said, *"...as the father has sent me, so send I you."* (John 20:21) He had earlier said, *"He who receives you receives me, and he who receives me receives the one who sent me."* (Matt 10:40) Therefore the church, to be an apostolic people, must receive her apostles and be in harmony with them. The church must embrace unity of spirit with their purpose, must honour them, and be submitted to their message and way of life.

We have learned that for Jesus to be appointed high priest, He first had to be made an apostle. This required him to lay aside His glory and yield Himself completely to the will of Another, so that He could carry the authority of and represent that Person completely. Of course, we are talking about things that are timeless, things that have occurred in eternity. There never was a time that this was not the choice and position of the son of God. He has always been, *"the lamb that was slain from the foundation of the world."* (Revelation 13:8, 1 Peter 1:20)

But there is yet one more lesson we must learn. Before Jesus was made an apostle, He was first – *a son*.

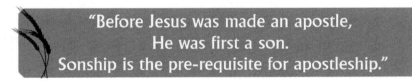

"Before Jesus was made an apostle,
He was first a son.
Sonship is the pre-requisite for apostleship."

Jesus as a Son

Sonship is really the pre-requisite for apostleship. There is something that sets a son apart from all others – he belongs. He is part and parcel of, not just the family, but the father. He is one with the father, and his view of things, and the desires of his heart, all have come from the father. In true sonship we have one who is like the father, one who is of the same essence and spirit as the father. In sonship we have one who has a heart for the father, and who will truly represent and stand for the father.

Allow me to digress for a moment. There is no sonship without the giving of the heart, just as the father's heart is for the son. In order of spiritual procession, however, it is the father's love which is first set upon the son, but the heart of a son has been made to respond to and embrace a father's love. The order of this procession we see reflected in the scriptures of Malachi the prophet: *"He (Elijah) will turn the hearts of the fathers to their children, and the hearts of the children to their fathers; or else I will come and strike the land with a curse."* (Mal 4:6)

My spiritual father, apostle Chuck Clayton, who hears the Lord say some of the most remarkable things at times, heard this: **"The reason we have not seen the fruit that we are looking for is that the fathers have not demonstrated their love to such a place that the sons are willing to lay down their own agendas."** The implications of this will need to be addressed by many people in ministry. I think one of the reasons for my own success in breaking through in the building of our ministry team based on such relationships, is that I did give my whole heart to my people, and persevered. I have had to correct and rebuke others amongst us for criticising and condemning each other, but I have not wavered in my belief in the validity of the genuine believers around me, no matter what their shortcomings.

The absence of this 'affection' of a father for sons in the ministry has been one of the great problems in the church. Too much emphasis has been placed, especially in some circles, on the need to be 'successful', to build one's own ministry, to pursue an ambitious understanding of personal giftedness, etc. In short, too many were raised in spiritual circumstances which taught them a different value system – one more like the dog-eat-dog business world where people strive for individual achievement, promotion, and personal advancement – but this was in the church! Over time a spirit of competition in the church has become lauded as 'a good thing', and few leaders had a heart for investing themselves in sons, or serving to make other people's ministries successful. But this is precisely the opposite of what the Spirit of Christ wants, and the opposite spirit of the apostolic church which His bride is called to be. Even a secular psychologist can tell you, there is no place for competition in a family! We need to stop being such fools.

Back to our main subject. To become an apostle, one must walk in a sonship relationship with the one who appoints him. No apostle has the heart that is required of an apostle unless he is a son to the one who is over him. Thus, Christ is the apostle of the father, and others have become apostles of Christ. Christ was a son to the father, and the 12 became sons to Christ.

We don't often stop to think of Christ as a father, but in more than one place the scriptures do refer to Him as such. The prophet Isaiah stated, *"...to us a son is given... And he will be called... Everlasting Father."* (Isa 9:6) We also read in the New Testament where the Son is quoted as saying,

"Here am I, and the children God has given me." (Heb 2:13b)

Thus the disciples as spiritual sons to Jesus would come to the place where, knowing His love for them, they came to love and trust Him so deeply they would yield their wills to Him, and become fully His apostles. Sonship is the spirit of apostleship, which like Christ, qualifies us for priestly service.

The church is not truly and properly expressing the life of God in this world unless we are walking in a spirit of sonship. Apostolic Christianity *is* sonship – each of us is meant to be in submission, not only to Christ whom we cannot see, but also in relationship with those He appoints to lead us, whom we can see and talk to, and who represent Christ to us. We must be sons to these our fathers, and in serving them and walking with them we discover the apostolic life and power of Jesus Christ.

This is what Christianity is all about – the spirit of Sonship. This is *apostolic* Christianity.

Authority Through Submission

It is most important to understand that true authority comes not only through *submission*, but also through *relationship*. It is not enough to be in submission to someone over you in the Lord; one must also have a right relationship with the person to whom one is submitted, if you would carry genuine spiritual authority.

I am referring here to the relationship of an apostle to the one who appoints him, if he is to be an apostle in any meaningful sense of the term, and if he is to carry true spiritual authority.

There are other forms of authority, but they are not apostolic. For example, there are institutional forms of authority in Christian organisations, but these are not the same as apostolic authority. Such authority should be respected, but it should not be confused with the personal apostolic authority of Christ, the head of the church, received by apostles so as to serve Christ and His people.

The Scriptures instruct us to respect everyone in authority, and go so far as to call governments and the like God's delegated authorities, but this is not the same as apostolic authority. For apostolic authority to occur, it must not only be delegated, but must also be the result of both the submission and relationship we have been speaking of between Christ and His servants.

True apostles are not appointed by denominational institutions or the convenient arrangements of men in ministry – real apostles are personal appointments of Jesus Christ alone, and result from a process of submission to Him, and long development of heart relationship with Him.

The apostle John quotes Jesus: *"I no longer call you servants, because a servant does not know his master's business. Instead, I have called you friends, for everything that I learned from my Father I have made known to you. You did not choose me, but I chose you and appointed you to go and bear fruit..."* (John 15:15-16). He said, *"I chose you and appointed you."* He also said, *"I have called you friends."* He went on to say, *"Then the father will give you whatever you ask in my name."* All of these statements are very personal, and quite relational.

I remember when the Lord Jesus appeared to me in 1997 and gave me a commission to take an apostolic message to the nations, there was something else He said that was even more important. I know it was more important because, not only was it His final statement to me, but somehow it was impressed upon me as if He had said it first, rather than last. What He said was, "Keep looking into the eyes of Jesus Christ."

To look into someone's eyes is the most intimate thing you can do. This is a far more intimate request than to simply look into things such as ideas, or even just to look into the face of someone. This calls for greater intimacy, a more personal connection. If I am to do well, or perhaps if I am to be able to do *at all* what I have been given to do, this intimacy is needed. We cannot say enough about the importance of right personal relationships for apostolic authority to be effective.

Here we must try and understand how personal and intimate is the relationship between God the Son and God the Father. Without deep intimacy in this personal relationship, God would not be God, God could not be Holy, and Christ could not save you from your sins.

This first apostle had to walk in a deeply personal and intimate relationship. Not just any relationship either, but the relationship of a son to a father, or else He could never have been an apostle, nor the saviour of the world. If we want to walk in apostolic grace, and exercise apostolic authority, we need to understand the relational nature and foundation of the faith we hold.

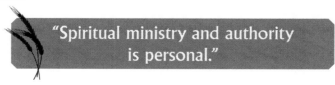

"Spiritual ministry and authority is personal."

This brings us to see that *ministry* and *authority* is personal. For a long time 'the church', as most of us have known it, has been largely institutional. In this we have lost the proper understanding of just how personal ministry and ministry authority is meant to be. We have grown up in denominational churches where authority to minister and hold leadership positions was conferred by institutional processes. Unless one completed the denominational training, and received the denominational approval through being sufficiently conformed to denominational norms, they were not approved for the work of the ministry, and could not carry titles such as Reverend or Pastor, and did not have certificates of ordination.

But the ministry given to Jesus Christ was not given to Him because he had the ability to do the work, such as the ability to teach, or the faith to work miracles, or even the willingness to suffer. No, it was given to the one person alone who had the relationship with the Father that truly counted.

Christ had to be a *son* over God's house. (Heb 3:6) Without this relationship of a deeply personal and intimate nature, a relationship involving the submission of the will to a father, there can be no apostle, and there is no personal mandate for ministry.

This personal and intimate relationship of full submission is acceptable in only one form, and that is *sonship*. It was necessary that Christ be a son to a father, or He could not be the Christ. Likewise it is essential that you and I walk in the same spirit of this sonship, or we can never truly be what we are called to be. We will never properly represent Christ as Lord or carry His authority unless we also are sons to a father.

This sonship has to be seen in practice, not just in theory. Anyone can say he is walking with God as a son, yet be deceived. It is in the way we walk with those over us in the Lord that shows whether we have the spirit of sonship in the heart, not just the imagination. As the Apostle John said, *"This is how we know who the children of God are and who the children of the devil are: anyone who does not do what is right is not a child of God; nor is anyone who does not love his brother."* (1 John 3:10) John further explained, *"For anyone who does not love his brother, whom he has seen, cannot love God, whom he has not seen."* (1 John 4:20) This is my point. Anyone who truly serves Christ will show it in the way he serves his leaders.

God did not establish an institution in the earth so as to bring salvation to us; rather, He sent His son. There had to be a man for this task – the second Adam. In the same way, Christ did not commission an institutional religious system to carry apostolic authority. Ministries and ministry anointings are gifts of grace, given to men and women who represent Christ. Christ's authority is conferred upon individuals for the ministry; these are personal appointments. God gives these things to people, not institutions.

Today, Christ in His ascension appoints apostles, prophets, evangelists, pastors and teachers for the service of representing Christ to His people, equipping His people, and providing leadership for His people. And like Christ's appointment by the Father, these appointments are *personal*. It is men and women who must arise to do the work of the ministry. But only those who learn the way of submission, which includes submission to others over them in the Lord, ever carry an *apostolic* authority. The Holy Spirit is leading us to find this relational intimacy, the true spirit of sonship, so that we can truly reveal God the Father and the Son in accordance with our call.

In the centuries prior to Christ there had been many High Priests of the previous order. But when Christ, the fullness of God's revelation came, He fulfilled all those things that had been previously established. They were merely types and shadows of the good things that were to come, and He replaced the temporary old covenant priesthood with a better one. That old priesthood no longer pertains as a means for anyone to approach God, not even Jewish people. It was declared obsolete, and has been taken away. (Heb 8:13) The previous high priests had been appointed by the law, but now there is but one High Priest over God's house – not a temporary one appointed by the law, but an everlasting one appointed by God's oath. (Heb 7:23-28)

Thus, a son appeared over God's house.

He was, and remains, *"faithful to the one who appointed him"* (Heb 3:2), and whilst Moses was faithful as a servant in all God's house, *"Christ is faithful as a son over God's house."* (Heb 3:6) This faithfulness 'as a son' is the required measure for the house of God in the new covenant. And sonship has another advantage – it creates a sense of ownership, but without covetousness, possessiveness, or selfishness. As sons we have an inheritance, so we gladly carry responsibility for God's house. It is 'ownership' without grasping and striving for selfish possession, gain, or advantage. We already own it all, and best of all, there is authority – the authority of a father – in the house. The spirit of sonship produces good stewardship.

This is why no apostle appears in Bible history before Christ. Christ was the first apostle, because apostleship, and the true apostolic faith of which it is the foundation, requires sonship. The spirit and grace of His sonship must be in us all.

Testimony

Trisha Bosel
Member of Peace Christian Church,
Rockhampton, Australia.

I joined the Peace fellowship in 1991, and am very grateful to the Lord for John's love, integrity, and non-compromising stand for Christ which have shaped my life and relationship with Jesus and God the Father, and brought me from religion and bondage to freedom and life in Christ.

Satan destroyed my father, and in the process our family suffered greatly. I carried a lot of woundedness in my heart which I had buried within. Coming to Peace has been a transforming journey for me primarily because of the grace that God gave John and his love for us all as he has led us on this journey. I was baptised not many months after joining Peace, and God has gently and persistently been restoring and sanctifying my heart.

To have a spiritual father has been central to my maturing as a Christian. God's love, gentle kindness, and patient compassion are evident in John, as well as the firmness to discipline & his intolerance to sin. I am very thankful for the correction I have received because it has kept me from evil. I have been affirmed and given opportunities to grow and mature as a Christian. A measure of John's love for us is also seen in the lives of the other leaders and their love for him, each other, and us.

When I understood that I was a son and not a servant in my Father's House, and that I had an inheritance, I was liberated from the servant mentality which I had had all my Christian life, and it totally changed my relationship with Father God. It was truly transforming.

Once when John spoke from his heart to us, he said that we at Peace were special to him, and that he held a deep affection in his heart for us. When John spoke this declaration of love to us, I experienced a deep sense of peace and security. When we were going through a difficult period in our fellowship many years prior, God had told me that John and the people of Peace were "inextricably bound together". While I didn't fully grasp the significance of this at the time, John had always taught us that the promises that God has given him are for us all.

In 1999 I was diagnosed with an aggressive tumour in my breast. The love and prayer I received from John and Hazel, the Peace leadership, and my whole church family, saved my life. I can never be thankful enough! I never knew I was so deeply loved as I was through that entire time. I was later told that the person who did the biopsy on the cancerous lump believed in miracles because of my recovery. John has taught us to love each other and to pray for each other and to be knitted together so as to fulfill Christ's prayer about oneness.

I know and experience the love of Christ and His forgiveness among my church family. This is so precious to me. And as a loving father, John desires the very best for all his spiritual children, and this is the formation of the likeness of Christ in each of us. To this end he sets before us the example of his own life as he passionately follows Christ, loves us, freely shares the rich revelation from God's word with us, exhorts us constantly to love each other, and to live holy lives for Christ our Lord.

Patricia Bosel.

CHAPTER 4

WHAT IS APOSTOLIC CHRISTIANITY?

*"He who receives you receives me, and he
who receives me receives the one who sent me."*

(Matthew 10:40)

Concerning the term *'apostolic'*, can I say this is a most important word –
one that is not like any other nor has an equal, even though, for example, it
is not uncommon to see conferences advertised as 'apostolic and prophetic'
conferences.

The Power and Meaning of the Word *Apostolic*

Originally the word apostolic stood alone, unlike any other word, and with
an awe-filled meaning so unusual and exceptional that it is quite difficult to
define; yet the meaning of the term is central and intrinsic to the faith itself.
This word 'apostolic' stands alongside the words 'Christian' and 'church'
and speaks of something absolutely huge, historic, and foundational.

And the word truly has no equal. Arthur Katz said that if we lose the
meaning of the word 'apostolic' this would threaten the loss of the meaning
of the faith itself. There is something wonderful here that we must really
come to terms with.

Because of the modern use of the term 'apostolic', we find the word being
used in different ways, and with two very different kinds of meaning. It has

one meaning when we put it alongside the word 'prophetic', for instance. In that case it is being used to simply describe a particular kind of giftedness, or a particular kind of ministry.

But it does have another meaning, with a greater depth altogether, when used in its classic sense to describe the indescribable. In this case, it refers to two things:

Firstly, to the timeless and immutable (unchangeable) nature of the life that God has given us as a people, in His Son, and which cannot be separated from that which is the faith itself. To this we will return.

Secondly, it also refers to the unchanging method God uses, whereby in everything He does (whether in creation, or intervening in the affairs of mankind, and also in the provision of our costly salvation) God's nature is such that He always seeks to express Himself through others and fulfil Himself in others. Thus, the Father sent the Son to speak on behalf of the Father and to do His works in the world, just as the Son had created all things on behalf of the Father in the beginning. Then, after Christ's work was finished, the Holy Spirit was sent to represent the Father and the Son. And this process must be reproduced in us. Christ must be fully formed in us, we must learn to represent and speak on behalf of the Father and Son, and we must by faith and prayer determine the will of God and open the way for the works of the Holy Spirit.

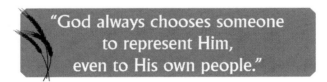

"God always chooses someone to represent Him, even to His own people."

This is God's *apostolic method,* functioning as a result of His apostolic nature. When the children of Israel cried out in Egypt for God to save them, He sent Moses. At that time He said to Moses, *"I have heard them crying out... So I have come down to rescue them... So now, go. I am sending you...."* (Exodus 3: 7-10). He has always chosen to have someone represent Him so as to accomplish His purpose in the world. Therefore He chose Abraham, David, Jeremiah, and many others. And He always chooses someone to represent Him even to His own people who know Him personally and who walk with Him – which is why He appointed apostles, and still appoints them today.

Each one of us without exception must not only walk personally with the Lord, but know how to receive the Lord in the leaders He appoints, and in the apostolic fathers He sends to us. Jesus said to His apostles, *"He who receives you receives me, and he who receives me receives the one who sent me."* (Matt 10:40)

The Nicene Creed

The early church fathers must have understood this. The Nicene Creed was produced after large numbers of church leaders, fathers in the faith, were brought together to discuss important issues in the years leading up to 325AD. They had gathered from all over the known world so as to agree on an understanding of just who was the Christ, because whilst in many places good doctrine was being taught, there were also heresies everywhere. They produced a wonderful statement known as the Nicene Creed, describing Christ Jesus as *"The only Son of God, eternally begotten of the Father, God from God, Light from Light, true God from true God, begotten, not made, one in Being with the Father."*

It is a fabulous statement, in which they included the following: *"We believe in one, holy, catholic (universal), and apostolic Church."* They used four terms to describe the church. The church is *one*; the church is *holy*; the church is *universal*; and the church is *apostolic*. They placed this word *apostolic* alongside other essential descriptors of the church. For them it was as important to say that the church was apostolic as to say that it was one, and holy, and universal. That makes the term *apostolic* a vital one indeed.

So what does *apostolic* mean? Notice they did not say the church is pastoral; nor did they say the church is prophetic, or evangelistic, etc. But the word *apostolic* used in a whole-of-church context such as this shows that the term has a greater meaning altogether – one that stands alongside terms like 'holy'. Please understand that whereas in Ephesians 4 the Scriptures speak of the Lord appointing apostles along with prophets, evangelists, pastors and teachers, this is describing a gifting, a duty, a calling, a responsibility, a work of service, that is given to individuals to represent Christ and minister His graces.

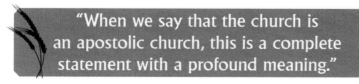

"When we say that the church is an apostolic church, this is a complete statement with a profound meaning."

But the term apostolic in the greater sense applies to the whole of the faith, to the whole of the church, and to a certain kind of grace that each and every one of us is meant to walk in –whether you are an apostle or not. So when we say that the church is an *apostolic church*, or that God's people are all meant to be an *apostolic people*, this is a complete statement with a profound meaning. To say instead, as we often hear, that the church is an 'apostolic and prophetic' people, is to miss the whole point of what it means to be apostolic.

Of course it is true we are indeed a prophetic people. We are all called to function in prophetic gifts as a naturally prophetic people, because we all are meant to live in, and minister out of, Holy Spirit enabled prophetic senses, graces, and abilities every day, just as we are also called to live and serve with apostolic type grace giftedness as well. But we must see there is another level of purpose altogether in the term *apostolic*, defining something that no other word defines, and so no other word stands alongside it as an equal. God's people may have prophetic and evangelistic and pastoral *functions*, but the church must have an apostolic *life*, which we all share – and that is a different thing altogether.

To support the importance of what is being said here, I quote from Arthur Katz, to whom I earlier referred. In the preface to his book *Apostolic Foundations*, Katz wrote:

> **"I have a very special respect** for the word *apostolic*. To lose its meaning threatens the loss of the faith itself. It is not a word that is easy to define, and yet there is something about this word and its meaning that is at the heart of the faith. It is an ultimate word, and it is a word that needs to be resuscitated, and not be thought of as merely a denominational identification. It is a word that pulsates with glory, and therefore we need to seek for and rescue the apostolic foundation – or we will not have a church worthy of that word."

> "Like every great biblical word, we will not find the definition in a dictionary. We need rather to be *apprehended* by the genius of what that word represents. It is a seeking out and restoring of all that was once authentic, all that was held dear, all that was believed, all that was understood, and all that was vital in the first church. There is something pungent about the word *apostolic* that brings to mind the heart, the spirit and the sense of the church when it was at its glory. The church was apostolic at its inception and needs to be so at its *conclusion*. Indeed, only an apostolic church can stand and overcome, and by that witness, testify to and penetrate an obdurate

and resistant remnant of Israel in the mystery of God at the end of this age."[1]

Katz continues to explore the subject in his Introduction to the same book:

"There is no word that should be more alive in our consciousness than the word *apostolic*. It is a word that says everything about the nature and the genius of the church, and all that God expects from it, and intends for it... It is a word that we need to apprehend and be apprehended by. It is a word that has fallen into disuse and needs to be restored, and that restoration is not going to be cheap – but it is worth *everything*.

"Nothing of any eternal consequence or immediate value can be effected in the earth independent of it... God is jealous over the word *apostolic*. The Lord designates Himself as the "High Priest and Apostle" of our confession. If the church is built upon the foundation of the apostles and prophets, then we need to appropriate the depths of the meaning of that word in order that we might be part of what makes that up, and the configuration of things apostolic that makes the church the church."[2]

To try and understand this idea so crucial to the faith has been the subject of my heartfelt prayer all these years. Just what does it mean to be *an apostolic people*? It was through asking this question, more than any other, which brought me to the understanding I now hold as to what we are meant to be as a people, and how we are meant to walk together.

The answers to this question have mostly to do with what we *are*, not what we *do*. It is not what activities we undertake, gifts we exercise, or institutions we build that define whether we have apostolic grace, and are truly an apostolic people. Rather, it is how we think and feel, i.e. the heart attitudes and values that we hold and act out of as Christians. In particular, it is about how we actually relate to God and *to each other*. If we can understand that, we begin to understand *apostolic* Christianity, and find that it is all about relationships. Apostolic Christianity is *relational* Christianity; and the apostolic faith is about relationships from beginning to end.

---

1   From the Preface to *Apostolic Foundations* by Arthur Katz
2   From the Introduction to *Apostolic Foundations* by Arthur Katz

> ## "The Lord is not only restoring apostles, He is restoring apostolic Christianity."

I began my search for this answer sometime in 1995. By this time I had been preaching for over five years a constantly growing message that apostles were being restored to the church, when suddenly I came to an astounding realisation – that the Lord was not only restoring apostles to the church, but restoring apostolic Christianity itself; that the apostolic *nature* of the church was to be restored; that all of God's people were meant to be an *apostolic* people.

This insight gave rise to a lot of questions. What does it mean to be *apostolic*? What does it mean for the church to be an apostolic *people*? And if something is to be restored to us, what is it that is missing? Or, what is it that is wrong with us? If we have not been apostolic, what have we been?

From 1995 until well past the year 2000, I kept peering intently into the things of the Spirit, and pondering this question. I kept my heart and ears open to the Lord seeking an answer, yet heaven seemed to be strangely silent for a time. But after a while I began to hear that still small voice as if speaking from behind me. It did not seem to be directly answering my question, but rather saying things of interest which I took to be additional pieces of information. I wrote them down, and kept asking the questions.

Eventually I had a list of things, all of which I felt the still small voice of the Spirit of God had given me concerning the nature of an apostolic people. But I thought of them as extras, rather than the main answer. And then the light dawned. These *were* the main things!

In a moment, I will share with you what the truth was that finally dawned, but in the meantime, let me explain why I was so slow to hear.

I had been looking for the wrong kind of answer. Like many people, I had been conditioned to expect a *power* answer when considering the term *apostolic*. I had on many occasions heard preachers proclaim that we needed to see a restoration of apostolic power and apostolic authority to the church. It usually meant that we, and the preacher, wanted to see signs, wonders, and miracles. We wanted to see multitudes come to Christ, and wanted to see towns, cities, and nations turned upside-down for Jesus – and we equated these things with obtaining apostolic 'power'.

But this is not the same thing as being an apostolic people, and a lot of people make this mistake. It is commonly assumed that being 'apostolic' is defined by the kind of things we do in ministry. If someone plants churches, or heals the sick, or sends out evangelists, or goes out as a missionary, it is assumed they must be apostles. If a church or congregation operates in things such as church planting and miracles, it is assumed they are an 'apostolic' church. But this is not necessarily so. Being apostolic is never determined just by the kind of things we do. In fact, there are many people who do these very things who are certainly not apostolic; some of them are not Christian at all.

No, whether we are an apostolic people and walking in apostolic grace is determined by what we *are*, and the way we *think*, and the way we *relate* – never by what we do. We are meant to be walking in apostolic *grace* as an apostolic *people*, sharing an apostolic *life*. What determines whether or not we are doing this is not found in external and physical things, but in internal and spiritual things – things of the heart.

But there has always been preaching urging the need for the church to walk in the grace and power of the early apostolic church. Where then is the apostolic power of the church to be found?

Ask yourself this question. Which person, amongst all who have ever lived, exercised the greatest power? Who, amongst all men and women who have walked the earth, carried the greatest authority? The answer is, of course, the one who walked on water, rebuked the wind and waves, turned water into wine, raised the dead, cleansed the lepers, gave sight to the blind, raised Lazarus when his corpse was already putrefying, and who was Himself ultimately raised from His own death and ascended into glory. His name is Jesus.

What was the secret of the power and authority that Jesus exercised? As we have already concluded in the last chapter, Jesus did not exercise an authority that was His own – He did not work in His own power. Rather, He carried the authority of another. The power was His Father's power, flowing through Him by the Holy Spirit, and made effective by His submission to the one who had authority over Him.

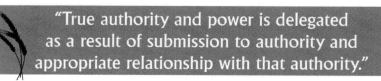

"True authority and power is delegated as a result of submission to authority and appropriate relationship with that authority."

In other words, true authority and power is delegated as a result of submission to authority, and appropriate relationship with that authority. This is how the most authoritative and powerful man, our Saviour, exercised His ministry. And this is how the church and every believer, and every apostle, prophet, evangelist, pastor, and teacher, must exercise their ministry too.

Authority and power is available to the church, but the full expression of apostolic power and authority will only come when the church as a people is again sharing an apostolic life, in submission to her apostles, with these apostles in submission to Christ.

Plainly, apostolic power comes through submission. And the best illustration of this is something that happened in the life of our Saviour, whom we have already seen is the greatest example of a man exercising the authority and power of God. The story recorded in the Gospels tells of a Centurion who had a servant who was sick. The Saviour was implored to heal the servant. When Jesus chose to go to the house, the Centurion's word to Jesus was, "Just say the word, and my servant will be healed." How did the Centurion feel so sure about this? He understood that because Jesus lived in submission to divine authority, he had the authority to command and release the power of that divine authority. The Centurion illustrated the principle when he said, *"I myself am a man under authority, with soldiers under me. I tell this one, 'Go,' and he goes; and that one, 'come,' and he comes."* (Matthew 8:9) What was the Centurion talking about? He was illustrating his understanding of how authority works, and showing his deep spiritual insight into the source of Jesus' power. He knew that his own authority to command soldiers came from himself being under the command of more senior soldiers. And he knew that because Jesus was also *"a man under authority"* (i.e. in submission to the authority of His Father) He had all the privileges to exercise the power and authority of the One to whom He was submitted.

This is the secret to apostolic authority, and its only true source. If the church desires to see again the fullness of apostolic power demonstrated by the early church, then we must again be a people of one heart and mind, walking in love with one another, in submission to the leadership of our apostles, with the whole Church, including those apostles, in submission to Christ. This is the way of God. This is the scriptural position, and we have no right to demand that the church operate in any other way.

All of this is confirmed in Luke's writing in the Acts of the Apostles. In the months following the day of Pentecost, and with the church having grown to be many thousands of people in Jerusalem, the following description was made of the life of that early church. *"All the believers were one in heart and mind. No one claimed that any of his possessions was his own, but they shared everything they had. With great power the apostles continued to testify to the resurrection of the Lord Jesus, and much grace was upon them all."* (Acts 4:32-33)

The phrase, *"With great power the apostles..."* is very telling. It follows on from a description of the state of the believers as a whole. There is a nexus – a bond, an invisible but definite connection – between, on the one hand, the extent of the authority, power, and achievements of apostles, and the quality of the submission, faith, and prayers of the people of God on the other.

The Critical 'Nexus' Between Apostles and Believers

I have long realised that for effective ministry, for victory in spiritual warfare and the progress of the gospel, the believers as a whole need the apostles, and the apostles need the people of God. Neither is sufficient in themselves, i.e. neither is self-contained, each is not complete without the other. Apostles who do not have a people in agreement, in harmony, praying for them, fighting together the fight of faith, agreeing with them, walking with them, cannot do very much. The work will be less effective and seemingly less significant. The apostle needs to be served, to be upheld, and to be strengthened, by a believing people. When we have such a people, God releases great power through apostles.

The apostle James was put to death by the sword, but in the same situation Peter was delivered because *"the church was earnestly praying to God for him."* (Acts 12:5) The apostle Paul in his letters was always pleading for the prayers of his people, not only for his own needs, but especially so that he could find freedom of speech and speak boldly, and make the gospel understood (Eph 6:19-20). Without such a people, an apostle is limited and can even be greatly hindered from succeeding in what should be achieved.

On the other hand, the people of God without apostles will be rudderless, open to every wind of doctrine, and led in many directions by well-meaning people who do not have the apostolic graces for the unity and overall direction of the body of Christ. Many denominations are under the leadership of such well-meaning people, who may be ministers of Christ, and may be very gifted and hard-working, but they are not apostles. Without apostles, the people too remain greatly limited, even hindered, often trapped and despoiled by the enemy. To make it worse, very often the tradition and religious institutionalism of denominations and other

Christian organisations prevent the people from seeing their need for apostles, and from recognising them when Christ sends them.

An Example Illustrating this 'Nexus'

I have a personal story which illustrates this nexus between apostle and people that I am speaking of. In the year 2000, Cindy Jacobs, an American well-known for her public ministry of prophecy and intercession, came to Australia to speak at a conference. She publicly brought a strong prophecy concerning a call to prayer over the political outlook in Australia. She specified about a dozen prayer points, but the gist of the prophecy was that the Australian church had to pray fervently concerning the next election, otherwise there was a danger that the wrong political party would be elected at that time. Without identifying any parties, she prophesied concerning the major parties that one, if elected, would help Australia go in the direction that was spiritually favourable for the nation, and this was in accord with what the Lord wanted. But if the other party was elected, this would take Australia on a spiritually adverse track contrary to our best interests.

What was wonderful was that the church everywhere seemed to really take up these prayers. All over the land people were praying in accordance with this word. A printed version of her prophecy found its way to us in Rockhampton, and we took up these prayers also. After some weeks, in a period when I was busy at home amongst our own people, the call of God came to me suddenly one day. I was to go to Canberra, our National Capital, and spend seven days in prayer in Parliament House so as to seek God for the knowledge of His will, and to believe God for the outcomes that He desired in the election which would soon be held .

So I went, and every day for seven days I was at the door of Parliament House when it opened to the public at 9 a.m. Once inside, I prayer-walked every part of the building that was accessible. I sat in the public gallery of the House of Representatives and prayed there. I then went and sat in the public gallery of the Senate and prayed, then to the main committee room and prayed in the public gallery there. After that I prayer-walked the roof of the building, and then all the surrounding streets. When after several hours I had finished all of this, I did it all again. Every day, two, three, or four times, I persevered with this process.

At times I felt led to include other prayers. I prayer-walked Commonwealth Avenue from Parliament House to the City Centre. I went to the old Parliament House and prayed through that building. I prayer-walked Anzac Parade, pausing to pray at a number of the memorials but in particular the Vietnam War Memorial. I went to the office of the Canberra Times and prayed and prophesied concerning how the media of this nation in the coming days will aid the gospel. I also went to the Telstra Tower on Black Mountain, from where there is a 360° view of Canberra and all its surrounds, and prayed over the nation from there, as well as from the Mount Ainslie Lookout. But most of those long hours I spent inside the Parliament building, interceding, pleading, listening, looking, longing for God to act – and believing too, which is the essential part.

I did not trust myself to really know the will of God concerning political parties and elections. Of the seven days, I spent the first four to five days seeking to know the Lord's mind. We all have our own ideas, and it is easy for us to assume what God wants. I knew I could not do this. I was not willing to pray simply in accordance with what I thought was good, nor in accordance with how I might have preferred to vote. I had to know the mind of the Lord. The four to five days I spent praying for the grace to discern what the Lord wanted was really important to me – my submission to His will and a clear inner witness I had to find, for conscience sake, and so as to be confident of the position I would have to take. Finally, I had to make a decision as to what I believed God was saying, and pray in accordance with that decision. I took out pen and notebook, and began to record what I heard as I listened and allowed Him to speak.

Here is an abbreviation of what He gave: The Liberal Party was to be the blue-ribbon party in politics. The Labor Party was to have no traction in the polls. The Democrats were to have their power destroyed, were to be divided, and have their numbers halved in the Senate. I was to pray for the National party to be given the balance of power in the Senate. In addition to this, there were many other points. Much prayer was needed concerning the staff that worked at Parliament House, not just the elected representatives but the cleaners, the security staff, and other public servants. There were prayers to remove the occultists and people with other special interest 'agendas,' and there were prayers to bring faithful praying Christians, dedicated intercessors, onto the staff of Parliament House, who would in turn pray much for the government, the nation, and the public service.

On this day the Prime Minister called the election, which was to be held some weeks later. Back home on election day, some of us spent the day in the prayer room. I heard the Lord say, "I have given you 90% of what you have asked for."

The Liberal party won the election, and indeed the Labor Party had no traction in the electorate, nor did they for a long time afterward. Not much else was visible on the day, but the Lord had said He had granted me 90% of what I had asked for. Just five months after the election, the Democrats in the Senate began the most incredible bickering among themselves – it was very public and seemingly irrational, and in a period of just weeks the power of the party was destroyed, half their senators had resigned from the party, and the Democrats had ceased to be a power in politics at all. In the following election three years later, through unusual circumstances, the National party had an additional senator unexpectedly elected which gave the National party the balance of power in the Senate.

The idea that the National party could have the balance of power in the Senate was the most unlikely outcome of all in Australian politics. It was embarrassing to even suggest that such a thing was possible. I know, because some months before that particular election, the Federal leader of the National Party, the Hon. John Anderson, was visiting Rockhampton and made a public statement to the media concerning roads. He and the television cameras just happened to be on the corner a few doors away. So we invited him in to visit for a few minutes. He said there were problems facing the National party because of the changing demographics of Australia. I told him that I had for several years been praying and believing that God would give the National party the balance of power in the Senate. He was somewhat embarrassed, and I was also, because we both knew this was not a rational position. He politely thanked me for my prayers. But within a few short months of that conversation, a subsequent election was held, and the National party did indeed win the balance of power in the Senate.

None of this is a comment on where things are right now, or what God might be saying about Australian politics today. All of this occurred several elections back, and things have changed. I am simply telling the story to illustrate a very important point with respect to the life of the church.

That point is this: I believe the reason the Lord called me to go to Canberra to spend time dealing with such issues and taking hold of God for grace was because the church was praying.

I believe when the church is praying and the people of God are in one accord, the Lord activates apostles and prophets. It might look like an apostle has done some great deed, or that a prophet has brought a mighty word, but I believe the best and greatest of the works of God through apostles and prophets come as a result of the people of God positioning themselves. I think that without the Cindy Jacobs' prophecy, and without the people of God believing and praying into it fervently and sincerely, the call to go to Canberra and deal with these things with apostolic authority would not have come.

We need to respect this nexus between the apostle and Christ's people and work to recreate the effectiveness of it. Apostles are needed to build up the body of Christ, and other church leaders need to look for them. We need to lay again the apostolic foundation. The church must seek to be in harmony with her apostles, and devote herself to walking in the way of the life and faith of the apostles that Christ sends. These apostles will serve to bring God's people into freedom, maturity, and our shared inheritance.

Freedom! – The first principle of apostolic ministry

I can't say for sure whether freedom is really the *first* principle of apostolic ministry, but for me it is. My role is to open the 'eyes of the blind' by revealing to God's people the spiritual freedom they have in Christ, and to help believers come into that freedom. I create freedom within my own ministry structures, and I always tell people, "You are free to come in, and you are also free to leave. But if you stay, my intention is to show you how to live for Christ, how to walk with God's people, and how to conduct yourself in the household of faith. This is not a free-for-all. Proper spiritual disciplines, respect for others, and submission to authority will bring you into true freedom."

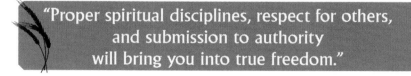

"Proper spiritual disciplines, respect for others, and submission to authority will bring you into true freedom."

Apostolic ministry, or an apostolic Church, requires authority and discipline, but without control. This is why all leadership structures and church life itself must be based on meaningful, healthy relationships in which authority is recognised and honoured. Building relationally is what apostles have been given the grace to do, but it is a learning, growing, maturing process.

I wrote earlier that in answer to my questioning, I began hearing the Lord concerning what it really meant to be an apostolic people, and ended up with a list of things which I afterwards came to realise was the main answer to the question. This is what He gave me.

The following list, "The Dynamic Qualities of an Apostolic People" has been revised and reproduced from chapter 11 of my first book, *The Apostolic Revelation*. Those things listed are the values and ethics which are foundational to the nature of the apostolic church. They are the true characteristics of an apostolic people. These are energising principles, and are clearly part of God's revelation for the life of His people. As we submit to Christ, and learn His way, the power of God flows through such a people.

The Dynamic Qualities of an Apostolic People

The word dynamic is used here purposefully. *Dynamic* refers to a motive force, something that is potent, and energetic. Here are described the specific qualities and the nature of the shared life of an apostolic people.

One Heart and One Mind:

An apostolic people is marked by a great desire for unity, although unity is not just an end in itself. The purpose of unity is not only to establish love amongst the brethren, but also to obtain intimacy with God and to bring the world to faith in Christ. Even so, the love and acceptance of one another is real. Apostles will bring unity to the church, both within each local fellowship, and across the body. This is one of the great purposes of apostles, and no mature apostle is without this burden – a burden for the whole body. The apostolic goal is the unity of the faith and the maturity of the church, spoken of in Ephesians 4:13, which is to be built upon the unity of the Spirit for which we are meant to strive and maintain.

Humility, Teachableness, Submission:

These values become our very life when we have the Spirit of Jesus. No one is able to change their own heart, but as we receive Jesus, we receive His Spirit, and are enabled by the Holy Spirit to live and think and feel as Jesus would. There cannot be such a thing as an apostolic people who are not teachable and in submission to their leaders. Without these qualities there can be no unity, and there can be no visitation of the Spirit in power. Without teachableness there will be no growth in grace, and without submission there is no genuine authority in the believer. Without these graces in the heart, truth cannot be received. Humility precedes both of these qualities, and is essential for apostolic power.

Honouring Leaders:

An apostolic people honours their leadership, not only because of the biblical command, but because this is a primary source of life and blessing which God has ordained. The ability to give honour is a mark of maturity, wisdom, and a pure heart. The impure always struggle to give honour, because it is against the nature of the flesh. In community, the mutual honouring of one another makes for a beautiful and peaceful experience of life. This is the wisdom that comes from heaven, mentioned in James 3:17-18, and is the opposite of the striving of envy and selfish ambition that disturbs many Christian fellowships and brings in every evil.

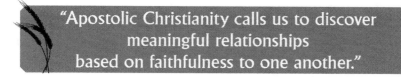

"Apostolic Christianity calls us to discover meaningful relationships based on faithfulness to one another."

Heart Relationship:

In traditional churches, relationship is often based on convenience. The relationship continues while it is convenient, but when it no longer suits, people walk away. Many Christians effectively live for themselves, and the result is that relationships are shallow. Apostolic Christianity calls us to discover meaningful relationships, based on faithfulness to one another. We are to become devoted to one another, as the apostle instructed, *"Be devoted to one another in brotherly love. Honor one another above yourselves."* (Romans 12:10) We are to be brothers and sisters, mothers and fathers to one another in the faith. Effectively, this is a relationship of the heart – we give our hearts to one another.

Accountability, Transparency, Openness, Honesty:

Amongst an apostolic people, there is accountability through relationship. We are to live lives of transparency with one another. For this to be effective, we have to come to the place where we trust others. The Bible says that love always trusts, but of course this can only be the experience of those in community, where the issues that divide have been worked through, our hearts are at rest, and we accept one another. In community, and the apostolic faith, individuals do not pursue a private agenda. We live for the good of other people, and we are honest about ourselves, our purpose, and our motives.

Love:

The early apostolic church was recognised by the believers and their enemies alike as being a people of amazing love for one another. They were fulfilling the law of Christ. The church's enemies were chagrined by the love the believers had for one another, and this love was foundational to the power evident in the early church. There is no other way to turn the world upside-down, and the apostolic church succeeded in doing this in one generation. This is the call of God upon today's church, to be an apostolic people in our generation, marked by the amazing, selfless, sacrificial love which is Christ in us.

Laying Down Our Lives for the Brethren:

Christ calls us to love one another, and to do so in the same way that He loved us. He loved us to the point of laying down His life for us, as He remarked to His disciples, *"Greater love has no one than this, that he lay down his life for his friends."* (John 15:13) The apostle John later wrote this challenging appeal, *"This is how we know what love is: Jesus Christ laid down his life for us. And we ought to lay down our lives for our brothers."* (1 John 3:16) This describes the spirit of apostolic Christianity. Do not be surprised if God calls some of His people to supreme sacrifice. More to the point, understand that the love of our hearts toward one another should be such that we would count the lives of other people worthy of sacrifice. This at least will call forth obedience to John's next statement, *"If anyone has material possessions and sees his brother in need but has no pity on him, how can the love of God be in him? Dear children, let us not love with words or tongue but with actions and in truth."* (1 John 3:17-18) This is the spirit of an apostolic people.

Not democracy, but community:

Democracy may be fine for nations, but it has never been God's plan for the church. Even Churchill remarked that "Democracy is the worst form of government except all those other forms that have been tried from time to time."[3] Instead, the church is meant to rise above mere democracy, and find community. Democracy cannot produce community, as we discussed earlier. An apostolic company functions through relationships and by its people knowing and trusting each other deeply, not through the politics of who can get the votes. In community, it is not the opinion of the majority that counts – it is the Spirit of God bringing peace to the heart that guides and speaks. The voice of just one member can be used by God to bring either direction, or correction, and the believers whose hearts are right with one another sense an inner witness to the truth. In the end, the anointed leadership of the community carries the responsibility for understanding the heart of the people and the mind of the Spirit, no matter through whom it is being expressed.

---

3   "Winston Churchill – Quotations," Jarrold Publishing 1997.

Rights, but no rights:

To be an apostolic people, we must give up our 'rights'. If we are not prepared to do this, we are not following the way of Christ, and therefore can never know His power. Christ was honoured by the Father and exalted to the highest place, specifically because He gave up His rights and trusted the Father instead. This is the message of Philippians chapter 2, where we are called to be like-minded and one in spirit and purpose with the believers, because we are united with Christ. We are called to look after the interests of others, as well as our own, and instructed to have the same values that Christ did when He made Himself nothing. Jesus did not count His equality with God something to be held onto, but humbled Himself to become a servant to others. Likewise, the believers of an apostolic community do not demand their rights, but trust the covering of God, and seek to be servants to their people. An apostolic people must be content to be 'nothing', and it is Christ who will exalt them in His way and time. This is the people who will inherit the apostolic promise, *"The God of peace will soon crush Satan under your feet."* (Romans 16:20)

The Plumb Line: Amos 7:7-8

"The Lord was standing by a wall that had been built true to plumb, with a plumb line in his hand. And the Lord asked me, "What do you see, Amos?" "A plumb line," I replied. Then the Lord said, "Look, I am setting a plumb line among my people Israel; I will spare them no longer."

In its context, this scripture is the word of the prophet Amos recording what was the final, unavoidable, judgement of the Lord over the Northern Kingdom of Israel, which had been hardened in sin, and despite all the Lord's mercies and repeated appeals and great patience, the end was now inevitable. And in the context, the wall referred to the way the Lord himself had originally built Israel. But a plumb-line was used in reference to pulling down as well as to building up, as we see in the use of these terms by Jeremiah in reference to the later destruction of Jerusalem (Lamentations 2:8).

It is common, however, to have preachers use these verses to bring a gospel message warning of God's judgments today, and to repeat the illustration of God setting in place a plumb line amongst his people. A plumb line is a tool used by tradesmen to ensure that what they build is truly upright and straight, which is why it is often used as an illustration of God setting a standard amongst his people, so as to judge what is crooked. And ultimately, of course, the plumb-line set amongst the people of God and in the world is the life of the Lord Jesus Himself.

But notice about the vision in the prophecy of Amos that when the Lord said this, he was standing by a wall that had been built true to plumb. Walls in Holy Scripture refer to the city of God, and this must apply to apostolic foundations in particular. And we need to note, that whilst there have been judgements of God that destroyed what hardened, idolatrous, apostate people had made of what He had given them, ie the Northern Kingdom, then later the Southern Kingdom of Judea and the city of Jerusalem in the time of Nebuchadnezzar, and again and finally the destruction of Jerusalem, the Temple, the Priesthood, the Sacrifices, the Levitical economy and Mosaic Judaism itself in fulfilment of the prophecies of Christ (and, no doubt, other judgments since), *He has never ceased continuing to build the real wall true to plumb, i.e. the City of God.* That is what we are, That is what the gospel of Christ makes us, Jew and gentile alike (For this, see Hebrews 12:22-24; Eph 2:14-15, 19-21; the gospel promises of Isaiah 58:12 & 61:4; and Amos' own prophecy of Ch 9:11-12 repeated and confirmed as a gospel word relative to Christ building his church amongst the gentiles in Acts 15:16-17, and Revelation 21:15, 19).

This can only mean that, in every generation of Christ's kingdom expanding in the world, no matter what false, religious, or apostate forms of the faith or the church there may be in the world, there will also at all times be built a true people — and this will be an increasingly extensive work in the world, in accordance with all gospel promises of the Old and New Testaments. In the light of this word spoken by Amos concerning God's purpose, then, we may find truth relative to the maturing of the church in the world — the bride without spot or wrinkle, the fully restored and mature church of Jesus Christ functioning with an apostolic life, and holding out the word of life to the nations. We can expect to see the church come more and more into the maturity of apostolic life as time progresses.

 *Testimony*

Carolyn Ponicke, Worship Leader
Peace Christian Church,
Rockhampton, Queensland, Australia.

I was raised in a Christian home and accepted Jesus as my Lord and Saviour at the age of 8. I have lived as a Christian ever since, though at times not very well. I had previously been a member of a traditional evangelical denomination. My husband Tony and I began attending *Peace* in January 1991, and since that time have been on a wonderful journey with John and our people in rediscovering the truth of apostolic Christianity. You can see that I have some understanding of 'traditional' Christianity, and all that goes with it.

We have been on this journey now for some 18 years, during which time there has been a stripping away of religion and tradition and a return to the truth of New Testament Christianity. Having experienced the old, and now the new, I know where I want to be, and that is right where I am. John is my spiritual Father and I am his 'son,' and it's great. I know that I am loved and accepted. I am encouraged and empowered to be all that I can be in the Lord. I am released into ministry, and exhorted to press further and further into God and become all I can be for Him. I love John deeply and will be forever grateful to him for all he has done. This includes the fact that John has been tenacious in his pursuit of the Lord, and this has brought real revelation. I feel very privileged to be part of the *Peace* leadership team and work alongside John in the ministry.

I have not always found this to be an easy relationship, mainly due to my own issues with authority, and father figures, and the wrong belief systems I had been living out of. In fact I used to be quite fearful of John, fearful that I would let him down and he would be disapproving of me. However this has not been the case. John has always been very gentle and gracious in his dealings with me, even if there was something that needed to be corrected. This is because we are in a genuine, holy, apostolic relationship. There is no lording it over anyone. For me there is no striving, no competition and no having to 'prove myself.'

As part of the leadership of *Peace*, I know we all honour, respect, and love one another, and this flows into our church life at *Peace*. There is genuine love shared among us. We are a community who care deeply about each other. I feel loved by the people of *Peace*, and I love them. We all want the best for each other. As I said before, I know where I want to be. This is home. I am safe and secure and being led by someone who truly loves, and wants to see the very best for me, and indeed the very best for all.

We are all meant to be growing into the likeness of Jesus, and in both John and Hazel I see the character and attributes of our Lord being modeled. I am truly privileged to be a part of this ministry, and part of what the Lord is doing in the earth today.

Carolyn Ponicke.

CHAPTER 5

THE APOSTOLIC GRACE OF SONSHIP

*"For those God foreknew he also predestined
to be conformed to the likeness of his Son,
that he might be the firstborn among many brothers.*

(Romans 8: 29)

It is the very nature of God to do everything through His Son. And in bringing us to Himself, He has declared us to be His sons also. The Spirit of Adoption has been sent into our hearts by which we cry "Abba, Father." (Romans 8:15-17, Galatians 4: 5-7)

In the message of the gospel, made especially clear by Paul after special revelation, but seen everywhere in Holy Scripture, we are not only *"predestined to be adopted as his sons through Jesus Christ,"* (Eph 1:5) but also *"predestined to be conformed to the likeness of his Son."* (Rom 8:29)

Made to be like Him

Sonship is in us. Even from the time man was created in the image of God, and certainly from the time we were born again and the Spirit of God's Son was given to us, this has been God's design for us, and His imprint upon us. We were baptised into Christ, and thus became one with all the believers. Ever since, the Spirit of sanctification has been striving within us, drawing us to Jesus, daily teaching us to love, so as to conform us to the image of the Son of God. There is absolutely nothing about the Christian life that does not have sonship written all over it.

If we are going to be conformed to the image of God's Son, at the very least this will mean that we must learn to think like Him, love like Him, act like Him, value what He values, and do what He does. Thus all of the values and attitudes of Jesus, the Son of God, are to be fully formed in each of us.

Jesus' Sonship

We should consider thoughtfully this fact: everything that Jesus did, He did as a son to a father. Why should we take special notice of that? Because this is the life, and the lifestyle, to which we are to be conformed.

> "Everything that Jesus did, He did as a son to a father – this is the life and the lifestyle to which we are to be conformed."

In following Christ, we should embrace His ways. He was not here to please Himself, not here to do His own will, but the will of another. The whole plan of salvation, including just how He should live and how He should produce fruit unto God, all was done under the guidance of another, in daily submission to His Father. There is nothing about the way the Son of God lived His life on earth, or how He lives in eternity, which can be separated from the life of the Father in Him. All His joys, all His pain, all His work, all His sorrows, and all His triumphs – His whole purpose for being – was wrapped up in His identity as a man who lived at all times as a son to a father.

Salvation is Sonship

We have to understand this *sonship*. We must come to appreciate the attitude and values of Jesus Christ, for to this we are right now being conformed by the Holy Spirit. If we reject this, we reject the purpose of God in our salvation. This is what salvation is all about, as the writer to the Hebrews said, *"In bringing many sons to glory, it was fitting that God, for whom and through whom everything exists, should make the author of their salvation perfect through suffering."* (Hebrews 2:10)

So let us be very clear. Sonship, and our conformity to this pattern, is what the Christian faith and our salvation is about in its entirety. To this outcome all of the Scriptures speak and direct us. It is a destiny that can only be achieved by walking in relationships – relationship with God in

Father, Son, and Holy Spirit, and as the Scriptures make plain, relationship with God's people as well.

The Holy Fellowship

For example, the apostle John included a striking statement at the beginning of his first epistle. *"We proclaim to you what we have seen and heard, so that you also may have fellowship with us. And our fellowship is with the Father and with his Son, Jesus Christ."* (1 John 1:3)

This is a thrilling Scripture, which not only clearly reveals that our fellowship with the saints and our fellowship with God the Father and Son is the *same* fellowship, but more. Like in other places in Scripture, the Holy Spirit has purposefully inspired the writers to interchange what we would have thought was the acceptable order when referring to Christ and the church. The purpose is to accentuate the truth that any fellowship with God the Father and Son must of necessity be also seen as fellowship with the saints. To reject the fellowship of the saints is to miss God and His purpose, and to leave ourselves spiritually vulnerable and poor, having misunderstood the riches of Christ and our true inheritance.

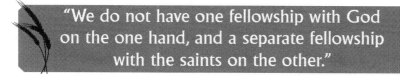

"We do not have one fellowship with God on the one hand, and a separate fellowship with the saints on the other."

One thing is very plain here. The fellowship referred to is but one fellowship. We do not have one fellowship with God on the one hand, and a separate fellowship with the saints on the other. There is only one holy communion – and when you are brought into this communion with God the Father and Son, you are in the communion of the saints. In this you have been brought into a relationship with brothers and sisters which is holy, and which cannot be defined as of less importance than our relationship with God, for it is God Himself who declares that we are all one with Him and with each other at the same time. There is only one 'oneness.'

This is strongly shown to be the case in Jesus' high priestly prayer for all believers on the evening before He went to the cross. *"I pray... for those who will believe in me... that all of them may be one, Father, just as you are in me and I am in you. May they also be in us so that the world may believe that you sent me. I have given them the glory that you gave me, that they may be one as we are one: I in them and you in me. May they be brought to complete unity to let the world know that you sent me and have loved them even as you have loved me."* (John 17: 20-23)

His Love in our Adoption

Perhaps a startling realisation for some would be to hear that God the Father loves us each as much as He loves Jesus. Many people do not stop to think about this, but this is the literal meaning of the work of God in our salvation. This is proclaimed in the very words of Jesus' prayer, *"you... have loved them even as you have loved me."* (John 17:23)

The Father does not love Christ with one kind or measure of love, and you and me with a different measure. He loves you in the same way as His Son, and to the same degree. Otherwise He would not have been pleased for His Son to suffer for us. In His eyes you are as cherished as Jesus, as wanted as Jesus, as rejoiced over and as passionately felt about as Jesus – and as acceptable in His presence as Jesus. This is what it means to be adopted as sons – you have the same status as Jesus the Son of God. As the great writer of the book of Hebrews said, *"Both the one who makes men holy and those who are made holy are of the same family. So Jesus is not ashamed to call them brothers."* (Hebrews 2:11)

The Blessing of Fellowship

We should not therefore despise the call to walk closely with our brothers and sisters in the faith, and we will find that grace and wisdom come to us from God when we choose to really walk with others. We are made rich by pursuing these relationships. Even more, when we love and serve our spiritual leaders, we find that great grace is given to us and our lives wonderfully enriched. I have long felt, ever since I was newly in the faith as a teenager, that 90% of the grace, blessing, providence, and answers to prayer that are meant to come to us, come if and when we are in right relationship with our brothers and our leaders. People who avoid relationships, particularly those who avoid submission to leadership, always struggle spiritually, no matter what they tell you about how well they are doing.

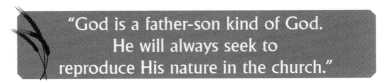

"God is a father-son kind of God. He will always seek to reproduce His nature in the church."

There are many examples in the Bible of personal relationships in the faith that follow a father and son pattern. In fact, we should be surprised if this were not so. God is a father-son kind of God. This being His very nature, He will always seek to reproduce Himself in mankind, and will surely reproduce His nature in the church.

Man's Way

But man is stubbornly and incorrigibly religious – this is part of our fallen sin nature. Consequently, when our minds turn to God, we think of pleasing Him in ways that seem right to men, and end up building the kinds of institutions that rise like the Tower of Babel as if they could be superior over all things. No wonder the Lord has 'confused our languages' by dividing religiously-driven Christians into many camps. Institutionalism is not the way of God, but of man.

God's Way

God's way was to walk with Adam in the Garden of Eden in the cool of the afternoon. God's way is to walk and talk, so as to develop relational intimacy. God's way is that of deep personal friendship, a desire to know and be known, a desire for the knitting of hearts, even with His own creatures. God's way is the way of love, and it can only be expressed in the kind of intimacy that comes from a friendship that has learned to trust, to honour, and to be at rest in the presence of another person – the kind of friendship where there is an acceptance of the other without an agenda of demands, judgements, and expectations.

But the church, when led by man, keeps producing institutionalism; for it has not understood the new covenant in Christ's blood, and is constantly turning back to the old in its practices. Thus we rebuild form and ceremony and institute hierarchical priesthoods, when all along God has been calling for relationships of the heart.

God wants 'real' sons, and He calls us to learn how to *be* real sons. This we do by the way in which we conduct our relationships in the church.

Levels of Spiritual Maturity

Certainly the church is a brotherhood, whether we are male or female; we are all brothers to Christ, and sons to God our Father. But we are also a family, and in this family, whilst on earth at least, we are meant to fulfil certain roles toward one another. Some are spiritually mature, and some are very young in the faith. There is a spiritual progression each of us is meant to pursue, from being infants, to childhood, to adulthood, and finally to the full maturity of being fathers.

The apostle John addressed the church in these family terms: *"I write to you, dear children, because your sins have been forgiven... I write to you, fathers, because you have known him who is from the beginning... I write to you, young men, because you are strong, and the Word of God lives in you, and you have overcome the evil one...."* (1 John 2:12-14). John used four Greek terms in this passage: *"teknion"* – meaning an infant, a Christian convert; *"paidion"* – a child, a half-grown boy or girl, an immature Christian; *"neaniskos"* – a youth, a young man (under 40); and *"pater"* – a father, parent.

This terminology gives us a picture of various levels of spiritual maturity and progress. We all understand there are newborn babies in the faith, those who need milk and not solid food (1 Cor 3:1-3, 1 Peter 2:2). There are also many who are still children spiritually, having never grown up, and still tossed here and there by everything that comes along (see Eph 4:14-16). But when we come to the other two designations John uses, we are in for some surprises.

He defines a 'young man' in the faith as someone who knows the word of God, who is strong, and who overcomes the evil one. This sounds to us more like a description of our leaders, of pastors and prophets, but according to the apostle this is just a young man. All children in the faith need to become such 'young men' as this.

But then, there are fathers! John described fathers as, *"those who know Him who has been from the beginning."* These are those who have reached a place of intimacy with the Lord and who have such a heart knowledge of God that they have entered into a position of rest. They have fought their battles, and matured. This is Abraham-like status. They have become the friends of God. And indeed this is what we each are called to – spiritual maturity! This brings us to that place where as sons, we have also become fathers.

The Goal of Maturity

What is the best way to attain this maturity in the faith? We know that maturity is the goal, for the maturity of the church has always been the purpose of the life work of every true apostle. Paul declared in Ephesians 4 that apostles and other fivefold ministers would continue to be appointed by Christ, in His ascension, *"until we all reach unity in the faith and in the knowledge of the Son of God and become mature, attaining to the whole measure of the fullness of Christ."* (Ephesians 4:13) Very clearly the overall picture in this chapter indicates that Christ remains in His ascension and continues to appoint apostles and prophets and other ministries until the church as a whole comes to this place of maturity.

What kind of maturity is this, and how can this maturity be measured? The Ephesians 4 passage reveals that the measure of this maturity is not only found in the unity of the faith, but ultimately by measuring up to the fullness of the stature of Christ. In Romans 8:29 Paul tells us we are called to this measure, when he stated that we were predestined to be conformed to the image of God's Son. Surely this is referring to the same thing – spiritual maturity!

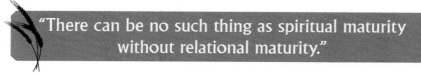

> "There can be no such thing as spiritual maturity without relational maturity."

Now the maturity spoken of is *relational* maturity. There is no other possible explanation for these many Scriptures. In fact, there can be no such thing as spiritual maturity without relational maturity.

Just Who then is Mature?

How do we determine just who is a spiritually mature person? Is it someone who has been a Christian for a long time? No, there are many who have been in the faith for decades but are still immature believers. Does having an extensive knowledge of Scripture, or having doctrinal wisdom, or being able to preach well, determine that a person is spiritually mature? No, anyone can gain knowledge, but knowledge alone puffs up. Many are articulate, but this does not guarantee character. What about someone greatly gifted in prophecy, one who can speak what seems to be the very words of God, and bring accurate insight into what God is doing today? Neither does this prove spiritual maturity, for the ability to prophesy is a gift, activated by faith not maturity. None of these things are a measure of spiritual maturity.

What if someone has great effectiveness in soul winning, with a great passion for the gospel, and is tireless in this work? Again, external works and facility in giftedness, even having heart passion in spiritual things, does not prove spiritual maturity. I knew somebody like this, a tireless witness for Jesus. He came to join our church, and was more enthusiastic than anyone around to share the gospel with outsiders, but he didn't stay very long. He hadn't dealt with his hurts, wouldn't deal with his insecurity, and so took offence easily and never settled into relationships. He didn't understand submission or trust of spiritual leadership. For him, it was all too hard to stay, and easier to just keep moving on. But moving on doesn't solve the problems, because the problems are within – and go with them. People like this keep coming up against the same issues everywhere they go. They remain spiritually immature, because they have not dealt with relational issues.

Relational Maturity is Spiritual Maturity

There is only one thing which is finally an effective measure of the degree to which a Christian is spiritually mature – that is the way in which he or she walks in relationship with other believers, especially with leaders who are over him or her in the Lord.

This is what we need to see in believers to be confident of their spiritual maturity. What kind of relationships does this person maintain? What kind of attitude to people? How easily offended? Do they avoid accountability? Are they honest, transparent, and open? Are they gracious towards others, and thoughtful concerning the needs of other people? Do they remain in committed relationships, and deal with issues as they arise rather than move on?

Notice how, in the biblical qualifications for elders laid out by Paul in 1 Timothy 3 and Titus 1, the quality of character, the family life, and the grace imparted to wives and children by the spirit of the church leader as a husband and father, was the main measure for determining whether a Christian fivefold minister had the grace and spiritual standing to be an elder in the church over the whole city.

The final measure, really the only measure of spiritual maturity, is found in the way we conduct ourselves in relationships in the house of God.

The Spirit & Power of Elijah

"See, I will send you the prophet Elijah before that great and dreadful day of the Lord comes. He will turn the hearts of the fathers to their children, and the hearts of the children to their fathers; or else I will come and strike the land with a curse." (Malachi 4:5-6)

This Scripture is placed in one of the most prominent positions in the Bible. It is very well-known, often quoted, and includes a prophecy, a promise, and the threat of a curse.

We should notice immediately that the prophecy is to be fulfilled at a very specific time in salvation history, but it has not been clear to many people just what time is being referred to. That is because there is confusion about the meaning of the term, the *"great and dreadful day of the Lord."* So before seeking what we could learn from it and applying it to ourselves, we must recognise and honour its actual meaning and fulfilment as a prophecy.

As a *prophecy* to *Israel*, it was fulfilled in the sending of John the Baptist ahead of the promised Messiah, our Lord Jesus Christ. That coming of the Son of Man was the fulfilment of many prophecies and promises to Israel, thus was the *"great day,"* and it also signalled the proximity (to them) of the pouring out of the Holy Spirit in Jerusalem, the covenant wrath of God coming upon Jerusalem, of salvation and deliverance for all those in Jerusalem who actually called on the name of the Lord (i.e. those who turned to Jesus), and the end of the Jewish age and the Old Covenant wineskin. Thus it was also the *"dreadful day,"* as well as the *"great day,"* because all of the things I have listed here are specifically described by the prophet Joel (2:28-32), including the *"blood, fire and billows of smoke,"* as what was to come upon Jerusalem, all part of the same great series of events in God's promised dealings with them at that time. And all this is quoted by the Apostle Peter on the day of Pentecost as being fulfilled at that time (Acts 2:16-21, see also v44). Joel himself, in the same prophecy, referred to *that* day in the same terms as the prophet Malachi, the *"great and dreadful day of the Lord."*

But concerning the final words of prophecy in Malachi, Scripture gives a consistent witness that this Scripture was fulfilled in John the Baptist.

In the Gospel of Luke we find the story of the angel Gabriel visiting Zechariah, who is to become the father of John the Baptist. Here the angel informs Zechariah concerning the meaning of John's life: *"...and he will go on before the Lord, in the spirit and power of Elijah, to turn the hearts of the fathers to their children and the disobedient to the wisdom of the righteous..."* (Luke 1:17). This Scripture is clearly related to, and is the plain fulfilment of, the prophecy of Malachi 4.

We find, too, the clear witness of the Lord Jesus that this is so. Jesus himself says, as recorded twice in Matthew's Gospel, that John the Baptist had indeed been this prophesied Elijah figure: *"And if you are willing to accept it, he is the Elijah who was to come"* (Matt 11:14) and later, *"I tell you, Elijah has already come..."* (Matt 17:12).

We notice also in the Malachi prophecy that when this 'Elijah' comes, he is to do a particular kind of work, and building on this, Gabriel tells Zechariah that John will have *"the spirit and power of Elijah"* to do precisely the work prophesied.

All this is clear. What might not be so clear to us all is that this grace, called *"the spirit and power of Elijah,"* is an <u>anointing</u>. What this means is that the same grace that had been given to Elijah to turn hearts in Israel back to God in his day, was given also to John the Baptist to turn the hearts of many in Israel back to the Lord.

But as soon as we recognise that this is an anointing of the Holy Spirit, given as grace, to do the Lord's work in building the house of God, we are on ground we can understand. Of course, if an anointing, then it is available in every age of the church, and if grace, then available to be sought after and obtained by faith in our Lord Jesus for the purpose of the ministry to which we are called. In other words, this grace is available to those who walk with God and for those who hunger and thirst after righteousness and the power of the Spirit in the ministry of the Word. This is encouraging to us all, and a firm Biblical basis for faith in prayer.

But there's more. This must have a particular application to *apostolic* ministry at the least, for it is most likely that Elijah and John are examples of the kind of ministry that ought to flourish in the church -- that of the apostle and the prophet. The truth is, in every generation, across all nations, we need many 'Elijahs.'

So if, as it was said, the spirit of Elijah rested upon John, and if Jesus can say of John to the crowd, *"if you are willing to accept it, he is the Elijah who was to come"* (Matt 11:14), then it is certainly possible for the 'Elijah' in this prophecy to also be for us a type for future ministries who may and do carry the same grace and anointing as Elijah. But to what grace and to which anointings does this refer? This is an important question, because the church as a whole, and apostles and prophets in particular, must understand so as to seek, receive, and walk in the graces being made available for the ministry today.

It has been common to equate the idea of 'the spirit of Elijah' with power, signs and wonders, and miracles. Elijah was the prophet of fire, who on more than one occasion called fire down from heaven, either to destroy his enemies or to convince Israel that God was indeed God. He closed up the heavens so that it did not rain, and he opened the heavens. He ran supernaturally ahead of chariots. He spoke to the Jordan and its waters parted for him. The ravens fed him in the desert, and the widow's flour and oil never ran out. He raised a widow's son from death. You can see why it has been common to simply draw the conclusion that the *"spirit and power of Elijah"* must be for miraculous powers to bring public witness to the ministry of Christ.

But the other 'Elijah,' John the Baptist, worked no miracle. There were no signs and wonders in his ministry, and it was in fact a requirement planned by God for his ministry that he not work any miracles. Therefore, since the angel said the *"spirit and power of Elijah"* would rest upon John, and it did, then that term cannot be referring to the power of miracles and signs. It must be referring to something else, which in fact it does.

Malachi 4:6 and Luke 1:17 both tell us what the spirit and power of Elijah is given to do. It is a grace to work great change in the hearts of men and women, and especially with respect to relationships. In particular, it is a grace which turns the hearts of fathers to their children, and of the children to their fathers. It has everything to do with repentance in relationships and heart attitudes, and in particular will bring great changes in restoring the proper values that believers should have in the house of God. This is particularly relevant to our day, because with the restoration of the gifts of the Spirit in the last 100 years on the one hand, and the modern technology of sound systems, music, cameras, publishing, and modern fundraising on the other, much of the church has become very performance oriented. These days it is easy to look gifted, to look anointed, to look successful, and not care about people or walk in any especially accountable relationship. But the spirit and power of Elijah, resting on apostles and prophets, is being given to turn the hearts of God's people back from outward form and performance to the love and relationships that truly empower the gospel. And Jesus is not returning for a church that is crass, hollow, and devoid of spiritual maturity by being performance oriented. He is sending apostles.

The prophecy of Malachi 4 makes it very plain that this great work of relational restoration at a heart level, brought about as a result of the work of the *"spirit of Elijah,"* will bring about a change of heart in the people of God, and to *"prepare"* them for the greater work of the Lord. This idea of being prepared immediately makes us think in terms of Eph 4:11-13, where *"he gave some to be apostles... to prepare God's people for works of service... until we all reach unity... and become mature, attaining to the whole measure of the fullness of Christ."* This Pauline passage is describing precisely the same work! This anointing is none other than the apostolic grace needed to reform the church, so as to bring those who are Christ's into a relational life, and to restore the proper heart that the leaders of the body of Christ should have (a fathering heart), and establish the proper heart in all the believers that they each should have (the hearts of children towards fathers).

This is, in our day, a great revival of the church. Not a revival in the classic sense of evangelistic crusades, but in the greater sense of a huge spiritual awakening which, at a grassroots level, spreads from house-to-house and heart-to-heart, month in and month out, year after year, across all nations of the globe, until there will have been a complete and total transformation of Christianity. This is a spiritual awakening of huge proportions, which has even now begun, and will continue until the church of these coming days can be said to be a truly mature apostolic people. And it is this people who will more fully succeed in carrying the gospel effectively to all nations.

The church in its inception was an apostolic people -- the believers enjoyed an apostolic life under apostolic leadership. The body of Jesus Christ on earth will again have such a life. The church is once again to be truly an apostolic people.

With respect to the maturity referred to in Eph 4:13, we need to understand this: the first apostles, in writing to the early church, urged them to go on to maturity. This means that even though the early church had an apostolic life, and were truly an apostolic people, they were not yet the fully mature church. Even though we uphold the early church as a model for us today, this model was not in itself perfection. They also were being urged by their apostles to go on to a more mature expression of the faith. We need to recognise an important truth here. In accordance with the Holy Scriptures, and in answer to the High Priestly prayer of our Lord Jesus in John 17:20-23, the church on earth must, is required, to come to the place where it has not only a restored apostolic life, but a fully mature one.

> "The church on earth
> must come to the place of having not only
> a restored apostolic life, but a fully mature one."

'Sonship' is an Apostolic Grace

The spirit of sonship is an apostolic grace. Paul said that by the grace he was given, he was a wise master builder. (1 Corinthians 3:10) Apostles have grace in particular for building the church *relationally*. Who then would we expect God to use both to teach and to model the relationships required, and in doing so provide the most outstanding example of apostolic life in the New Testament. Paul of course.

Of all the apostles, and there were many including the 12 that walked personally with Jesus in the three years of His ministry (I am speaking of the eleven plus Matthias), which one of these in particular does the New Testament really *reveal* to us – making much of his personal life, his love, his doctrine, his accomplishments, his passion, his revelation of Christ, his suffering, etc. It happens to be the one who is the greatest model – a model representing Christ in ministry, bearing exactly the right apostolic fruit of Christian love and ministry in father and son. Paul poured his love into sons, not just to create followers or workers, but to re-create the great grace he had been given in the lives of others who were true sons.

In writing to Timothy (2 Timothy 3:10,14), the Corinthians (1 Corinthians 4:16-17), the Philippians (Philippians 2:16), the Thessalonians (2 Thessalonians 3:7,9), and others, Paul teaches us, as well as them, that we are to imitate his doctrine and his way of life. His way of life included the necessity to pour his fathering love into sons in the ministry.

The Scripture says, *"Remember your leaders, who spoke the word of God to you. Consider the outcome of their way of life and imitate their faith."* (Hebrews 13:7) Tell me, of whom could we apply this instruction more than of Paul? We would be fools to claim we follow his doctrine but ignore, or neglect, or reject, his way of life in ministering as father and son, as if this were not central to the whole message of Christ, and the focal point of true ministry.

Whose letters, more than anyone else's, are we given in Scripture to study? Whose revelations? More than all the apostles, Paul was given great personal revelation in the Gospel and of the doctrines of Christ! (2 Corinthians 12:17) And it was this man who then produced, directly as a result of the grace he was given, the one relationship in Scripture which is probably more preached about than any other in history – that of Paul and Timothy. He has provided a wonderful model for us, and we need to follow the example and pattern given!

Paul said, *"Join with others in following my example, brothers, and take note of those who live according to the pattern we gave you."* (Philippians 2:16)

Gerry Viray, Senior Pastor
All for Christ Church,
Taguig, Metro Manila, Philippines.

One of the things I have observed is - linking with a father is so exciting!

Why did I enter into this father and son relationship. Some years ago, I got this impression from the Spirit that He was about to do far greater things in my life and ministry, but I needed to do something. Take a father in the faith. It was very clear, take a father in the faith. I began to pray for a father. I considered the two that were on my mind at that time. One was a Filipino pastor, and the other was John. After some time, I felt led to ask John to become my father.

Ever since that time I felt tremendous things happened. One is increased anointing in my life. Also, I began to receive revelations about father and son relationship. I felt that the greatest miracle in Jesus' life and ministry is not His resurrection from the dead but His death on the cross. The Lord opened my understanding that the reason He died is in obedience to His Father. That the way to greatness is really in submitting yourself to a father and love him, respect and honor him. I realized I can only become a good father if I will be a good son like the Lord.

When we were able to purchase our church property worth P6.5M, I felt in my spirit that it was because now as a son I have inheritance.

As a son to John, I felt that his heart has become very close to my heart also. I want to share about it whenever I have opportunity to do so. In fact, in our pastoral group here in Taguig City, two pastors asked me to become their father. The teaching is now well accepted here in our city as other preachers are also preaching it. I have also two other sons from other places as well.

I feel such love to John and to the sons I have today. I have decided that whenever he is here (in the Philippines), I will see to it that I will be with him. I am praying that God will continue to give me understanding of how to raise up sons and daughters who will love the Lord and serve Him faithfully.

A son (and proud of it),

Gerry Viray.

CHAPTER 6

THE SPIRIT OF SONSHIP

"I hope in the Lord Jesus to send Timothy to you soon...
I have no one else like him, who takes a genuine interest in your
welfare...
but you know that Timothy has proved himself,
because as a son with his father he has served
with me in the work of the gospel."

(Philippians 2:19-20,22)

Sonship! It is, quite simply, the way God prefers to do business. If you mean business with God, you really need to learn what it means to be a son to a father in the body of Christ. This is especially important in these days, for even though God was pleased to bless our denominationalism and institutionalised ways in the past, all this is changing. To go on with God, and not remain stuck in some rut, or backwater, we have to be prepared to listen to what God is doing, and be prepared to accept change.

God is taking the time to fully restore to us the apostolic graces so as to establish in the church an *apostolic life*, by which we become truly an apostolic people. If then you want to walk in the greatest possible measure of God's blessing, you will need to learn how to be a son in the ministry of Jesus. It is not difficult; it is a case of being willing. Do you really have the heart that a son should have? Do you have Christ's heart – willing to be nothing, willing to be a servant, willing to be humbly natural in relationship with other people?

Paul wrote to the Romans and said he was aware that when he came to visit them, he would *"come in the full measure of the blessing of Christ."* (Romans 15:29) This indicates that, even for an apostle, it is possible to walk in something less than the *full* measure of the blessing of Christ, otherwise Paul wouldn't have been so foolish as to waste his words on a meaningless statement. But there are many people today – even many people in ministry – who do not walk in anything like the full measure of the blessing of Christ, because they don't walk in appropriate relationships.

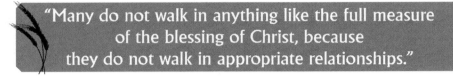

"Many do not walk in anything like the full measure of the blessing of Christ, because they do not walk in appropriate relationships."

Paul knew what it was to be a father; he knew what it was to maintain the deeply personal, caring, selfless, intimate relationships with others that the ministry of Christ calls for. He knew he had obtained grace, and was walking in it. Paul's record is plain, and not just with Timothy, but also with Titus, the Thessalonians, the Ephesian elders, Philemon, and the list goes on. The letters of Paul are alive with his love for people, and with a record of his deep personal involvement in healthy, caring, accountable relationships with many of them.

You could argue that Paul himself did not have a spiritual father, even though he was a father to others. There are some people who appear like this, but the heart of a son is not absent from them – there simply was no one for them, no one able to fulfill that role. Yet in saying this, we might be mistaken, for we are arguing from silence. We do not know what happened during most of the years of their earlier lives. Paul sat at the feet of Gamaliel, Moses was very submissive to his father-in-law Jethro, Elijah we do not know about, but he loved Elisha and obviously had meaningful relationships with many people. Think about the very large numbers of men in those schools of the prophets, and his earlier grief over the fact that Jezebel had put so many prophets to death.

But we also notice another phenomenon. These fathers who went before, and who raised great sons to walk in victory, suffered a great deal more than their sons. It is true that a Christian leader who does not have the protection and blessing of a spiritual father can make great headway, can break through to spiritual victory, can open the way for other people – but it is costly. Whereas, for those who are sons to a father, they do not have to make the same mistakes, they do not have to pay the same price, they seem to learn the lessons needed from being taught by fathers rather than from suffering, they obtain greater success at a younger age, and one more thing, they seem to obtain a greater co-operation and support from the people of God.

The examples seem clear enough. Moses was constantly opposed through his 40 years of leadership, with plenty of grumbling and resistance to fuel his frustrations all the way along, which only served to exacerbate his anger. Yet Joshua, from the time that Moses laid his hands upon him and transferred some of his authority, was a huge success. He greatly enjoyed the support of the people, and led them into their inheritance (which, by the way, is the whole purpose of spiritual leadership).

And this is typical. Those who are sons seem to find the way easier. In fact, the whole generation that followed Joshua were sons, having been raised in the desert, and thus were entitled to their inheritance, for they had the attitude of sons. It is always sons who receive inheritance.

We see the same pattern with Elijah and Elisha. Elijah was a man who fought great struggles, who must have known loneliness, a man of the wilderness, hiding out from the authorities, under threat of death, sometimes running scared, but he held on and broke through for victory. But Elisha, the son who received Elijah's blessing and mantle, was a man of the towns and cities, a man honoured, a man received everywhere with holy fear and respect, a confidant of kings, a social man who travelled about the communities of Israel. The contrast is huge.

These kinds of fathers suffer to make a way for others, and it is a very great benefit for those who become sons – whose way has been opened for them. A modern comparison might be that of the great evangelist, Billy Graham. He prayed and believed, worked hard and maintained great integrity for many years, and built with others a ministry of genuine worldwide impact. In doing so he went places no one else has gone. His son Franklin, obviously also a man of great integrity, is one who has benefited from being a son to a father. For Franklin Graham, there are great benefits in spiritual inheritance, but he is not the only one benefitting. The church also is much benefited, and greatly enriched, when true sons follow great fathers in that fashion.

We should not make the mistake of thinking this only applies to well-known fathers, or to people who build large ministries. The principles are true and pertain to every leader and father in the faith. In small churches and ministries everywhere, the grace flowing would be more powerful, the ultimate outcomes for the believers much greater, the blessings more evident and more freely obtained, if the ministries were to be established through loving fathers and led by true sons. This would bring the people of God into their inheritance, which in its greatest expression is always a shared inheritance in the saints. (Ephesians 1:18)

> "It is not the quality of the fathering, but the quality of the sonship that counts."

We must also understand that any grace and blessing that flows does not really come from a spiritual father as such, but from God who is pleased with what He finds in the heart of a son. We have a maxim we share with people: *"It is not the quality of the fathering, but the quality of the sonship that counts."* It always comes back to what is in the heart. Someone I know tells the story of a young pastor who said, "I'm going to get me a famous father." This fellow will find, if he pursues with this attitude, that this will not advance him in the faith, for there is a pride and a grasping covetousness that is revealed here. This is not what sonship is about at all.

Sonship is about the giving of our hearts to serve another, to someone who loves us and we choose to love them, and we make ourselves accountable to them. We desire to receive blessing from them to be sure, but our service is not based upon what they can do for us; it is all about what we can do for them. Even if we are established in our own ministry, we are here to serve the ministries of others.

So it is not about how great, how gifted, how influential, or how anointed a spiritual father might be. Most people will have very average spiritual fathers. It is all about how we love, serve, honour, and support them.

Some people have not had a spiritual father, in the sense of someone in leadership who personally cared for them or mentored them, yet they have still received all the blessings of sons. How is this so? I remember meeting a pastor at a luncheon years ago. He had a large church in Victoria, Australia, of some hundreds of families. There were various pastors around the table all chatting over the meal, but I was listening to what this brother had to say. He struck me as someone who had a deep wisdom, a genuine insight into the church and the ways of God. I felt that he could have only had this grace from being a son in the ministry. I asked him, "Surely you have walked with a spiritual father, haven't you?" He replied in the negative. He said that he had always wanted to have a spiritual father, but could never find anybody in his evangelical denomination who would give him the time or the relationship.

The conversation continued around the table, and I kept hearing him say things in a way that revealed he had a great grace. I felt he must have loved a spiritual father, so I made this remark again. But again, he assured me, he had not had such a relationship.

After a while, he began telling us about his family. He had a number of brothers, and his father had been a pastor. He said that on Sunday mornings his father used to leave home early to walk to church, so that he could place Christian literature in letterboxes on the way, for which he would take a different route every week. He said that he always went with his father on these walks. He said his brothers always went with their mother in the car, instead of walking with their father, but for him, he just always wanted to be with his dad. Right there was the key! The spirit of sonship had been in the heart of this man all along, which is why he had been given great insight by the Lord and was rich in grace.

This is one of the reasons King David's life was so spiritually rich. Who but someone full of grace could write those Psalms, and be such a man after God's own heart? David's heart of sonship was proven, not just in his relationship with his father Jesse, but with the man who became his leader, his father-in-law King Saul. David was brought into Saul's house, married Saul's daughter, made the captain of Saul's armies, and fought the king's battles.

Spiritually, David was a great son. Despite the fact that Saul, enraged with jealousy, deranged as a madman, and troubled by an evil spirit, just wanted to kill him, and sought to do so again and again, David never changed in his heart towards Saul. He loved him, honoured him, and only ever wanted to fight his battles for him and make him a success. And when Saul was dead from battle, David lamented for him and held him in high honour. David was a true son, which was part and parcel of just why the Lord declared him to be a man after God's own heart. (1 Samuel 13:14, Acts 13:22)

Notice that David's cause was not harmed by having such a lousy spiritual father as Saul. Things were so bad that David, to preserve his own life, had to remove himself from Saul and hide in the wilderness. But David never removed his *heart* from Saul. And the result of this faithfulness is that David was not only finally made the king of all Israel, but that God chose to make a personal covenant with him. And what was that covenant? That David would not lack a son to sit upon his throne forever – and ultimately his 'son' was none other than the lion of the tribe of Judah, the promised Messiah, the king of glory. (2 Samuel 7:11-16, 1 Chronicles 17:10-14) His faithfulness as a son ensured the blessing of God upon his lineage to come.

That is inheritance, and more: this is also typical of the posterity that is given by the grace of God to those who have the heart of sons. Remember, this is Christ's heart – God is a son.

Such Clear Biblical Examples!

The Scriptures of the old covenant were commonly referred to as 'the Law and the Prophets.' You will remember that Jesus referred to them in this way; this was customary. (Matthew 7:12) So it is helpful to note that within the collection of books of the Old Testament known as the Law, and again amongst the books known as the Prophets, as well as in the Scriptures of the New Testament, we find three outstanding examples of father-son relationships which have been placed there by the Holy Spirit. Thus all major segments of the Word of God bear witness to this truth.

I am referring to Moses and Joshua, Elijah and Elisha, and Paul and Timothy. These are not the only examples of such relationships; really there are many others. But these three are generally well-known to all Christians, and they are outstanding examples of the way in which we are all meant to walk with, learn from, serve, and honour our leaders and spiritual fathers. The New Testament position is that all these stories were written down under the inspiration of the Holy Spirit as examples for us to follow (1 Cor 10:11), and that these Scriptures are to be used for teaching, correction, and training in righteousness. (2 Tim 3:16) To reject these examples as a model for life for every Christian is to reject the very witness that Scripture gives us concerning the way in which we are to walk in our salvation.

Transfigured with Christ

When Jesus went up what Peter called *"the sacred mountain"* (2 Peter 1:18) with His three leading disciples, and was there transfigured in glory before them, two men appeared with Him in that glory. These were Moses and Elijah. The Scripture says that the three of them i.e. Moses and Elijah with Jesus, were discussing the things that were to come, and what He was about to accomplish. One has to wonder why it was necessary for this discussion to take place at all. One would have thought the will of God was settled in eternity, that Jesus knew the will of His Father, and that Moses and Elijah would have little to do with it. But if Godly men from the past, Old Testament patriarchs or prophets, were to appear with Jesus in this glory and discuss with Him His purpose, why these two? Why Moses and Elijah, for there are others that might seem more suitable for the task?

Why not Abraham, who is both the father of faith and the friend of God? Why was he not there? What about David, the one with whom God made covenant to seat a son upon his throne forever – the son that was none other than the Lord Jesus who was on the Mount of Transfiguration? David foretold with great detail in the Psalms the complete passion of Jesus. Why was he not there with the son of this glory? Or why not Daniel, wise man and confidant of kings and rulers who was, according to the angel, the most highly esteemed of men? Why was the most highly esteemed not there? Why not Isaiah, sublime prophet, astounding writer of the sweetest Scriptures and numerous prophecies of the Christ? Or why not Jeremiah, who had suffered for years with heartbroken agony over the people of God, longing for their salvation?

The answer is simple enough. Of all the ministries of prophets, priests, and kings in the Old Testament, there were only two who not only raised a son in the ministry to be like them, and towards whom they were a true father in the faith, but they also successfully passed to this son their own anointing for the ongoing purpose of the ministry, and for the care, leadership, and protection of the people of God.

The reason Moses and Elijah were on the Mount of Transfiguration, discussing with Jesus the things to come, was because these two, more than all the figures of the Old Testament, most accurately represented and prefigured the ministry that was to come under the new covenant in Christ's blood. The coming new order, the ministry of the body of Christ (1 Peter 2:5, 9), was to be a relational ministry. The body of Christ, which was the coming *new wineskin,* would have a nature and structure that was *relational.*

The Ministry to be Established in Relationships

This new ministry was to be established in fathers and sons. Mature leaders, men and women, were to be fathers and mothers in the faith. They were to love, watch over, care for, and raise sons and daughters in their own 'likeness.' They were to desire and plan to pass on to their 'sons' their own portion of grace and anointings for ministry. Then their sons, raised in this way under the discipline of fathering authority, would have two portions – their own, and their 'father's' added to it. Thus, each believer could find a true double-portion of the Spirit, through love, in holy relationships, as it ought to be. For each believer is, by definition, a first-born son (Hebrews 12:23), and a double-portion is meant to be the inheritance of the firstborn.

This concept of father-son relationship in ministry, which both Moses and Elijah modeled, is the precise style of ministry for which the body of Christ has been designed, and which the new covenant actually calls for.

Yes, we are brothers in the Lord – and so were Paul and Timothy, just as surely as Elijah and Elisha were. But we must learn to walk together as fathers and sons if we would obtain the fullness of the blessing and the powerful grace of manifold anointings for ministry.

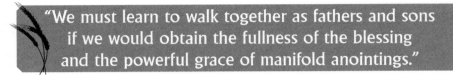

"We must learn to walk together as fathers and sons if we would obtain the fullness of the blessing and the powerful grace of manifold anointings."

God is father and son by nature. The task of the church and every believer is to reveal God to the world. It is not possible to reveal God without revealing His nature, and this is why He sent His Son. We each are meant to reveal the Son of God, and to show the love of God. We are meant to reveal to others this great salvation which has the power to bring everyone who believes into intimate friendship, as well as into sonship, with God. It is a relational salvation, designed to bring each of us into a relational body. How is this going to be shown to the world, if all we ever show are our institutions?

We cannot point people to a building or to a denomination and expect them to recognise God. These things are not relational in themselves, and so cannot show forth God's glory or His nature. There is but one thing that does show the nature of God, and therefore shows the glory of God, and that is the kind of personal relationships in which the sons of God walk.

Relationships Show God's Nature

If we are to show forth God's nature, our relationships must reflect that nature. If God is indeed a father-son God, then He must produce in us a fathering and a sonship about the way in which we walk with each other. When unbelievers see our relationships, and they see the love, the honour, the trust, the affection, the intimacy of relationships, the deep sense of community, the acceptance, and the inner rest, then will they be looking at the goodness of the Lord and recognise the truth.

Jesus Himself made it so plain when He prayed and asked the Father, *"that all of them may be one, Father, just as you are in me and I am in you. May they also be in us so that the world may believe that you have sent me... May they be brought to complete unity to let the world know that you sent me and have loved them even as you have loved me."* (John 17: 21-23)

So as to clarify what Jesus' prayer tells us, here is a summary: In order for the world to believe that the Father sent the Son to be the saviour of the world, all believers, including you and I, need to be one in the same way that God the Father and God the Son are one.

This 'oneness' alone is what gives the church the dynamic power we are meant to have in the world. Paul proclaimed, *"the gospel ... is the power of God for the salvation of everyone who believes."* (Rom 1: 16) But the truth of this gospel is revealed to unbelievers by the love of God they see in us. They will see His glory and trust His power when their eyes are opened by what they see in our relationships. Jesus said, *"By this all men will know that you are my disciples, if you love one another."* (John 13: 35)

> "These relationships are of supreme importance to the power of the gospel in the world."

In the ministry of Christ, we must walk together as fathers and sons, brothers and sisters, and mothers and daughters – but not just in outward form, or just using the language: that doesn't work at all. I remember Juan Carlos Ortiz saying years ago, *"We call each other brother because we are not."* It is not names, titles, or the right vocabulary that advances the cause of Christ. We must walk in relationships of the heart, as God Himself does. These relationships are of supreme importance to the power of the gospel in the world.

We All Have Many Fathers

Some people object and say that we only have one father, that is, our heavenly Father – and they seem to imply that it is offensive to God for us to say or think that we have any other fathers. But actually, we all have *many* fathers, and this is God's doing. God is not afraid of fathering. He knows we need plenty of it, and He designed the whole human race to have a need for fathers and fathering, which He provides in many ways.

Following is a Biblical list of some of those that God Himself has given us specifically to be fathers in the faith:

Firstly, there is the Lord Jesus. This will surprise some, but in addition to God the Father, the Bible refers to God the Son as our father also. The prophecy of Isaiah concerning the Christ states, *"For to us a child is born, to us a son is given, and the government will be on his shoulders. And he will be called Wonderful Counselor, Mighty God, Everlasting Father, Prince of Peace."* (Isaiah 9:6) And the book of Hebrews quotes Jesus saying, *"Here am I, and the children God has given me."* (Hebrews 2:13)

Then we must consider the place of Adam. Adam was created by God to be the father of us all, the spiritual father of the whole human race, and essentially the first apostle. But Adam fell, and consequently, instead of being a source of blessing to all his children, he became the source of our curses. Spiritual fathering does have huge ramifications. But the solution to the damage caused by a fallen father is not to reject fathering. Good fathering is still needed.

Thus the Lord had to raise another father for the whole of the human race. Ultimately, this would be Christ, the second Adam. But Christ was not to come for a long time, so in the meanwhile another father was needed. God chose Abraham to be the father of faith for the whole race. Adam is the source of a curse for every person born into this world, but Abraham is the source of blessing for everyone who believes. His first name was Abram, which meant "exalted father." God changed his name to Abraham, which means, "father of many nations." He was childless, and to become the father of faith his faith was to be proven in believing the promise God gave that he would have a son. His faith was further tested on the question of whether he would be prepared to offer that son to God. All the developments of Abraham's life and walk with God surrounded issues of fathering and sonship, and he became the father of faith. It is God Himself who calls Abraham our father, and declares you and me to be his offspring: *"He is our father in the sight of God."* (Romans 4:16-17)

Similarly, Isaac and Jacob are our fathers also, having walked in the faith, and provided for us a clear voice to listen to, and having left us a spiritual inheritance.

King David is our spiritual father too. He is known in Scripture as the Shepherd of Israel (2 Samuel 5:2), but not because he pastored a congregation, or was available for counseling. Rather, by the life he lived, the grace he carried, the way he watched over the nation, his heart for God, and the ministry of the Holy Spirit through him in prayers and psalms, he has become for us all a truly great father in the faith. His role as such a father continues to this day. We sing his words, we pray his prayers, we are taught by his wisdom, we emulate his spirit. The grace he discovered has come down to us as our inheritance. Thus each one of us learns from him, and becomes to God, like David, *"a man after my heart."* (Acts 13:22)

In the same way, many such as Elijah, Elisha, Isaiah, Jeremiah, Daniel, and others are fathers to us, for this is what God made them; this is their God-given role.

There is yet another truly great father that all of us, without exception, share. That is the apostle Paul. Peter, John, and James are fathers to us also, as we continue to read their words, receive their witness, and trust their wisdom. They each help to mould our thinking and our faith. But Paul holds a special place, and by God's grace has become an outstanding spiritual father to the whole of the Christian Church for the last 2000 years. He declared himself to be such a father in Christ, and that those who followed his leadership and heard his words were his precious children. He said, and says to us still, *"... my dear children... in Christ Jesus I became your father through the gospel. Therefore I urge you to imitate me."* (1 Corinthians 4: 14-16)

> **"God, our true father, provides the fathering we need, and He does much of this through other people."**

These words are certainly powerful, and the truth of them, and the intent of the Holy Spirit behind them, is quite obvious. We need fathers, and God has provided them. At the very least every believer must accept that God Himself has made both Abraham and Paul, these two at the very least, fathers to His people. But we must understand that it goes far beyond this. God, our true father, is the one who provides for us the fathering we need, and He does much of this through other people, for we need the witness of those who have walked where we also need to walk.

Further, in the history of faith more recent than the Biblical record, we have such great heroes of the church – like Luther, Zinzendorf, Wesley, and others too numerous to mention. These also are our fathers. They suffered for us, they opened the way for us, we have been made rich in inheritance because of them, and their voice continues to speak to us today. They became the fathers of many nations, thus walking in the inheritance of their father Abraham to whom this promise was given. In a great sense, they are the fulfillment of God's promise to Abraham, wherein God said He would make Abraham the father of many nations, and that all nations would be blessed through him. So these promises made to Abraham are fulfilled by the very process in which many believers, as sons of Abraham, become fathers to Abraham's children everywhere. This is a great blessing!

Then we each have many fathers whom we have personally known. There is the one who first discipled us in Christ, or the pastor of the church we were first in, and many others since – Sunday school teachers or Bible college principals, for example. All along the way there was someone to whom God gave grace to father us. So many were fathers to us, but we did not have the language or the understanding to recognise them for what they were to us in Christ.

As I look back over my more than 40 years in Christ, I see now the fathers I did not recognise then. I have made it my business to go back and acknowledge them, to honour them, and to obtain their blessing. The blessing of a father is a powerful approval, and an impartation of favour and spiritual power.

Does this mean then that a father is superior and a son is inferior in spiritual standing? No, for father and son are to be of one spirit, therefore equals, as in our doctrine of the Deity – you can't be a father and call someone a son, without this being at the very least a calling of that person to become what you are, to stand where you stand, to become one with you in essence. This is why the Pharisees were so shocked about Jesus, because He claimed to be equal with God by declaring Himself to be the son of God. (John 5:18)

To understand this better, perhaps we can illustrate it by saying that, since we need to serve someone as a son, we need then to have someone willing to serve us as a father. Each one serves the other, and thus they fulfill a very important role towards each other. One takes the 'office' of son, and the other takes the 'office' of father. This must at least be somewhat similar to the Godhead, for God the Father and God the Son are of exactly the same 'age' – neither has seniority over the other, except in the roles in relationship and in submission to authority that they fulfill towards one another. The Father is Eternal God, The Son is Eternal God, and they are co-equal in power and glory. Yet the Father is a father to His Son, and the Son is a son to His Father.

But Christ was 'not ashamed' to be called our brother, and in the process acknowledged His own 'many fathers' (that comment might offend, but please follow the explanation).

Christ's favourite name for Himself was 'the Son of Man.' Literally, this means the son of Adam, or the son of the human race. In coming as our Messiah, He also came as the son of Abraham and the son of David. To say He was not ashamed to call us His brothers is to say He is not ashamed to acknowledge His 'fathers' either.

In coming as the Son of Man, Christ became the second Adam, so as to represent the whole of the human race in offering His life in our place for sin. Since He was also the son of Abraham, then in removing the curse of the law that was against us by His death, He made us also sons of

Abraham, thus guaranteeing our inheritance and access to faith. (Galatians 3:14) The greatest blessing of Abraham that we inherit is that our faith is counted as righteousness. Christ also came as the son of David, to fulfill the covenant that God had made with David to establish his throne forever, and to give him a son who would reign upon the throne of David forever. (1 Chronicles 17:10-14, Luke 1:32)

To this day Christ is known as the Son of David. He is also known, and this is quoted regularly in churches everywhere, as *"a shoot... from the stump of Jesse"* (Isaiah 11:1) and as *"the root of Jesse".* (Isaiah 11:10) Paul quoted Isaiah, *"The Root of Jesse will spring up, one who will arise to rule over the nations; the Gentiles will hope in him."* (Romans 5:12) These are examples of fathers of which we could say Christ is 'not ashamed'.

The Scriptures cannot be broken, and the words of Christ concerning Himself, as well as the words of the prophets and apostles, should now seem quite clear. Those in the body of Christ who are negative about 'fathering,' and who push the line that 'we have only one father' and 'God in heaven is my only spiritual father' need to reconsider their position. I am not speaking like this to those who have honest questions, but to those who seem bent on opposing what God is saying and doing out of scepticism, fear, or hurt. These Scriptures refute the lie of those who refuse to see that there is such a thing as valid relationships that have the beauty of Christ in them, and which God has not only ordained, but given us the most incredible examples of in every part of Scripture. The intransigent denial of some does not come from spiritual wisdom or genuine honest enquiry before the Scriptures in the Holy Spirit. It more than likely comes from past hurt, insecurity, lack of trust, pride, personal agendas, independence, arrogance, jealousy, or selfish ambition.

But What About Matthew 23:9?

A commonly asked question that arises from time to time is concerning what Jesus meant in Matthew 23:9, when He said, *"And do not call anyone on earth 'father,' for you have one father, and he is in heaven."* I have included hereunder the full text of Matthew 23:1-13, since this is a very important question to answer, and we must consider the context in which Jesus spoke.

"Then Jesus said to the crowds and to his disciples: ² "The teachers of the law and the Pharisees sit in Moses' seat. ³ So you must obey them and do everything they tell you. But do not do what they do, for they do not practice what they preach. ⁴ They tie up heavy loads and put them on men's shoulders, but they themselves

are not willing to lift a finger to move them.

[5] "Everything they do is done for men to see: They make their phylacteries wide and the tassels on their garments long; [6] they love the place of honor at banquets and the most important seats in the synagogues; [7] they love to be greeted in the marketplaces and to have men call them 'Rabbi.'

[8] "But you are not to be called 'Rabbi,' for you have only one Master and you are all brothers. [9] And do not call anyone on earth 'father,' for you have one Father, and he is in heaven. [10] Nor are you to be called 'teacher,' for you have one Teacher, the Christ. [11] The greatest among you will be your servant. [12] For whoever exalts himself will be humbled, and whoever humbles himself will be exalted.

[13] "Woe to you, teachers of the law and Pharisees, you hypocrites! You shut the kingdom of heaven in men's faces. You yourselves do not enter, nor will you let those enter who are trying to." (Matthew 23:1-13)

Firstly, in Bible interpretation we are never to take one verse or phrase and turn it into a doctrine or a binding legalistic dictum. Neither are we meant to only ever apply the narrowest meaning possible to any single phrase of Scripture. The essential principle of Bible doctrine, or concerning anything if it is to be established as a general truth, must be confirmed by the whole tenor of Scripture. The rule is, 'every truth is established in the mouth of two or three witnesses'. (Matt 18:16, 2 Cor 13:1) For a truth or doctrine to be established as primary, or absolute, there must be at least two or three clear instructional passages of Scripture which establish or speak to that truth.

Matthew 23: 9 is but one witness. What we must do, so as to obtain a full understanding of the mind of the Lord, is to consider the Bible as a whole, and to receive the witness of every reference in Holy Scripture to the subject.

This statement of Jesus cannot be inferred as meaning that the use of the word 'father' is forbidden, since the term is used so freely by the apostle Paul, and also by the apostle John, and others. Paul's witness is that the Corinthian church was poorer for having had only a few fathers (1 Corinthians 4:15), and the apostle John twice referred to fathers, amongst others, to whom he was writing (1 John 2:13-14). Therefore there is a proper and appropriate use of the term 'father' in the body of Christ, as applied to the maturity or ministry of certain believers.

Probably the most helpful thing to note here is that Jesus did not prohibit anyone from fulfilling the role of a father in ministry as far as providing care, comfort, encouragement, leadership, maturity, wisdom, teaching, correction, rebuke, etc. These are fathering roles, and Scripture commands leaders to fulfill them. (2 Tim 4:2, see also 1 Tim 5:1-2) Rather, Jesus places prohibitions on being called by these names *as titles of honour*, and on applying to other people these terms *as titles of honour*, in particular when it is all for ostentation, and show, and when it is all outward religious form and ceremony, and hypocrisy, as it was with the Pharisees.

Jesus was not ruling out the functions of spiritual leadership, but was ruling out the fleshly and prideful human desire to seek status and fleshly distinctions of honour through proud titles.

We should note that everything Jesus said in Matthew 23 was directly relevant to the specific practices of the religious leaders and Pharisees of His day, and His speech followed on from the activities of the Pharisees in Matthew 22. Matthew 23 records seven 'woes' spoken by Jesus concerning the teachers of the law and Pharisees (although R.V.G. Tasker points out, "These 'woes' are not so much curses as expressions of sorrow, and a better translation would be 'Alas for you' rather than *Woe unto you*."[1]) and Jesus' instructions in verses 8-10 were made specifically in the light of the extreme controlling, arrogant, honour-seeking and prideful behaviour and religious practices of the leaders of His day. He was addressing very particular and specific cultural, social, and religious actions that were an abomination at that time, and which are a spiritual danger in every age.

Special greetings in the Jewish culture were a required courtesy, and to fail to greet a person considered superior in his knowledge of the Law was a serious insult, and the marketplaces referred to, of course, were a very public place. The religious leaders of Jesus' day greatly coveted these titles of respect, and at the same time, they were very controlling masters of their students, and had to be venerated in many ways. The title 'Rabbi' means "my great one." The statement, *"And do not call anyone on earth 'father'"* was most likely a reference to the 'Ab' ("father of the Sanhedrin"), who was second in charge. The Prince of the Sanhedrin (Ha-Nasi) sat in the midst of elders. On his right sat the Ab, and on his left the Chacham (sage). It has been said that 'Jesus meant the full sense of this noble word for our heavenly Father. "Abba was not commonly a mode of address to a living person, but a title of honour for Rabbis and great men of the past" (McNeile)[2]'.

This is significant, because the common tradition of the early church

1   Tyndale New Testament Commentaries: Matthew, The Tyndale Press, 1969.
2   Robertson's Word Pictures, Commentary on Matthew 23:9

was that Matthew's Gospel was first written in Aramaic for the many
Jewish Christian readers of the early years, and translated later into Greek.
Certainly Jesus spoke in Aramaic, so even if the Gospel was written in
Greek, it is still only a translation of what Jesus said. So 'pater', in Greek,
is not the term Jesus personally used, which only serves to strengthen the
thought that perhaps the word 'father', as we know and use it, is not even
intended in this passage.

In fact, none of the three terms Jesus used here were really common
words (i.e. 'Rabbi', 'Ab', and the word translated as 'teacher' in the NIV in
verse 10 – this latter word was also a specific term, meaning 'master' or
'guide', and is not the one used by Jesus in Matthew 23:8, which did mean
teacher). Rather, these were special words used by religious leaders as
reverential titles, and that by people preening themselves in public. Really,
without criticism intended, this is more like the use of titles such as 'Very
Reverend' or 'Archbishop' than the simple use of terms as references to
roles and calling, such as the use of teacher or spiritual father in the New
Testament, and as used by Christians today. This will mean that there will
be a proper use for words like pastor, apostle and prophet, and an improper
use.

None of these statements by Jesus are meant to imply that there should
be no lines of authority in the church, or that we should not recognise and
honour people in positions of leadership and authority amongst us. Nor
does the Lord Jesus intend by these statements to set aside all natural and
civil order. This is simply a rejection of the use of titles to gain honour,
and by which men and women pursue prestige, or posture themselves so
as to be greater than others. It is particularly abominable for anyone to
put themselves in the place of Christ, lording it over others, assuming
authority or power to control the lives of others, or doctrine, or give dictate
to the consciences of Christian men and women, as the Pharisees did. True
apostles and leaders of the faith are instead the humble servants of all.

But the father-son relationships that this book speaks of are not like
this. Rather, they are Godly, Christian, and biblical, are called for by the
gospel and service to Jesus Christ, and have been modeled for us. What
are they like? They are non-hierarchical, non-controlling, voluntary, with
voluntary accountability, full of affection, with mutual humility, serving
one another, mutually honouring, based on friendship, love and care,
and with no controlling ownership in one another's ministries; there is
freedom of conscience, yet with a submissive spirit. A full discussion of
the relational biblical authority that an apostle has, and does not have, was
taken up in Chapter Five of my earlier book, *The Apostolic Revelation*.

The same principles apply to spiritual fathering.

The Three Great Biblical Models of Father-Son Relationships

Every truth, the Scripture says, is established in the mouth of two or three witnesses. God has provided us the three witnesses that we need to establish a great truth. Yet this is not just a truth, it is a practical biblical doctrine for the way life should be lived in service to God through Jesus Christ.

There are great lessons to learn from each of these three examples – that of Paul and Timothy, Moses and Joshua, and Elijah and Elisha. And yet all three stories also hold a common theme.

The graces and principles that we see common to all three stories are that:

- faithfulness in service to a spiritual leader reaps great reward;
- persistence over the long haul of the many years of our life is what brings about the greatest outcomes;
- the love and the heart of a son for a father, along with fidelity and service, is really the key ingredient , i.e. the son must give his heart to a father;
- to follow, and continue to follow when all others fail, is an essential component of sonship;
- there is a flow of authority and grace from father to son, which is no doubt apparent incrementally from time to time, but which has astounding consequences at the end;
- and it almost goes without saying, God is very pleased to bless such heart relationships.

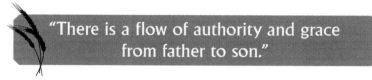

"There is a flow of authority and grace from father to son."

For every spiritual leader, God wants to provide faithful followers, sons, individuals uniquely matched to their needs who will stand with them no matter what. This is what God will do for everyone He calls and appoints, if only the hearts of the fathers would be turned toward their children. Of course, the sons to begin with don't always look like they are matched to the need. I have numerous sons, and a team of wonderful men and women, young and old, who stand with me no matter what, and have been with me for many years. One of these, Michael, was a young man finishing university in 1992, when he came to me with a question. He had just finished his degree, and the industry advice was for him to move to a much bigger city for the sake of his career in that profession. In his heart he really wanted to stay in our city so as to remain in the church. We prayed together about what he should do. Immediately and clearly, the Lord gave an unanticipated instruction. Michael was called to future prominence in world mission, and the Lord wanted me to employ him as an assistant in the church in preparation for his future ministry. I had not been intending to employ anyone, and he had assumed he would follow a professional career. But it seemed exactly right, his parents felt the same, and so I had a young apprentice.

I discovered that Michael, even though a university graduate, was not great at spelling, and had no office experience. One of his first duties was the regular daily emptying of the waste baskets. Yet, in a very short period of time, Michael became amazingly adept at everything. Gifted and skilled, a natural multi-tasker, he became my office manager, accountant, staff trainer, building and grounds manager, personnel manager, bookshop manager, troubleshooter, research assistant, ghostwriter, and technical producer, all at the same time. And over the years Michael became greatly skilled in prayer and discernment, in spiritual warfare, and in preaching and teaching even though he was never appointed a pastor. He has become a great apostle, is today a vital member of my apostolic team, and I can send him anywhere and trust him completely. He is the director of our world mission, and is now also the principal of our primary and high school. Michael was my first 'Timothy,' and I am very glad that we heard the Lord that day.

Still, Michael had to work through issues, and stick with me no matter what, and I had to be very patient with him through certain periods. But our love and commitment to one another has brought great rewards in the service of Christ, and in the joy of our own hearts also. I tell the story to illustrate my belief that God will attempt to provide every leader with such Timothys, if only they as fathers will turn their hearts to their children.

Furthermore, every follower of Christ needs to attach themselves to a leader, so as to love and serve them, and pursue the relationship. I am not here speaking only about young Christians, or of the bulk of the Christian public who are members of congregations. I'm speaking concerning every Christian. This includes every leader, every apostle and prophet, and every pastor and evangelist. No matter how old you are, or how long you have served Christ, how well established your ministry, how much authority you walk in, or how much grace you have to lead others; you will need to be a son. You must put yourself in the way of this grace. Without continuing to walk in the submission of a son to a father, no one has all the grace they need and can have in Christ.

Let's now look for a moment at these three examples individually.

Paul and Timothy:

Paul's love for Timothy, and Timothy's faithfulness to Paul, is legendary. Paul wrote to Timothy (2 Timothy 1:2-4) speaking of how beloved Timothy was, how much he longed to see him, how he remembered his tears, and how full of joy he would be when finally he saw him again. These are heartfelt expressions of deep emotion. This was the heart of a father speaking of the son he loved, and in whom he found great joy. It is crucial to the ministry of Christ that all of us in spiritual leadership have such depth of emotion, such personal care and feeling for others – for sons, for our compatriots, and for our leaders. We must love with deep longing and great joy over them.

Paul said, in writing to the Philippians (2:20) that he had no one else like Timothy. He described Timothy as being a kindred spirit, being like-minded. This is what such relationships are meant to bring about – a deep agreement of spirit, a common knowing and understanding of the ways of Christ, and depth of fellow feeling about why we are here and what must be achieved. At the same time, a common love is shared for those to whom we minister and for whom we care. This is the critical element in building apostolic leadership teams for the ministry of the church in these days. This cannot be achieved without the giving of our hearts in father-son relationships, that we might know and love them, even as Jesus knows and loves us.

Paul writes to the Corinthians as his own dear children, burdened for them. He urges them to imitate him, seeing he is their father in Christ. They needed a visit from him to refresh them in their understanding of the way to live for Christ, but he could not come. He writes, *"... therefore I urge you to imitate me. For this reason I am sending to you Timothy, my son whom I love, who is faithful in the Lord. He will remind you of my way of life in Christ Jesus, which agrees with what I teach everywhere in every church."* (1 Corinthians 4:16-17)

It's obvious, isn't it? They needed to see Paul's way of life more clearly, but he could not go, so the solution was to send Timothy. Not only would Timothy remind them faithfully of what was in Paul, but they would actually see it in Timothy. The grace of father and son is one grace.

Moses and Joshua:

The story is remarkable for a number of reasons, and not least because there is such a clear transfer of authority to lead a whole nation into their inheritance.

Joshua served Moses in a personal, devoted way all those 40 years in the wilderness. Joshua never left the tent of meeting. (Exodus 33:11) He was very defensive of Moses' authority and leadership. (Numbers 11:28-29) He led the army in battle on Moses' behalf, but we see from the remarkable story in Exodus 17 that the spiritual power to win battles came from Moses' prayers.

> "There will always be a direct spiritual connection between
> the winning of spiritual battles by the hands of sons,
> and a father's walk with the Lord."

You know the story of Moses on the mountain with hands raised, with Aaron and Hur assisting him, while Joshua fought the Amalakites in the valley. While ever Moses' hands were raised, Israel prevailed in battle, but whenever Moses rested his arms, Amalek prevailed. Aaron and Hur sat Moses on a rock, and held his arms high until Joshua totally defeated the Amalakites. These stories are written to illustrate spiritual truth. There will always be a direct spiritual connection between the winning of spiritual battles by the hands of sons, and a father's walk with the Lord. Joshua could never have defeated Amalek if it were not for Moses. The enemy was put to the sword, but the grace to do so was obtained on the mountain top.

Sons are needed to serve fathers, but they cannot prevail without their fathers. A son who achieves victory in battle should never overlook the truth that grace flowed because he walked in relationship with a spiritual father. Not only does God choose to bless such relationships, but the relationship itself is the very key to a son remaining connected to the power of God. Of importance to note here is that in Exodus 17:14, the Lord gave Moses an instruction, *"Write this on a scroll as something to be remembered and make sure that Joshua hears it, because I will completely blot out the memory of Amalek from under heaven."*

Moses was instructed to write the scroll of remembrance concerning what occurred, but specifically to make sure that Joshua heard it all. The real significance of this is not that Joshua should remember that he destroyed Amalek with the sword, but that he should understand and remember that the grace to do so came through Moses. Apostolic authority and power always flow through submission and relationship. Joshua was to have a perpetual reminder, not only of the Lord's word concerning Amalek, but of the place that Moses played in the victory. It was, first and foremost, Moses' victory, but a victory in which Joshua could rightly rejoice as a shared inheritance.

Late in life Moses sought the Lord to appoint a man to replace him. He knew his stewardship was now concluding, and he cried for a man to be appointed who would lead Israel into their inheritance. And the Lord's reply? Lay your hands on Joshua, and give him some of your authority. (Numbers 27:15-23) He was not given all that Moses had, but still it was much of what Moses had, and everything that Joshua needed. At this point in history, not everything that Moses had could pass to Joshua, for some responsibilities were to be taken up by the High Priest.

So Moses commissioned Joshua with the laying on of hands before all the people. Deuteronomy 34:9 tells that Joshua was filled with the spirit of wisdom specifically because Moses had laid his hands upon him. It was for this reason the Israelites listened to him and did what the Lord commanded. Striking, isn't it?

When a man was needed to lead Israel, God chose the one man who had been a son. I'm sure that in the vast numbers of the camp of Israel there were many gifted men, many powerful men, many full of wisdom and understanding, many with great capacity for leadership and wisdom in every circumstance of life. But God chose Joshua, for he was a son.

And after the death of Moses, God spoke with him, *"No one will be able to stand up against you all the days of your life. As I was with Moses, so I will be with you; I will never leave you nor forsake you."* (Joshua 1:5) This kind of promise can only ever come to a son. The words *"as I was with Moses, so I will be with you"* are very telling indeed, and reveal the continuity of God's favour through faithfulness in relationships.

The church everywhere needs such sons who, by fighting battles alongside a spiritual father over many a long year, will ultimately be qualified and given the grace and opportunity to lead the people of God into victory and their inheritance.

In the coming days we will see the church on earth come into a great inheritance. This inheritance can be obtained when the people of God are led finally by those who have been faithful sons.

Elijah and Elisha:

I will speak more of Elijah and Elisha in a later chapter showing how and why to pursue spiritual fathers. But for now, consider these observations. From their story we find that grace for ministry can be given in double portion, but it was given to a son who pursued relentlessly and would not leave the side of his spiritual father.

The story does make one thing very clear. To obtain a true double portion inheritance of the anointings, grace, and power of the Holy Spirit for ministry, one needs two fathers – one in heaven, and one on earth. I have on many occasions heard faithful believers pray in church prayer meetings, crying out for *"a double portion of the Spirit."* But I have never yet heard of anybody with a testimony of having received an answer to this prayer. There is a reason – they were asking the wrong father.

The Bible contains only one record of a man receiving a double portion anointing for ministry. We should take note of just how he obtained it. In his case, his spiritual father asked him, *"what can I do for you"* (2 Kings 2:9), and in reply Elisha asked Elijah to grant him a double portion of his spirit. We shall consider this more later, but for now I make this one point. To obtain a double portion anointing for ministry, you will need the agreement of both your Father God in heaven and your spiritual father on the earth. It is God alone who gives the anointing, and it is God alone who has the final sovereign decision over whether it is given or not, but it seems to be also dependent upon obtaining the agreement and approval of the spiritual father with whom you have walked.

But some people will object. They will say, "I don't need a spiritual father, I have Christ alone." Or they might say, "Abraham didn't have a spiritual father, and I am the son of Abraham. I walk in the footsteps of my father Abraham as the New Testament says. Therefore if Abraham can be the man of faith and the friend of God without having a spiritual father, so can I."

People who think these things have only half the truth. It is true that Abraham might not have had a spiritual father in the sense of which we speak today, i.e. a permanent ongoing relationship of accountability and spiritual leadership. But to assume that Abraham was therefore independent and without submission to another is complete ignorance and overlooking the facts. Abraham was not an independent man, and there is something quite astounding, even surprising regarding him. Even though God called Abram and gave him truly great promises (Genesis 12:2-3), which committed God to making Abraham into a great nation, blessing him, making his name great, and causing him to be a blessing to all peoples on earth, we have to note this fact. Until Abraham met Melchizedek, the priest of God Most High, and recognised him as being over him in the Lord, submitted to him and paid to him the tithe, after which he received Melchizedek's blessing, absolutely nothing had happened in Abraham's life.

Abraham had the initial promises, but no more. Yet after receiving the blessing of Melchizedek, God came to Abraham and made covenant with him, and then made many more promises as part of that covenant. Amongst those promises was the promise of a son.

It was from the time of receiving the blessing of another man, one who was over him in the Lord, that all the things that we know were of great moment in Abraham's life, and in the history of salvation, began to happen, including the promise of a son. Thus, from the very early history of justification by faith we see the principle that for the fullness of inheritance to come to us who are the Lord's, we must receive the blessing of another person, someone who is over us in the Lord, as Abraham did. You are called to walk in the footsteps and in the faith of your father Abraham. You will need to emulate his faith in this matter also.

Perhaps someone else will object and say, "I'm a follower of Christ. I do not need anyone in my life but Jesus. I will only do the things that He shows me to do."

Let us then consider Jesus. Born the sinless Son of God, He grew in wisdom and in favour with God and man. When He turned 30, the time had come for Him to begin His ministry, for in Jewish culture a 30 year-old man had become a fully mature adult, and in the family business the word of a son of this age was binding upon his father. Up until this time He had conducted no public ministry, and performed no signs or miracles.

Before He commenced ministry, Christ also had to submit to another man, someone who was, so to speak, 'in Christ' before Him – someone who was in the ministry and had the approval of God, but someone who, in a sense, had spiritual seniority. It was necessary for Jesus to receive the blessing of God from someone like this before He commenced His own ministry. He went to the one who had been sent ahead of Him especially for this purpose – John the Baptist, who was baptising in the Jordan River.

You can see the significance of this already. John said to Him, *"I need to be baptised by you, and do you come to me?"* Jesus replied, *"Let it be so now. It is proper for us to do this to fulfil all righteousness."* (Matthew 3: 14-15) Jesus knew that it was essential. Even though He was the sinless Son of God, He must submit to the grace of God that had been given to another, the one who came before Him. Thus He sought and received John's laying on of hands and blessing. This being fulfilled, the heavens opened, and the Spirit of God descended upon Him bodily. It was upon His submission to another that Jesus Christ, our Saviour, received the fullness of the Spirit in preparation for ministry. This will be a requirement for each of us as well.

> **"It was upon His submission to another that Christ received the fullness of the Spirit in preparation for ministry."**

Without submission there is no true authority, and without relationship there is no fullness of blessing. Each one of us, every believer, every five-fold minister, is meant to find the fullness of grace and blessing through relationships, through submission, and through honouring other believers, but especially those who are over us in the Lord.

What is the 'spirit of sonship'?

Just what is the 'spirit of sonship'? We have said that it is an attitude, and a value system. What is a value? Values are those things that we hold in our hearts as fundamental beliefs concerning what is right and wrong, concerning how we should live, and how the world should work. Our values are shown not in what we say we believe, but in how we react, how we spend our time, how we treat people, the decisions we make, the use of our money – basically, the way we actually live will reveal just what are our true values.

Christ's values are shown by the way He lived, and especially by the way He served His father. The 'spirit of sonship' is the operation of the grace of Christ in our hearts whereby we learn His values and walk in them, especially in our relationships with other people and with regard to how we follow and serve our leaders as spiritual fathers.

Of special note here is that the 'spirit of sonship' is the same in the heart of fathers as well as sons. These are not values that only sons must walk in; these are the values of all, including everyone who has matured as a father in the faith. In fact, no one ever really becomes a father without first being a son. And even then, every father remains a son to someone else. Sonship is common to us all. There are no qualities in Jesus that are not in His father also – the values and attitudes to service of both God the Father and the Son are the same.

Entering into such a father-son relationship, where as a son we give our hearts to a father, very often immediately opens the way for grace to flow. We have often found, with pastors and others who are already mature in ministry, that when they become a son to a father, they immediately become fathers also. It is an amazing domino effect. Men and women who were never recognised before as fathers in the faith, immediately become seen as such by their followers after they become 'sons.'

The Values of Sonship

What are the values of sonship? This is that set of values that includes love, loyalty, faithfulness and fidelity, honouring, a sense of belonging to other people, spiritual unity i.e. being one with others, caring for leaders, a genuine sense of family, excitement and joy over others, longing to see them, honesty and transparency in heart relationships, mutual serving, mutual honouring, genuinely having a heart for other people. And all of these attitudes and values are directed in particular to serving those over you in the Lord, and to walking with a spiritual father. You will accept the responsibility of walking in healthy and accountable relationships, and will recognise and honour spiritual authority.

I have said that fathers can pass their anointings to their sons, and this is one of the great benefits of father-son relationship. Unfortunately Elisha's anointing went with him to the grave, for he had not passed on his prophetic authority and grace to another before he died. This is perhaps because his disciple Gehazi, the one who most likely was being trained for this position (as we see in 2 Kings 4), fell from his calling through greed and disobedience, brought about by independence and lack of submission. There was something very wrong with his heart, and in 2 Kings 5 we see Gehazi judged.

Needed are faithful sons of good character. Christian history has many cases of such prophets and others who died without passing on in a personal, relational way the grace and anointings they had found. Was it that they did not understand fathering? This is very likely. Was it there were no trusted sons in the house? This is also possible.

Personally, my plan is to pass what I have to as many as possible, and to pass it on early. I believe an apostle's call is to help make other people successful. I must obey this call, and raise sons for Christ's glory. This is like using one candle *to light another candle*.

The Heart of a Son

A son should not see his father as a 'ticket to success,' or just as the means for his advancement. Yet it is not uncommon for both ambitious pastors, and driven believers, to make this mistake. I have had a few people who have come to me with a wrong spirit. They like what you can do for them, and they think that you are going to lift them up and push them forward in ministry, – but they are not motivated by love for you and the brethren; they are driven by ambition. And pride.

Occasionally someone comes along who looks supportive and caring on the outside, but is driven by something worse – lust (in its original meaning of the word). Lust means an inner craving, or grasping, or covetous desire to take hold of things that other people have, to satisfy their inner needs. In a lustful person, their pleasure is taken, often without them realising it, by having the unseen and unsavoury effect of draining other people, or even swallowing them up. Paul went so far as to say, *"If you keep on biting and devouring each other, watch out or you will be destroyed by each other."* (Galatians 5:15) and further on he said, *"Let us not become conceited, provoking and envying each other."* (Galatians 5:26)

James spoke of this also, *"But if you harbour bitter envy and selfish ambition in your hearts, do not boast about it or deny the truth. Such "wisdom" does not come down from heaven but is earthly, unspiritual, of the devil. For where you have envy and selfish ambition, there you find disorder and every evil practice."* (James 3:14-16) People driven by these kinds of lust have the effect of leaving the people they cling to debilitated, life sucked from them, energy drained away, the vision dimmed, and motivation dulled. We have to beware of those particular believers, whether false or fleshly, whose enthusiasm for the ministry is lust. There is a dangerous and powerful spirit that works through such people.

Jesus said of His disciples, *"Have I not chosen you, the 12? Yet one of you is a devil!"* (John 6:70) Of this original group that he named apostles (Mark 3:13-14), only 11 became sons. The other was a dead weight, no doubt a burden on Jesus' heart, yet he had a necessary role to fulfil. And my experience has been that, even where I have had people to contend with who feigned sonship but were driven by lust, whilst the pain of the process I never enjoy, there are very positive outcomes. We learn a great deal, we mature. Sometimes people like this are the unwitting key to the maturity of people around us who learn and see. There are great victories to be had even when the Lord allows us to be exposed to debilitating evils for a season.

But our purpose is to raise sons, not devils. And sons have a different heart, or at least those who are willing to learn and change do come to have a better view of things. Whilst a father is a source of blessing and security for a son, a spiritual son cannot afford to have as his primary motivation what his father can do for him. Our primary motivation, as in all things, must be the love of Christ in us causing us to love others. Therefore love for a spiritual father, and what benefit we can be to him and others by serving him, is the motivation of a true son.

We had a remarkable testimony a few years ago from a pastor who is a son to me. He and his wife are in their 60s, and he was a Baptist pastor for over 40 years. He became a son to me some years before, and we had very fruitful visits to his city. He and others had been coming regularly to our conferences in Rockhampton. He had always been convinced of the apostolic message, and unashamedly spoke of me, and was very generous financially as well. But one year he had a transformation, even though what was in him before was good.

My spiritual father, Chuck Clayton, came to Australia for our 2005 Apostolic Summit, and when he first arrived and stood in the door of our building, was suddenly given strong impressions and visions from the Lord for us. In particular, God was about to do a new thing in the hearts of our people – whereas before they had believed the message and supported the vision because they accepted my leadership and believed that what I was doing was good, now there would be a great change in their hearts. From this time, God would cause the vision and the message to be in them as if it was their very own, and Christ would gather them under his arms as a hen gathers her chicks. They would believe the message and run with the vision, not just because the vision in me was true, but because it would now also be in them.

A few days later, in the middle of the series of Summit meetings, during the worship the spirit of the Lord completely changed this brother's heart. His testimony was that whereas up until that point he saw the apostolic message and the ministry of the apostle, meaning me, as being of great benefit to him and to his people, so that he enjoyed walking with me because it was so beneficial to him, now he saw things completely differently. Now he could see that the message and the apostolic ministry God had given me was so important, that he must devote himself to serving me, so as to lift me up and help me. It was no longer a case of what I could do for him, but what he could do for me.

This gives a picture of the motivation of a true son. This is what we see in Christ. This is what we see in Joshua and Timothy most clearly. It is not that a son does not have needs, or does not have ultimately their own calling and purpose in life. Of course they do. But a son does not see his father's purpose and his own purpose as two different or separate things. We are family; we are working for the same inheritance; we are here to serve other people – and our love has grown to the point where we love to give and to serve. It is a fulfilment of that insight Jesus shared, *"It is more blessed to give than to receive."* (Acts 20:35)

Testimony

Jenny Brown
Member of Peace Christian Church,
Rockhampton, Australia.

I have been giving considerable thought as to what spiritual fathering has meant to me, and what impact it has had on my day to day life, and my spiritual walk with the Lord.

Only recently did I see and understand the benefits that spiritual fathers have brought into my life, when the two pastors I have served under were brought together. I was able to catch up with my first 'spiritual father" at a recent speaking engagement that he had in our town. As a young Christian I didn't know how to express myself well to him, but I knew that he cared about me. I could see the love in his heart to those around him, and although he didn't know me well, knowing that love gave me confidence to follow Christ, trust in him and know his leading.

John Alley is now my spiritual father, and knowing him has continued to give me that confidence and assurance in my walk with Christ. But there was a time, before John came into this understanding of fathering and sonship and he was able to share this revelation of love towards us, that other "christian" friendships took and destroyed the confidence I once had.

Those friendships totally disabled me. I lost confidence in every aspect of my life and if someone spoke of the good in me, I could not believe it. I had a low opinion of myself, thinking I was of no value to anyone, and it was a tough, lonely time, hanging on to the hem of Christ and his words, and the truth he had spoken into my life in the past. For a period of at least 4-5 years, I daily struggled with the effect of lies that had come from the lives of others, and their effect on my family also.

The affirmation of father/son/daughter relationship has the healing power of the love that Christ desires to establish in the church. The strength and power of that love will fill lives, they will overcome, they will know and be confident of who they are in Christ. Once again, I am free to follow Christ without condemnation, and I have great confidence in the truth that God is my Father and He loves me dearly.

Thank you, John, so very much, for the chance to express my heart about this amazing gift that God has given the church through the Apostolic Heart of Christ.

Love, Jenny.

CHAPTER 7

THE WINESKIN OF THE NEW COVENANT

'He told them this parable:
"No one tears a patch from a new garment
and sews it on an old one.
If he does, he will have torn the new garment,
and the patch from the new will not match the old.
And no one pours new wine into old wineskins.
If he does, the new wine will burst the skins,
the wine will run out and the wineskins will be ruined.
No, new wine must be poured into new wineskins.
And no one after drinking old wine wants the new,
for he says, 'The old is better.'"'

(Luke 5:36-39)

Father-son relationship is the new wineskin of the church that Jesus spoke of. This new wineskin was especially designed for the family of God that would be brought together in Christ, for the new wine could not be poured into the wineskin of the old covenant. But how can relationships be the new wineskin itself?

The Old and the New

Firstly, we need to understand just what the old and new wineskins are. The old wineskin was Judaism, and the new wineskin is the body of Christ. The old wineskin was established as a result of the covenant God made with His people at Mt Sinai, but sometime later He promised that a new covenant would be made. (Jeremiah 31:31-34, Heb 8:8-12) The old covenant did not meet the needs of the people, and God found fault with the people. (Heb 8:7,9) The new covenant is the one given us in Christ's blood. (Luke 22:20)

With the old covenant was established a priesthood and a High Priest. With the new covenant also was established a new priesthood, and a new High Priest. The old covenant had been ratified and the priesthood authorised by the giving of the Law at Sinai. The new covenant was ratified by the outpouring of the Spirit on the day of Pentecost, and the new High Priesthood, that of the Lord Jesus Christ in the order of Melchizedek, was appointed not by law, but by God's oath. (Hebrews 7:20-28)

The old covenant required a priesthood, a tabernacle, furnishings, offerings, and many other things – a lot of physical things. The new requires nothing physical at all – our salvation is by faith alone, without physical religious trappings. The new covenant does have a tabernacle, but it is spiritual, in the heavenlies, and not made by man. The new also has a holy priesthood, spiritual offerings, and with the sacrifice of Christ, a better blood. These features of the new might sound similar to the old, but this is only on the surface. There is a total, permanent, and overwhelming difference between the old and new covenants, both in structure and in outcomes. A thorough reading of the Epistle to the Hebrews, from Chapter 4:14 to Chapter 10:23 will greatly clarify all of this.

Everything under the old covenant was physical, external, visible, and temporary, whereas under the new covenant everything is spiritual, internal (of the heart), seen and understood by faith and not by sight, and permanent. The old is the shadow, and the new is the substance. The old is temporary, the new is eternal. The old has outward appearances, but the new is the real.

The old has been done away with – it has perished because God declared it obsolete. God removed it and it will never be restored. (Hebrews 8:13) The new is permanent, guaranteed in the blood of Christ in whom we have an eternal hope, and He has entered the heavens on our behalf, eternally living to make intercession for the saints.

With this very brief overview, let me point out the one really significant thing about a wineskin. The purpose of a wineskin is to contain and preserve a valuable commodity so that you can keep it, store it, transport it, and dispense it. A wineskin holds something that is otherwise difficult to store, and makes it available to us and usable by us. If you have a bottle of water, it is not because you want the bottle, but because you want the water. If I give you the contents of a bottle of water to take home, but because I want to keep the bottle I pour the water out onto your hands, the water will no longer be useful to you. There is no less water in the world, but it is no longer available or useful, because you have no container, and it all spills.

And this is the role that a 'wineskin' fulfills in the purposes of God. Some kind of 'wineskin' is essential if God is to fully make available His goodness, presence, life and power to His people in the greater way He wants to.

Jesus spoke of only two particular wineskins, the old and the new. Each of these wineskins had a purpose. This was to effectively receive and hold the revelation, life, and grace of God, indeed the very presence, power, and blessing of God, and to bring these holy things into the experience of God's people to make them available and useful to them.

Thus God designed the wineskins, old and new, for great purposes. The greatest purpose of all has always been for God to come and live amongst His people.

"The greatest purpose of all was for God to come and live amongst His people."

But in the old covenant everything was external and physical. The revelation of God on the mountain was so physical it was terrifying. When everything had been set up in the camp according to the Law i.e. the tabernacle, the altars, the offerings, the priesthood, the sacrifices, etc, God Himself came and lived in the camp. The glory of God came and took up residence in the tabernacle. From that time they saw the presence of God, marked by the cloud of His glory over the tent. But note: even the presence of God was only of a physical nature. It held promise, but only as a shadow and hope of things to come. It was never the reality. The presence of God was not in anyone's heart. Even the offerings did not cleanse the consciences of the believers. Thus everything under the old covenant, including the presence of God in the camp, was physical and external. And this is why God found fault with it all. It did not meet the needs of the people, and was only ever temporary.

What was the old wineskin then? It was the people of Israel as a nation, with established religious practices by which they could draw near to God, but waiting for a greater revelation of God in a new covenant. When the slaves came out of Egypt they were a mixed multitude (Exodus 12:38), for not all had descended from Abraham. But at Mount Sinai, with the giving of the covenant and the Law, they became a people. A wineskin is always a people. It was a form of community, but the community was external; a new nation was established in the world with a shared political and religious life.

The same principles apply for the new covenant and the new wineskin, except that all its features are spiritual and of the heart – not of external things which are shadows, but of internal things which are real.

With the outpouring of the Holy Spirit on the day of Pentecost, 'a people' was formed. Under the new covenant, the people of God were not formed as a political nation, but a spiritual body with a powerful common life. The followers of Christ were now a spiritual nation of priests, offering spiritual sacrifices. We are built into this community, not by external things, but purely by the work of God in our hearts. A new law has been given – the Law of Love. As before, the presence of God comes and takes up residence in the camp, except this time the camp is in the hearts of all believers, for we are encamped together as one people by the Holy Spirit. The Holy Spirit indwells each person, but He also lives in the whole body together. Community has been formed, but it is of the Spirit, and is internal and spiritual.

Why is all this relevant to our subject? Because whilst under the old covenant the wineskin was institutional, under the new covenant the wineskin is *relational*. The old created a community for God's people, but the community was only in external form. That wineskin was comprised of external forms and ceremonies in a physical nation that kept the people in a group, called to hear and respond to the word of God, and remain under His blessing.

Now in the new wineskin, people are built together also, but it is not external things that hold them together. It is the grace of God in the heart. This is why the church is never an institution, and an institution is never the church. There are many organisations in the world that call themselves churches, but do not necessarily have the shared life that has genuinely joined the hearts of the believers together. There are many people who attend churches on Sunday mornings who are joined to some organisation, but whose hearts are not necessarily joined to one another. They say they believe the word of God, but they live in a spirit of independence. Where this occurs, this is not the form of Christianity that was given at Pentecost.

In summary, the new wineskin is the building together of God's people by relationship in such a way that they are a true community, and God can live amongst them by His Spirit. This is not the same thing as each individual member being full of the Holy Spirit.

Each of us individually is a temple of the Holy Spirit, and we are each to be filled with the Holy Spirit and have a knowledge of God. But there is a corporate experience of Christianity that is greater than this. Individuals full of the Holy Spirit are not in themselves a wineskin, even though they have received blessing and of course do contain new wine – the Holy Spirit, the word of God, the power of the gospel, and the gifts of the Spirit. In short, the life of God is in us. But the purpose of a wineskin is to so build all the people of God together in one entity, that God can come and live by His spirit amongst us corporately. A wineskin is formed when the Holy Spirit can take hold of a people corporately and so build their lives together as one people that they become a people of one heart and one mind, and God lives amongst them by his Spirit. This is what happened at Pentecost, and this is what Acts 4:32 and Ephesians 2:22 refer to.

Under the Old Covenant, Israel was that entity whereby God came and lived in the camp. But Israel in that sense was only a physical nation, and God's presence was only a physical presence in the midst of the camp.

Under the New Covenant, the believers corporately are a nation or kingdom of priests offering spiritual sacrifices, and God is looking for times and places when His presence can reside amongst His people – not just on the one-by-one basis that each of us individually has an experience of the indwelling Christ, but in a corporate sense. For there to be an experience of the presence of God living amongst His people corporately, there has to be a unity of believers. Lives have to be built together in community. They have to love one another, and walk together.

> "It is the building together of lives in spiritual unity,
> with genuine intimacy of relationships,
> that forms the new wineskin."

It is the building together of lives in spiritual unity, with genuine intimacy of relationships, that forms the new wineskin. Then God can take up residence in the camp, and we would see a corporate manifestation of the life, power, and presence of God amongst us. Ephesians 2:22 gives us the promise of this, as does 2 Corinthians 6:16. God has always wanted to live amongst His people.

By definition then, a wineskin is a structure specially designed to receive, contain, and make available to us the life, power, grace, and spirit of God in a greater or corporate way. A wineskin is always a God-given means by which He builds His people together to form a single entity. For the new wineskin, this is a spiritual entity requiring oneness through love, acceptance, heart unity, and honouring; in short, committed meaningful relationships.

Now that we have some understanding of what the wineskin is, and we understand the specifically relational nature of the new wineskin, we can make a clear application. Since it is only when our lives are joined together and we are truly one people from the heart that we have a 'wineskin' that God can fill by His Spirit in a corporate way, then it is true to say that father-son relationships in the ministry are the new wineskin of the church, seeing they are the strong, biblical pattern for the relationships of the church.

I am not saying that father-son relationships have become a new wineskin just in this present age, or just in this current move of the Holy Spirit. No, father-son relationships and the like have always been the new wineskin of the church, even from the day Jesus said that God was building a new wineskin into which He would pour His Spirit in the age of the gospel.

And when we see father-son relationships as the new wineskin, it is everything we have said the church should be. It meets our needs, and provides for all the following:

- gives us relational instead of institutional Christianity
- allows for the genuine spiritual leadership of apostles, prophets, and others as fathers in the faith, rather than hierarchical government
- allows for the restoration of the apostolic and prophetic ministries as foundational to building the church aright
- facilitates the removal of the spirit of competition from our hearts, which is very damaging in churches with an institutional life, but is removed by the very values of apostolic relationships
- shows forth the father-son nature of God in the life of the church and ministry
- restores the very personal, and heartfelt love that should be evident amongst church leadership, as it was in the New Testament
- and many other benefits too numerous to list. This is what this whole book is about. And essentially, it is the fulfillment of the Scripture: *"Once you were not a people, but now you are the people of God;"* (1 Peter 1:10).

Making a Straight Path for the Lord

After 400 years of silence between the last of the Old Testament prophets and the coming of John the Baptist, yet with the witness of Malachi 4:4-6 still sounding as a beacon of hope, what did we get? The voice of one crying in the wilderness, *"Make ready the way of the Lord, make straight paths for Him."* (Mark 1:3) How do we make a straight path for the Lord? By turning the hearts of the fathers to their children, as the angel of the Lord said! Speaking to Zechariah of his son, John, who would soon be born, he advised, *"...he will go on before the Lord, in the spirit and power of Elijah, to turn the hearts of the fathers to their children and the disobedient to the wisdom of the righteous – to make ready a people prepared for the Lord."* (Luke 1: 17) There must always be, in the ministry of Christ, the heart of fathers for sons, and of sons for fathers, if a people are to truly live and walk in the Spirit of the Lord.

This is now the crucial factor for the church life of the future. Such heart relationships in the Body of Christ are essential if the church is to come to the maturity into which the Holy Spirit is leading us. This is a maturity in love and relationships; it is a restored apostolic Church with a revived apostolic life, for which apostles and prophets are now being raised to provide the leadership required, and to revive both the anointings and the life examples needed. Their task, and the great task of every apostle, is to turn the hearts of church leaders to become those of fathers caring for their children, to teach the five-fold ministry how to love each other, and to bring the hearts of all God's people to love and trust their leaders.

From the time of John, the true ministry of grace has always been a ministry that requires the hearts of fathers for their sons, and sons for their fathers, and this we see with Jesus and the 12. In the day of John the Baptist and Jesus, the move of God was not in the institutional temple service in Jerusalem, but in the relationships formed out in the field. It was in the 'wilderness' they made straight the paths of the Lord. And ever since, it is in the relationships we form in Christ – where love and honour of one another is not just a means to an end, or a 'Christian' requirement, but a way of life – that we open the true way of the Lord, and make a straight path for him in dealing with the hearts of men and women. As Paul said, *"you are God's field."* (1 Corinthians 3:9)

The religion of the 'temple' today, i.e. the institution, is a sham. There is a lot of outward show, and not much substance. But that is, of course, what you get if, after being offered the reality, you turn back to the shadow; and these were only ever shadows. Now we have the Christ, and the way of love; we are called to walk with Christ and find more of Christ by loving others. When you can have Christ, the light of life, the glory of the father – who in their right mind would want the mere shadow?

Shirley Fisher
Member of Peace Christian Church,
Rockhampton, Queensland, Australia.

I came to Peace in 1993. I had been in Church most of my life, but was always looking for something I lacked. I thought I understood the love of Jesus and who He was, but I had no personal relationship with Him, or any understanding of the love of a Heavenly Father.

My relationship with my own father wasn't what it was meant to be. My father was a good and kind man, but he was a product of his upbringing – his father died when he was young, and his mother showed him no love. Consequently he didn't know how to give or receive love. I grew up never being sure of his love, and never being affirmed or blessed by a father.

One day I asked John to pray for me regarding some other matter, and I mentioned how I felt. He prayed for me, affirmed me and gave me a father's blessing. This broke something off my life and I felt more confident and free than ever before. I realised then what it was that was missing in my life. I now had an identity.

John is what I believe a father should be – loving, kind, and gentle, but at the same time firm and strong, and not afraid to discipline those he loves. I have seen him give correction on a couple of occasions and it was done with such love and gentleness.

I am so blessed to have such a father in the house. It gives me a feeling of security to know we are loved by someone who sets a living example of how we should live and love one another. Many people who come to visit us comment on the love they sense among us.

I feel a great privilege to love and serve John and Hazel as I know many others do. To me that is what it means to be a true son.

Shirley Fisher.

CHAPTER 8

GENERATIONAL BLESSING

*"May God Almighty bless you and make you fruitful and
increase your numbers until you become a community
of peoples. May he give you and your descendants
the blessing given to Abraham,
so that you may take possession of the land
where you now live as an alien..."*

(Genesis 28:3-4)

All our lives we have heard the word 'blessing'. The subject of blessing is mentioned in the Bible about 600 times, and its opposite, cursing, about 200 times. That makes this subject a major theme of the Scriptures.

I once heard someone say that the church in his time has learned a lot about curses – e.g. what curses do, how to cut them off, how to counteract curses, etc. – but we hadn't taught the church enough about blessing. We take blessing for granted. I decided to seek the Lord for an understanding of blessing, and within a few days received this powerful message.

We come across the concept of blessing from the first chapter of the Bible. On day five of creation God made the fish of the sea and the birds of the air, and blessed them and said, *"Be fruitful and increase in number and fill the water in the seas, and let the birds increase on the earth."* (Genesis 1:22) Ask yourself this question: since God had made these creatures perfect and complete, in a perfect environment, and gave the command by which they lived, why then did He need to also bless them?

We notice immediately that the blessing here has a lot to do with producing fruitfulness and increase. This is true of what a blessing does in our lives also.

On day six of creation God made man, male and female, in His own image. Then He blessed them: *"Be fruitful and increase in number; fill the earth and subdue it. Rule over the fish of the sea and the birds of the air and over every living creature that moves on the ground."* (Genesis 1:28) Again, why was the blessing needed? Man had been made in the image of God, and God had breathed into him His own breath by which man became a living soul. Man was placed in a perfect environment, and all his needs were supplied. They were healthy, the garden was perfect, and there was no sin, and no sickness or disease. They were the way God wanted them, and the Lord would come every day to walk with Adam in the cool of the afternoon. In the light of these perfections and graces being present, why did man also need a blessing from his creator?

Well, just what is a blessing? The answer is found in the following definition: **A blessing is a pronunciation which imparts spiritual power, opening the way for us in life, giving us approval and confidence, and power for us to succeed; it is grace to enable us to become what we are meant to become, and to achieve what we are meant to achieve.**

To amplify that, a blessing is a form of words, specifically a pronouncement, often by someone with authority, that gives you permission to succeed, and power to personally advance in life and fulfill your God-given purpose. It is an approval that will aid your success. It will sustain your life. It will enable you to overcome obstacles, to rise to become what you were meant to become, and to achieve well in doing what you are meant to do.

Do you not think that you just might need a blessing? And man, having been made in the image of God, also has the power to both bless and curse. Jesus said that we were to bless even our enemies. (Luke 6:28) Paul said that we were to bless and curse not. (Romans 12:14) The power of blessing is meant to be expressed by each of us in the service of the Lord Jesus Christ. Every family, every home, every business, every church, every pastor, every leader – each one of us – needs a blessing, and can give blessing.

What then is *generational* blessing? This is a term that defines a certain kind of blessing – one which flows from one generation to the next. A generational blessing is that which passes from father to son, a blessing which, when carried by one generation, can and should be passed on to another. Very often, if you do not receive that blessing by impartation, it is lost.

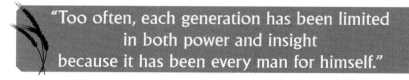

"Too often, each generation has been limited in both power and insight because it has been every man for himself."

This has often been a problem with the church. We have lost the art of blessing, because we have forgotten its most specific form in generational impartation i.e. the blessing of the fathers. Too often, each generation has been limited in both power and insight in its struggle for the gospel, because it has been 'every man for himself,' so to speak. Therefore each succeeding generation did not rise as much as it might have done had the church only understood how to walk together as father and son.

I heard someone say that the most anointed place in any city or town is the graveyard, because so many Christians, like Elisha, have taken their anointings to the grave – for they did not know how to pass them to their spiritual children, or even knew that they could.

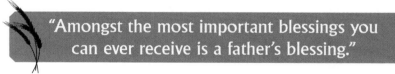

"Amongst the most important blessings you can ever receive is a father's blessing."

Understand then, that amongst the most important blessings you can ever receive is a father's blessing. And by extension, the leaders Christ appoints as the shepherds of the flock, especially when mature, have an important role to play as fathers in the faith.

Sue's Blessing

I was the visiting speaker for a conference in a large provincial city in Australia, when at the conclusion of one of the meetings a young woman of about 35 years of age approached me.

She said her name was Sue, and that while she had been sitting there, the Lord had told her that I had something which, if she asked me for it, I would give it to her. But, she said, "I don't know what it is." I said, "Well, that makes two of us; I don't know what it is either. However, let me pray about it for a moment."

As soon as I began to pray, I realised what it was, although this was a completely new thought to me at the time. Sue had never had the blessing of her father, and the Lord wanted me to lay my hands upon her in prayer, stand in the place of her dad, and give her the blessing that she had never received as a daughter. I told Sue what I thought, and she just knew that was it! She knew what was missing in her life.

So I began to pray for her, and poured out my heart in prayer as if this was my daughter. If this was my little girl, what would I want for her in life? I prayed every good blessing I could think of for her: good health, long life, wholesome friendships, trusting relationships, financial prosperity and protection, and above all, fruitfulness in the service of Jesus Christ. Over her life I declared my approval, that she was a wonderful daughter. I commanded over her life blessing in Jesus' name, and gave her my blessing as a father too.

Sue had been estranged from her natural father; he was not speaking to her, and she had never received his blessing. But within two weeks of me praying for her, her father was reconciled to her, and then he gave her his blessing as well. Soon after, Sue, who had been single, married a pastor. I continue to receive regular news from them, and hear of their joy and fruitfulness in the Lord.

There are many like Sue, for whom something is missing, even though they often do not know what it is. And as well as your natural father, you will have had spiritual fathers over the years too. You need, and should want, and be eagerly desirous of obtaining, the blessing of your fathers – because the blessing of a father gives life.

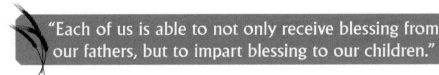

"Each of us is able to not only receive blessing from our fathers, but to impart blessing to our children."

We all need to learn how to receive blessing, but also how to generate blessing. That is, we must receive it, and we must pass it on. Each of us is capable, not only of receiving blessing from our fathers, but of imparting blessing to our children, both natural and spiritual , and to everyone around us. You are a source of blessing. Many people are meant to be blessed through your words, and by your approval.

What a Father Gives His Children

There are so many things we derive from our fathers. I am speaking now specifically of what God has designed to come from our natural fathers, but these truths are paralleled by that same holy design in the spiritual families of the body of Christ.

Every son and daughter needs to hear the voice of a father, for a father's voice speaks love, affirmation, affection, approval, motivation, correction, success, permission to succeed, blessing, identity, courage, and security. Let us consider briefly some of these.

A son or a daughter gets their sense of <u>identity</u> in the main from their father. The question of 'Who am I?' is answered in a child's heart by their interaction with their father. It has been said that 85% of what a person thinks about themselves comes from dad.

A father supplies the <u>motivation</u> that a child needs, and gives the discipline by which a child overcomes a lack of motivation.

It is a father that gives his son or daughter '<u>permission to succeed</u>'. This 'permission' is written subconsciously upon a child's heart by what a father says, and by the attitude he takes to them. Some face life with confidence, and some struggle. It is the father who has the power to speak and release in a child this subconscious inner sense of approval that tells them they have permission to succeed in life.

A father's <u>love</u> and <u>encouragement</u> is of supreme importance in the lives of his children. From a father comes that sense of <u>approval</u> and <u>affirmation</u> so crucial for happiness, peace, well-being, strength, and purpose. The love and encouragement that affirms and approves speaks into every area of a child's life. Thus a child's identity, motivation, and permission to succeed, as well as their sense of security, are all reinforced by approval. Even in the church, 80% of pastoral care is encouragement.

There is nothing so wholesome as a good sense of <u>security</u>. It is a father's love, protection, and discipline that establishes an effective sense of security in his children. This helps to keep them from the need to 'perform' to please others, a weakness that can be spiritually debilitating and produce religious good works rather than faith, and which also hinders them from finding trust and intimacy in relationships.

In addition to all this, from dad comes <u>inheritance</u> and <u>generational blessing</u>. Aside from a natural inheritance, which will vary from family to family, a Christian father of great faith and obedience to Christ can leave a powerful spiritual legacy for his children, which is of great worth and effect.

It is most important that a father speaks into the hearts of his little sons and daughters, surrounding them with acceptance and approval. Out of this comes security, identity, and motivation, so that the hearts of children are blessed, enlarged, lifted up, and directed into a prosperous future by a father who loves and speaks.

What having a father does for a son!

While I was travelling in a car with some young pastors one day, they began to discuss the value of having a father in the ministry, and compared it to having a good dad.

They made the point that under the ministry of a father, your value seems to appreciate (this is a financial term, the opposite of depreciate). They said that when dad is by his side, a small boy becomes a big man. Having a dad really releases a son, for a father energises. Walking with a father builds confidence. You can face anything when you know that your dad is behind you. It is wonderful when you know your father believes in you. This is what spiritual fathers do for men and women in the service of our Lord Jesus Christ. We are not meant to walk alone.

God is a good father

When Jesus turned 30 years of age, the time had come to commence His public ministry. He came to the Jordan to be baptised by John. We discussed the purpose of His submission to John in an earlier chapter. After He was baptised, and came up out of the water, not only did the heavens open and the Holy Spirit come upon Him bodily in the form of a dove, but something else occurred as well. God spoke with an audible voice.

It is not often that God speaks from heaven audibly. One would think that if this occurred, so as to be written in the public record of Scripture, God must have said something of supreme importance. In fact, the Father was to later say the same thing on the Mount of Transfiguration, which means He declared it twice. The content of that statement is recorded in the New Testament seven times – which shows it to be a matter of the utmost importance. What did He say? *"This is my son, whom I love; with Him I am well pleased."* (Matt 3:17)

Why did God the Father speak like this? Because He knew the importance of a father's voice for a son. Jesus was about to commence His ministry. He was about to face the wilderness and the onslaught of Satan's temptations. Look at the words the father spoke. *"This is my son"* – that is affirmation of identity! *"whom I love"* – that is affection! *"with him I'm well pleased"* – that is approval!

What was God doing? He was being a good father! Even the Son of God, our Saviour, needed to hear the voice of His Father.

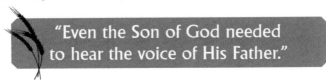

"Even the Son of God needed to hear the voice of His Father."

We all need to hear the voice of a father, but of course there are some who have not known such a voice. There are too many that have only known cursing, or disaffection, or disapproval, and so have been wounded. There is in the heart of many of these what is often called an orphan spirit, or an orphan heart.

By this term, I am not referring to an evil spirit. The term has been used by others, notably Jack Frost, who later rephrased the terminology as "orphan heart." A term such as this is needed to refer to the state of heart we find in many people who, through broken trust, or betrayal, or lack of parental care and affection, or other such experiences (but just as often through their own perceptions rather than actual fact), struggle with emotions such as fear, insecurity, and low self-worth – and who carry attitudes of mistrust concerning authority figures and others, and sometimes find difficulty maintaining relationships especially where intimacy or transparency is required.

People who struggle like this often have perceptions of life that we might equate with orphans – a sense of not belonging, not being loved, not approved, insecure, untrusting, wary of father figures, or just not knowing how to relate to a father figure, etc. These things are not usually on the surface, but hidden in the thoughts and feelings of the heart. They affect behaviour and attitudes, and warp the values out of which people live. Often people do not know why they act or feel as they do. Very often people like this do not remain in churches when confrontational issues arise, especially if they are challenged personally in some way. Instead of maintaining relationships, facing the issues within their own hearts, and becoming mature, they take offence and leave to join another church. And sooner or later, the cycle will repeat itself.

This kind of hurt is found everywhere. No wonder that fatherlessness is such a curse.

A father's blessing helps establish a faith system in the heart, but quite apart from the approval, security, identity, and the rest that comes with a father's love, spiritual power also flows with the blessing. When a father speaks approval and blessing, placing upon you the blessing of God as well as his own, spiritual power flows.

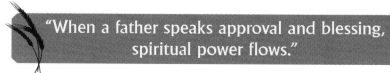

"When a father speaks approval and blessing, spiritual power flows."

This is not just something relevant to the ancients, neither is it something to be obtained for yourself alone. You must also develop a faith that says "I can be a blessing." Imagine how rich the house of God will be when every believer understands their purpose in life to be a source of blessing to others. This is why we are to accept one another as Christ accepted us, and why we are to honour one another. There is within each of us some measure in which the voice of God the Father speaks when we choose to bless.

We must therefore place upon other believers our love, affection, and approval, choosing to honour them, and giving them the sincere and forthright acceptance of our hearts. Then will the whole body be a healthier, happier, and more holy people.

Abraham's Blessing

I said earlier that virtually all blessing is generational in nature. Even the blessing of salvation by faith in Christ our Saviour has a strong generational aspect to it. You will remember that the Bible puts a great importance upon the blessing of Abraham being passed to Isaac, then to Jacob, then to his 12 sons – and then proclaims that the blessing of Abraham comes to every believer in Christ. What exactly is the blessing of Abraham?

When God called Abraham, that call would establish Abraham as a source of blessing for the whole world. The Lord said to Abraham: *"I will make you into a great nation and I will bless you; I will make your name great, and you will be a blessing. I will bless those who bless you, and whoever curses you I will curse; and all peoples on earth will be blessed through you."* (Genesis 12: 2-3)

Notice how often the concept of either receiving or giving blessing occurs in this call. Everything surrounding the purpose of Abraham had to do with blessing, not just for himself, and not just for his own children and their ongoing natural generations, but ultimately for every family and nation in the world. But the blessing of Abraham is generational in nature, so to be received, it must be received by those who are sons to Abraham. If it is not received generationally, it cannot be received at all.

It is easy to see that, historically, the physical descendants of Abraham were able to obtain this blessing, for they had been born with certain natural inheritance rights. Historically, any Jew could look to the heavens, know that he was a son of Abraham, believe and therefore be of the faith of Abraham, and thereby claim the grace of this blessing in his life and family.

But the whole purpose for setting aside the old covenant and bringing in a new one was that the blessing of Abraham would be available to everyone. The Gentiles could be included as sons of Abraham. In fact the gospel makes it clear that no one is considered to be a Jew, no one considered to be of Israel, just because they are a physical descendant of Abraham. *"For not all who are descended from Israel are Israel. Nor because they are his descendants are they all Abraham's children. On the contrary, "it is through Isaac that your offspring will be reckoned." In other words, it is not the natural children who are God's children, but it is the children of the promise who are regarded as Abraham's offspring."* (Romans 9:6-8)

The descendants of Abraham are considered by God to be those who have the same faith as Abraham, whether Jew or Gentile. Thus Abraham is certainly a source of blessing, but it is for all those who believe and walk with Christ. Now the meaning of Galatians 3:14 is made more clear, *"He redeemed us in order that the blessing given to Abraham might come to the Gentiles through Christ Jesus, so that by faith we might receive the promise of the Spirit."*

So through the cross of Christ, because of the sonship of Jesus, you were adopted into a family. You became sons. Through the cross you belong to Abraham's family, and by being made Abraham's seed, for you are now in Christ, Abraham's blessing can flow to you.

Now you know why we have such a vital interest in the nature of the blessing that was given to Abraham, and which then flowed to Isaac, and then to Jacob. It is because, in establishing a New Covenant, Christ has paid the price by which you receive a very particular blessing, as well as all the blessings that were given to Abraham.

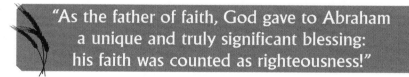

"As the father of faith, God gave to Abraham a unique and truly significant blessing: his faith was counted as righteousness!"

As the father of faith, God gave Abraham a unique and truly significant blessing: his faith was counted as righteousness! The very means of salvation, that which is called *justification by faith* – i.e. salvation by grace alone, through faith alone, in Christ alone – was first established by God in the faith of Abraham, and is the blessing given to Abraham. This is why he is the father of faith, and our father in the sight of God.

Isaac's Blessing

Now consider the outcomes in Isaac's life of the blessing which Abraham passed to him. There is no record in Scripture of how Abraham went about this, but we know he did, because Isaac, when later blessing his son Jacob, specifically passed on "the blessing given to Abraham." (Genesis 28:4)

Like Isaac after him, Abraham would have laid his hands upon his son, and spoken words of grace and power. Those words carried a very tangible divine power. With them, the favour of God, the power of covenant, and the unchanging purpose of God in human history, was transferred to the son.

Consequently, we see outcomes. The Lord appeared to Isaac – because the blessing is not impersonal; it is highly relational. Abraham was the friend of God. Therefore, if you inherit Abraham's blessings, you will also walk in friendship with God. The Lord confirmed to Isaac the oath He swore to Abraham, and again emphasised that this was for Isaac and his descendants. (Genesis 26: 2-5) Later in that chapter we read, *"Isaac planted crops in that land, and the same year reaped a hundredfold, because the Lord blessed him. The man became rich, and his wealth continued to grow until he became very wealthy."* (Genesis 26:12-13) That is a very powerful blessing. He became rich because the Lord blessed him – and that blessing came with the original blessing given to Abraham. Abraham had become rich in the land. His sons and his grandsons became rich in the land as well.

Of vital interest to us is that in the Jewish mindset, or in Jewish thought, there is no inner struggle between the idea of someone being spiritual, and someone having a lot of financial blessing, i.e. having a lot of wealth and property. But many Christians do struggle to reconcile these ideas, as if you cannot be holy and have money too. But we don't get that from the pages of Scripture – instead, that is a misinterpretation of Scripture. I am not suggesting that everyone should be self-indulgent with wealth, but I believe we are meant to handle wealth for the sake of the Kingdom of God. (see 2 Corinthians 9:8-11)

I am saying there ought not be a struggle in your heart over the issue of just how much God is allowed to bless. The blunt fact from the text of Scripture under consideration here is that Isaac became very wealthy *because* the Lord blessed him.

One truth should be very clear. Wealth does come from the blessing of the Lord (Proverbs 10:22), and furthermore, the capacity to build wealth is found in the blessing of Abraham (Deuteronomy 8:18). The power to prosper and do well is also to be found in the blessing of our fathers, if they will understand so as to command this blessing for us. Isaac benefited from the blessing of the Lord and the blessing of Abraham. Jacob, though he had to flee from his brother Esau to live with his uncle Laban, and obviously had little in his hands when he arrived, nevertheless, all that he did prospered, so that over the years he became very wealthy in his own right. He had received Isaac's blessing, Isaac had passed on to him Abraham's blessing as well (Genesis 28: 2-5), and he had the Lord's blessing. (Genesis 28: 13-15)

Isaac's Sons: Esau & Jacob

Now the story gets really interesting when we come to Isaac's sons. Isaac received blessing from his father Abraham, so he is now carrying an anointing that protects him, that gives him success, that multiplies wealth, and the grace of God is upon his life and his home. This does not mean that Isaac and Rebekah do not have struggles. They have lessons to learn, there are issues that arise in the family, and they have to deal with it, just like you and me. Into this family are born twin boys, Esau and Jacob.

We will now see the tremendous significance of the blessing, from the struggle played out over the lives of these two boys in Isaac's family.

Esau was loved by his father, but Jacob by his mother. Esau was born very hairy and red, and became a man of the fields and forests – physically a strong man. He loved to hunt wild game, and his father loved to eat it. But Jacob preferred finer pursuits. He was a man who knew his way around the kitchen, and cooked fine meals, it seems. So we have two boys who, as they grew up, were not at all alike.

One day Esau came home tired, weary, and famished. Jacob, however, had been home at the tents, cooking. Esau came in, and there was a bowl of lentil stew. It was red in colour, and Esau said to Jacob, *"Quick, let me have some of that red stew! I'm famished."* Jacob replied, *"First sell me your birthright."*

Esau replied with fateful words: *"What good is the birthright to me?"* So Esau swore an oath, and sold Jacob his inheritance, his birthright, for a bowl of stew. For this, he was also called "Edom," which means red, as his descendants the Edomites were. (See Genesis 25:29-34)

This had been a great test in Esau's life, in which he failed. There had always been something wrong with Esau's spirit, which was why at their birth the Lord had said, *"the older will serve the younger."* (Genesis 25:23)

Esau's actions greatly displeased the Lord. The Lord heard those foolish words, *"What good is the birthright to me,"* and the Scriptures conclude, *"So Esau despised his birthright."* (Genesis 25:34) Thus was the judgement of God over Esau – this man would never receive the blessing.

Dire Warning

We are told to warn every Christian believer about this, so they do not also commit this kind of ungodly sin and miss the grace of God. *"See to it that no one misses the grace of God... See that no one... is godless like Esau, who for a single meal sold his inheritance rights as the oldest son. Afterward, as you know, when he wanted to inherit this blessing, he was rejected. He could bring about no change of mind, though he sought the blessing with tears."* (Hebrews 12: 15-17)

Why does the New Testament describe Esau as ungodly – and use Esau as the classic example of a kind of godlessness that we must avoid, and warn all our people to avoid? Esau is considered an ungodly man for despising his inheritance. And we find that is precisely what many Christians have done as well.

Wherever believers have rejected their God-appointed spiritual leaders, wherever they have not honoured their spiritual fathers, and wherever they think little of the vision, or the prayers, or the heart's cry of pastors for the holiness of God's people, those believers have despised their inheritance.

How many believers do you know that belong to a church somewhere, but do not have a great respect for their pastor or their leader? They go along on Sundays, and sit, perhaps participating casually; they listen, but perhaps only lightly, or cynically, or proudly, perhaps believing they have superior knowledge, greater ability, or more astute spirituality. They are despising their inheritance, and don't realise just how poor they are.

Not all preachers in the world are big-crowd-gathering people. Most of us teach as best we can to bring our people into the grace of God. But in many churches there are numerous 'believers' who don't care about the ministry, or think little of the preacher. Sometimes the Pastor is appreciated as a person, but the message he preaches is not highly esteemed.

Then think of those who go home critical of what was said. They take offence, and don't think highly of the one who watches over their souls. Or they say to their friends, *"Well, he's a good pastoral carer, but not much of a preacher"*. Casual comments like that are common enough, but what does it mean? There is no respect, no honour for their father, and they have despised their inheritance, their birthright.

Blessing flows from the mouth of a father, but these are sins, like Esau's, that despise the source of that blessing. Therefore there is no blessing. Are you guilty of this? Then you have been despising the source of your inheritance, and have therefore been selling your inheritance for a bowl of stew.

Can you now see how we have lived? We have lived inappropriately. We have had wrong attitudes. We have not appreciated our leaders. We have not respected them, or honoured them. We have not lifted them up, or supported them – and what we didn't realise all the while was that we were impoverishing ourselves – just like Esau, who despised his inheritance. The Bible calls that *godless*.

Think about this. There is a sense in which Esau is the anti-type of Christ. Why so? Because Christ is the beloved son of the Father, who inherits everything the Father has. The Father's love is set upon Him, and Christ cherishes the father. The Father says to Jesus, *"Ask of me and I will make the nations your inheritance, the ends of the earth your possession."* Christ loved His inheritance, and embraced all that His Father appointed Him to. We are meant to emulate the attitudes of Christ to our inheritance. But of Esau, God says, *"Esau I hated".*

On the one hand we see Jesus, the son of God's love. On the other we see Esau as the anti-type of Christ – the one man in the Bible whom God says He hated – even though he was the son of Isaac, and the grandson of Abraham. God did not hate David for scheming, adultery, and murder. He did not say he hated Saul, even though He tore the kingdom out of his hands, gave it to a better man, took His Spirit away from him, and rejected him.

No, but there is one man of whom this is said. And it takes a lot for God to say He hates someone. What was it about Esau that was so disturbing to the God of salvation? He despised his inheritance!

When you despise your inheritance, you despise your father's house, you despise what your father has, you despise your father, and you despise everything your father stands for. Can you see what a dangerous place it is when you put yourself into the mindset, thinking, and heart patterns of despising your inheritance? This is a godless thing to do!

When you were born again, you were born into God's house. You have around you a family, and God always appoints leaders. There will always be somebody who carries the grace for fathering. There will be for every believer a birthright here, an inheritance amongst these people. We are not to grow to despise what other people who are over us in the Lord have to offer. It is godless to think *little* of your inheritance. It is godless to 'sell it off' for next to no value in our thinking. And many amongst us have done this kind of thing by the attitudes taken to humble pastors and other fathers in the faith.

Yet look how much we love, honour, and revere the fathers of other generations. We greatly honour the Luthers, the Wesleys, the Zinzendorfs, and the Livingstones of church history, and great men and women of past ages, but we have no such great honour and respect for those who are with us, who have the responsibility for raising us as sons and daughters in the faith, and giving leadership to the church today. We think little of them. But they are the ones that need our love, respect, honour, support, and agreement, even more than those who have gone before. They need the love and support of sons and co-workers now.

I know there will be many exceptions. I am only speaking in principle about what often goes on in institutionalised forms of Christianity where the organisation is all-important, but the average pastor is nothing much in the eyes of people.

A Fountain of Blessing

There has been too much of this kind of thing, and people have not understood an important key to their blessing. The mouth of that Godly man or woman, the pastor, the leader of the ministry, the apostle or prophet, is appointed by God to be a fountain of life to you. The scriptural principle, *"Honour your father and your mother, that it may go well with you,"* permanently stands, and is restated by the apostle Paul in Ephesians 6.

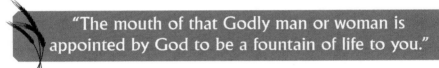

"The mouth of that Godly man or woman is appointed by God to be a fountain of life to you."

You need to know how to honour the mouthpiece of God. Your church might be small, and you might think you have a very ordinary pastor. Or perhaps you think nothing new is being taught, and you are not learning much. I'll tell you what is meant to happen. You are meant to give honour. When you recognise who your father is, when you honour and love, when you bless and respect, and when you are willing to serve, you will receive. When you are willing to be a son in the house, willing to love, serve, and honour a father, God opens the fount of blessing.

There will come a day when God will open the mouth of your pastor or spiritual father because you will have positioned yourself by the giving of honour. From the very pastor that might not have appeared to say anything new in a year, but was doing his best week after week teaching the word of God – suddenly one sentence might come from him, and power will fall upon you. And even if you do not notice it in that moment, nevertheless grace will spring up in you. You've just received inheritance! Blessing has just been released to you.

The Nature and Value of the Blessing

Don't be godless like Esau. His actions set in train some fateful events, for a seismic shift was to take place in the family.

As Isaac became older, he grew frail and blind. His days were passing, and he knew there was something he must do before he died. He must pass on the generational blessing that he received from Abraham, his father. Before it was too late, he must impart the blessing to his son, and command his own blessing upon him as well. And Isaac's beloved son, the one he intended to bless, was Esau.

Isaac called Esau in one day and said, *"My son... go out... to hunt some wild game for me. Prepare me the kind of tasty food I like and bring it to me to eat, so that I may give you my blessing before I die."* (Genesis 27: 1-4) But Rebekah, who loved Jacob and knew God's word concerning him, overheard at the flap of the tent. She had probably been listening for this moment for a long time.

While Esau was out hunting, Jacob's mother quickly cooked the meal the way she knew her husband was expecting it, and then dressed up Jacob as if he was her other son. A goat skin covered his arms and neck, because Esau was so hairy. Esau also had his own distinctive body odour, so Rebekah dressed Jacob in Esau's clothes so that the smell of Esau was with him. Then she sent Jacob in to Isaac, carrying the meal. And Jacob said, *"My father."*

The dear man, elderly and blind, heard Jacob and asked, *"Yes, my son. Who is it?"* Jacob replied, *"I am Esau your firstborn."*

After some further exchanges, his father said to him, *"Come here, my son, and kiss me."* Then we read in the text of Genesis 27, *'When Isaac caught the smell of his clothes, he blessed him and said, "Ah, the smell of my son is like the smell of a field that the Lord has blessed. May God give you of heaven's dew and of earth's richness – an abundance of grain and new wine. May nations serve you and peoples bow down to you. Be lord over your brothers, and may the sons of your mother bow down to you. May those who curse you be cursed and those who bless you be blessed."'* (Genesis 27:27-29)

Now listen, this blessing is power! In that moment power was transferred to Jacob, and it mattered not that Isaac thought he was Esau. He laid his hands on his son, and blessed him. At that point grace, privilege, favour, and power, were conferred upon Jacob.

Immediately after, Esau came in with the game he had hunted, prepared a meal, and brought it to his father. Oh, suddenly there was great distress in the camp. His father asked him, *"Who are you?"* *"I am your son,"* he answered, *"your firstborn, Esau."* At this, Isaac trembled violently. (Genesis 27:32)

It may be hard to imagine just how shaken up that old man was. This was a terribly disturbing and deeply emotional shock, a heart-rending grief, to both Isaac and Esau. Trembling violently, Isaac asked, *"Who was it, then, that hunted game and brought it to me? I ate it just before you came and I blessed him – and indeed he will be blessed!"* (Genesis 27:33)

When Esau heard his father's words, he broke down with a loud and bitter cry. This is one of the most emotive stories in the Bible. He cried bitter tears, and said to his father, *"Bless me – me too, my father."* But Isaac said, *"Your brother came deceitfully and took your blessing."* Esau said, *"He has deceived me these two times: he took my birthright, and now he's taken my blessing!"*

Then Esau asked his father, *"Haven't you reserved any blessing for me?"* But Isaac replied, *"I have made him Lord over you and have made all his relatives his servants, and I have sustained him with grain and new wine. So what can I possibly do for you, my son?"* Esau said to his father *"Do you have only one blessing, my father? Bless me too, my father!"* *Then Esau wept aloud.'* (Genesis 27:37)

The Scriptures tell us that because this man had despised his inheritance, when he wanted the blessing he could not obtain it, even though he sought it with tears. (Hebrews 12:17) That information is written in the New Testament for one reason, and one reason only – to warn *you* not to despise *your* inheritance, and thus fail to obtain your blessing. That makes this very serious stuff indeed.

These sons knew how important it was to get their father's blessing. By comparison, Esau thought nothing of selling off millions of dollars worth of financial benefit for a single bowl of lentil stew – yet he highly valued and yearned for the blessing. He had lived for the day when he would get that blessing. He thought nothing of giving away in a moment his inheritance, was very dismissive of his birthright, but he had never wanted to lose the blessing – and he was a shocked and desperate man trying to obtain, in the end, *some* blessing from his father. Why? What was the difference?

The inheritance was wealth and material goods, but the blessing was the favour and power of the Almighty. The blessing was grace – it was favour, success, protection, well-being, and blessing on his posterity. His future, and the future of his children, and his children's children, and their children's children, were dependent on that blessing. But God would not let him have it, because he had despised his inheritance. This is the sin of being godless.

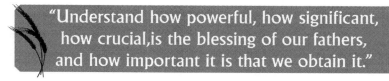

"Understand how powerful, how significant, how crucial, is the blessing of our fathers, and how important it is that we obtain it."

I want you to understand the gravity of this matter. I want you to understand how powerful, how significant, how crucial, is the blessing of our fathers, and how important it is that we obtain it.

You may never have had the blessing of your natural father. I myself never formally received the blessing of my natural father, and yet I have always known his blessing. My father was not one who ever prayed with me, but he loved me, and somehow his love came upon me and blessed me. I know you can obtain the blessing of your natural father, at least to some degree, without it necessarily having been a formal impartation. But obviously it is far more beneficial for blessings to be purposefully and consistently placed upon sons, with heartfelt prayer and deeply expressed love.

How I Obtained the Blessing of a Father

Some years ago, soon after I had discovered these truths about spiritual fathers and generational blessing, my wife and I heard some news. An old friend of ours had cancer, and was dying. We had not seen him in a long time. He was much older than we were, and lived in Canberra, a city far from where we lived.

When I was a teenager, soon after I had become a Christian, my family moved to Canberra and joined the church where he had been a member for a long time. A month later, another family moved from another city, and joined the same church. The eldest daughter in that family was Hazel, who within a few years would become my wife. We were each 17 years old at the time. This was the church where we married, and from where we left to go to Bible College to train for the ministry.

In that church was a man whom we all knew as 'Mac.' At the time he was in his 40s, a great-hearted man full of good humour. He was the organist and bandleader in the church, and a great leader of men. He always had the most wonderful testimony, and was always talking about Christ, and the Scriptures, and the blessings of fellowship he knew with the Lord.

Everybody loved him. He always seemed to be the centre of everyone's affection, and much of church life seemed to gravitate around him in one way or another. But he was not the pastor. In that denomination in those days, pastors, even though loved, remained just 1, 2, or 3 years, and were then moved on. But this man and others remained year after year, and provided great stability. Even after we left, if ever we returned home, we always looked for Mac, and it was never the same if for some reason he was not present.

This was the man we heard was sick and dying. I said to Hazel, "We will be returning from Adelaide in a couple of months. Why don't we come home through Canberra and visit them? We have not seen them in such a long time."

That night in my sleep, I heard the Lord speak clearly. "That man," He said, "was your father." I woke with a sense of awe. I had never realised; we had not known. In all those early years, we did not have the understanding – we did not have the use of this vocabulary. Now I understood. In those years, whilst one pastor after another came and went, the Lord saw to it that someone in that spiritual family had the anointing and grace to be a spiritual father – someone carried the grace to command the blessing of a father upon His people.

This changed everything, and I heard the Lord say, "When you go to Canberra to visit him, you *must* get his blessing."

Two months later we arrived, and I made an appointment to visit. I took with me a gift, for I knew that a gift opens the way for the giver. Mac loved to read the Scriptures, so I bought him a translation that I felt he would not yet have. I wrote of my personal appreciation for him at some length in the front of that Bible, and made every endeavour to express honour toward him.

We knocked on the door, and were invited in. I had half expected to see him sick and weak, but there he was, in his dressing gown but beaming, happy, full of life, just like before – and he immediately expressed the joyful faith of a man with a great experience of Jesus.

I explained what I wanted. We had learned of fathering, and of generational blessing, and had come to realise that clearly, he had been our spiritual father. Would he bless us? Would he lay hands on me and bless me for the work of the ministry to which I had been called, and bless our own lives also? I had been wondering whether he would understand, being of an older generation, but no, he understood fully. So we knelt, Hazel and

I, and his wife knelt with us, while Mac poured out his heart in prayer, and laying his hands upon us, he blessed us.

Not long after, Mac went home to be with Jesus.

For me, I knew I had a call to preach this apostolic message of sonship the length and breadth of Australia, as well as to all nations. I knew that I would still do that work of the ministry whether I had this man's blessing or not. But I also knew that if I obtained his blessing, it would be that much easier. And at least some of the grace in which I now walk is the result of the fact that I have listened to God, honoured my fathers, and received their blessing.

Jacob's Blessing – What Did He Get?

Now we must consider briefly the wording of the blessing spoken over Jacob by Isaac. The content of these words is important to you, because these are your blessings also. This is the blessing that came from Abraham, who was blessed to be a blessing to you. Abraham blessed Isaac, Isaac blessed Jacob, and Jacob blessed his sons. This is generational blessing, but not just any generational blessing. This is the generational blessing that comes from Abraham, who is your father in the sight of God. Therefore, these are your blessings.

How can you obtain the fullness of these blessings? I suggest that you ask your fathers, both natural and spiritual, to lay hands on you and declare that these are your blessings.

These blessings, along with every blessing, are brought to you by the gospel of Christ. The ordinances that were against you, and which prevented you from obtaining these blessings, were nailed to the cross, and in Christ you are brought into the fullness of the blessings of Abraham. (Galatians 3:6-9, 13-14, Ephesians 2:13-19, Colossians 2: 13-14)

Therefore, we are to be thoughtful about the words that Isaac spoke over Jacob, and believe for their fulfilment in us. It was from these words being spoken that a powerful, covenantal, and eternal blessing passed to and rested upon Jacob, never to be removed. Here are the words again. Isaac said, *"Ah, the smell of my son is like the smell of a field that the Lord has blessed. May God give you of heaven's dew and of earth's richness – an abundance of grain and new wine. May nations serve you and peoples bow down to you. Be lord over your brothers, and may the sons of your mother bow down to you. May those who curse you be cursed and those who bless you be blessed."'* (Genesis 27:27-29)

This doesn't sound like a lot of words, does it? But concerning these words and Jacob, when Isaac replied to Esau he virtually said, "I have given him everything, what else is there for me to give you?"

In these proclamations, then, is to be perceived every blessing, strength, and favour from God there is. These words are loaded with purpose, and if you follow these terms through the Scriptures, words like 'smell,' 'field,' 'grain,' and 'new wine' are all weighted with meaning, and open up the promises of Scripture. For example:

"Ah, the smell of my son" – We are the aroma of Christ to God. He loves the smell of His son, and we cannot come into His presence without the smell of Christ upon us. But because we do, we have His favour, we have access to His presence, and He lavishes upon us every spiritual blessing in the heavenlies.

"a field the Lord has blessed" – the apostle Paul said, *"you are God's field"* (1 Corinthians 3:9)

"May God give you of heaven's dew" – dew is a symbol of the Holy Spirit. This is an outpouring of grace, of salvation, of intimacy, and of power. This is salvation. Heaven's dew is the giving of the very life of God to you, with every crowning blessing upon what you do.

"and of earth's richness" – prosperity, good health, long life, joy, etc. These are the riches of the blessing of peace, i.e. of *shalom.*

"an abundance of grain and new wine" – this is harvest, this is fruit for our labour, and in the body of Christ this is the harvest of souls. The threshing floors are to be filled with grain (Joel 2: 19, 24), our joy is to know no bounds (Psalm 4:7), the new wine of the life of God is to fill our days, our homes, and our churches (Proverbs 3:10, Hosea 2: 20-23).

And as if that is not enough, Isaac called Jacob back a second time, and blessed him again. He said, *"May God Almighty bless you and make you fruitful and increase your numbers until you become a community of peoples. May he give you and your descendants the blessing given to Abraham, so that you may take possession of the land where you now live as an alien, the land God gave to Abraham."* (Genesis 28:3-4)

There is no limit to the power and the richness of these blessings, and by faith we are to make them ours.

And every one of us has the capacity to speak blessing to others.

Peace for My Children

Every night that I am home, I go to each of my four youngest children, who are still at home, lay my hand on each of them, and speak blessing over them. I speak the Lord's name, I ask God for His favour, and for grace. I speak wisdom and success over them. This takes a few minutes for each of them, but I see to it as often as possible that I bless them, and bless them, and bless them again.

I have promises from the Lord. One is, *"All your sons will be taught by the Lord, and great will be your children's peace."* (Isaiah 54:13) Another is Psalm 112:2, *"His children will be mighty in the land; the generation of the upright will be blessed."* I am not leaving the fulfilment of these promises to chance. Promises are fulfilled in response to faith. I have been promised blessings, and therefore I declare those blessings over my children.

At the same time, my children will not grow up with any doubt about the fact that their father loves them, cherishes them, and approves of them. And as well, they grow up with an example before them – they have the blessing of seeing their father as a prayerful man.

Blessings are to be *Commanded*

It should be made clear that a blessing is not really a prayer, and is not a prophecy. A blessing is a *pronunciation* – that is, we give blessings, we release blessings, we bestow blessings, by command.

Certainly, when we are about the business of blessing others, we do pray, and we do also prophesy over them. I pour out my heart at length in prayer for people, and all through there will be thoughts, words, and insights, all of which are prophetic, and which I will proclaim. But in the end a blessing is a command. I must command blessing over those to whom I minister, as God does, and as the apostles did.

Psalm 133 gives us a clear witness here, *"For there the Lord commanded the blessing."* (Psalm 133:3 NASB) If we think again about the apostolic proclamations of grace and peace to the churches, these were commands. The apostles were not wishing nice thoughts upon them; these were not just sentiments. They were declaring and releasing: read their words, such as, "grace to you, and peace to you, from God our Father," as strong commands.

Therefore, pray earnestly for your children, prophesy over them by all means, but do not fail to command the blessings over them that you have the grace and faith to so command.

Finally, remember also to *release* the blessing. This is a very practical piece of information, but when you impart a blessing to someone, there must be that moment of faith in the heart that releases it. There has to be that inner sense in our hearts in which we give it. You want the other person to have what you have, and in your heart you willingly release it to them, as you believe.

Testimony

David Alley, Pastor
The Mountain Christian Centre,
Mount Morgan, Qld, Australia.

I believe I have a truly great blessing, because my spiritual father in the ministry and my dad are one and the same person. I used to dream about how great it would have been to have spent 3 years with Jesus as the disciples did, and to have served Him as a 'son.' Another great blessing would be to spend all of your life with your spiritual father. Usually this is not possible either. However in my case, growing up in the home of my spiritual father has been an 'ultimate' blessing, because of the love and wisdom that has been imparted to me, and because of the very natural way this has involved the giving of my life and the receiving of love in the ministry.

As my father has walked through challenges, and grown in stature, I have been able to share in these things too. I have been able to stand with him, contribute to his endeavours, and believe with him through the trials. This has not been for his benefit alone, because grace has always returned to me. As a maturing son in the ministry, my heart is to see Dad succeed in all that God has called him to.

In thinking about spiritual sonship, I realize that the greatest blessings Christ gives come not from looking for what can be received from a spiritual father, but from putting ourselves in a position to serve. Jesus words come to mind, where He said: *"He who wants to be great in the kingdom of God must be the servant of all."* Obviously, this is best worked out within the context of relationship, especially the sonship relationship. And I find that the more I am able to love, serve and honour my spiritual father, the more I am blessed as a result.

I have come to realize that every good thing I have, or every quality I possess, has come because of the grace of God and the relationships I have. I have nothing in life of any quality that I can claim to be mine alone. It makes a lot of sense that by loving, honouring, and being the best son I can be, I am building a heritage for myself and for my sons and daughters as well.

When properly examined, this was the way Jesus lived his life too. Jesus was a perfect Son to a perfect Father. All good things that exist have come out of that relationship.

David Alley.

CHAPTER 9

THE APOSTOLIC BLESSING

*"Jude, a servant of Jesus Christ and a brother of James,
To those who have been called,
who are loved by God the Father and kept by Jesus Christ:
Mercy, peace and love be yours in abundance."*

(Jude 1-2)

The Command to Bless

At the conclusion of the last chapter, I said that a blessing is not really prayer or prophecy, but a *pronunciation,* in that blessings are bestowed. They are commanded.

I have learned that the Lord requires me to command blessing over those to whom I minister, as all the apostles did. Apostolic authority is given for this purpose, as much as any other. I find it is my duty to bless, and to be about the business of helping to enrich, strengthen, and protect the lives of others.

The Old Testament Priestly Blessing

The Lord commanded Moses to give a certain form of words to Aaron the High Priest and his sons, which they were to command over Israel every day. These words are very well-known, and often used as blessings in church services the world over.

'The Lord said to Moses, "Tell Aaron and his sons, 'This is how you are to bless the Israelites. Say to them:
"The Lord bless you and keep you;
the Lord make his face shine upon you and be gracious to you;

the Lord turn his face toward you and give you peace."'''
So they will put my name on the Israelites and I will bless them.'
(Numbers 6: 22-27)

Again you could ask why this blessing was needed. Israel in the wilderness had the covenants, the promises, the priesthood, the tabernacle, the offerings and sacrifices, the ark of the covenant, and the cloud of glory. The presence of God was in the camp as well. Yet here God commanded that those who represent Him to His people, those who have authority to lead and serve the people, were to place His blessing upon them. And they were to do this every day.

The Lord said this was a placing of His name upon His people, and as a result, He would bless His people. It is very clear. God gives responsibility and power to anointed leaders to place God's blessing upon God's people.

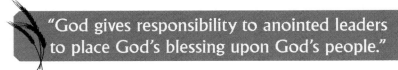

"God gives responsibility to anointed leaders to place God's blessing upon God's people."

Do you think we have less power and less grace under the new covenant than they had under the old? As you know, in the gospel, in the body of Christ, we have more power and a greater grace – and everything that was of any benefit to Israel under the old covenant is included in the new, as well as better and more precious promises. (Hebrews 8:6)

The New Testament Apostolic Blessing

Seeing that under the old covenant specific words were given which, when spoken by the priests over God's people, were a source of life and power and blessing, then we should ask; is there any such form of blessing under the new covenant? Are there any words that were given to the apostles, or used by apostles, to release blessing over the house of God?

Of course there were, and it will be no surprise when I tell you what they are. We find them recorded in epistle after epistle. We find them at the beginning of the epistles, and also at the end.

These words are *grace* and *peace*! There are a variety of ways in which the apostles expressed them. There was no set formula, because the apostles had the authority to command these blessings, and freedom of expression in doing so. They nevertheless stand out as primary apostolic commands over the life of the churches and the believers. Here are a few examples:

"To all in Rome who are loved by God and called to be saints: Grace and peace to you from God our Father and from the Lord Jesus Christ."
(Romans 1:7, see also 1 Corinthians 1: 2-3, 2 Corinthians 1:1-2, Galatians

1:1-2, Ephesians 1:1-2, Philippians 1:1-2, to 2 Thessalonians 1:1-2, and others)

> *"To the holy and faithful brothers in Christ at Colosse: Grace and peace to you from God our Father."* (Colossians 1:2)
> *"To the church of the Thessalonians...: Grace and peace to you."* (1 Thessalonians 1:1)

Paul ends the Ephesian letter with, *"Peace to the brothers, and love with faith from God the Father and the Lord Jesus Christ. Grace to all who love our Lord Jesus Christ with an undying love."* (Ephesians 6:23-24) Other writers also made these proclamations, including Peter, John, Jude, and the writer to the Hebrews. The apostles were always saying "Grace to you and peace from God our Father."

There are probably no more powerful words in all the faith of Jesus Christ than these two, except for His name. These words represent the primary anointings of God upon His people – for protection, for strengthening, for peace and well-being, and for their being helped and kept in the faith. We often talk about the power of God to not only save, but to keep. These blessings are primary expressions of His keeping power.

And when we take a closer look at the priestly blessing in Numbers 6:24-26, we find that grace and peace are the primary components of the Old Testament blessing as well.

The Impartation of Peace

Years ago, when people often came for personal prayer and pastoral counsel, I developed the habit of ending every prayer with a specific request of the Lord. I would conclude by asking the Lord for His peace, place it upon their minds and hearts, and release it to them. After I had done this many times, we discovered that a grace had been established, and every time I prayed that way the tangible presence of God came upon them, and great peace would flood into their hearts and minds. One brother was delivered of evil spirits and baptised in the Holy Spirit when I simply released peace to him. Others were healed of great anxiety.

People began to comment that peace had touched them powerfully. And I found that it was totally reliable, in the sense that this wave of peace came consistently whenever I prayed and released it. It seemed I had been given the authority to place His blessing of peace, and that it was not just a form of words; it was actual power.

What I discovered, without looking for it, was the powerful blessing of 'Peace' (or 'Shalom') – and it was tangible. What does 'tangible' mean? It means it is evident to our senses, and makes an immediate and practical difference in people's lives, and in all kinds of circumstances.

Jesus said to His apostles, *"When you enter a house, first say, 'Peace to this house.' If a man of peace is there, your peace will rest on him; if not, it will return to you."* (Luke 10:5-6) You cannot speak like this unless you are discussing something tangible. Some might have thought this was just an expression of goodwill, but Jesus was in fact referring to the use of the grace and power we have been given for the purpose of ministry!

The Grace Anointing

Similarly, when we come to the apostolic use of the word 'Grace,' we find the same powerful and effective release of anointings, blessings, and favour from God. This is why the apostles were always saying, "Grace to you."

I have discovered that very often the most powerful prayer I can pray is, "Lord, grant me grace." When I have to address pastoral issues, for example, where there is a problem in a family, I will pray a simple prayer, "Lord, I ask for grace for that family." Or suppose I have to address a disciplinary matter, or have some problem to solve, I'll say, "Lord, give me grace to solve that problem." And it is amazing the difference that praying that particular prayer makes. Grace is a powerful word that seems to greatly move the heart of God. It almost seems like He cannot resist, as if His heart is very tender when He hears that word. He responds, He answers. And so we receive the help of God.

Apostolic Covering & the Apostolic Blessings

I treated the subject of apostolic covering at length in my last book, *The Apostolic Revelation*. Apostolic Covering is a hugely important subject, a vital grace in the body of Christ, and was the central thesis of that book. Here, I simply want to say that apostolic covering is a form of generational blessing – the most important form of generational blessing in the life of churches, in the lives of the fivefold ministers of Christ, and for the Kingdom of God.

In particular I want to enumerate four distinct covering blessings which are found within the apostolic ministry in its relationship to pastors, churches, and other ministries.

1. An apostle's blessing:

Every fivefold minister, every Christian ministry, and in particular every church or congregation, needs the blessing of an apostle. When someone is attempting to do great things for Christ, or build a ministry even in response to a specific call from God, the absence of apostolic blessing will mean that you will struggle more; you will not flourish as readily as you might.

For example, the evangelist Philip might appear, at first glance, to have gone off on his own to Samaria where he had phenomenal results. (Acts 8) But in fact he had been under the leadership of apostles, obviously knew their blessing, and when the work sprang up so fruitfully, those apostles were brought in to lay hands on people and bless the work. Like him, no one should endeavour to build a ministry for Christ Jesus without obtaining the specific blessing of an apostle.

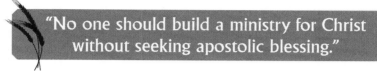

"No one should build a ministry for Christ without seeking apostolic blessing."

In this day, churches everywhere should be receiving the visit of apostles. At this initial level, any apostle can be used by the Lord to give an apostolic blessing. For example, Paul was planning to visit Rome, a church over which he had no governmental authority, yet he wrote, *"I long to see you that I may impart some spiritual gift to you, to make you strong."* (Romans 1:11) There is an initial blessing that every ministry must receive, to put in place the strength and protection and other grace provisions that are needed, so that the work might flourish.

It has been noticed in times past, for example, that where house churches start up but remain independent, although they might seem to go well for a while, they then often stagnate, sometimes badly. But where an apostle is received, and he declares over that work that this is the Church of the Lord Jesus Christ, and he receives them under Christ, and blesses them, and in this way links them to the whole body – that house church will maintain a good life.

2. Apostolic Covering:

Apostolic covering is established where a pastor, church, or other ministry forms a permanent and ongoing relationship with a specific apostle, so as to be accountable, remaining under apostolic leadership, supporting the work of the apostle, and receiving his ongoing input. It is a tangible relationship, with a lot of blessing, joy, and mutual honouring involved. Through the anointings of grace received as an apostle, he places the covering of Christ over that ministry. This makes a great difference in the spirit realm for them, and properly establishes an appropriate level of protection and blessing. The apostolic covering helps to bring in good things, and keep out bad things. That is, it is a source of both blessing and protection. Every ministry needs apostolic covering, but this requires the leader and the ministry to establish a committed relationship with an appropriate apostle i.e. an apostle that has the grace for this particular work.

3. Father-son relationship in the ministry:

This is the third level of apostolic blessing, and goes far beyond, but is an extension of, apostolic covering. At the first level of blessing, only a prayer of impartation is called for, and the blessing is released. At the second level, apostolic covering is established by a prayer, but maintained by accountability in a committed relationship as well as ongoing prayer. But at this third level of apostolic blessing, the blessings come almost purely as a result of the depth of relationship.

At this level, the apostle who has provided covering has become greatly loved, and he himself loves. Tenderness of heart, intimacy of relationship, and depth of trust, have all been established. There is a sense of sweet unity, a deep sense of true belonging; they have become family. The pastor and the apostle care deeply for each other. They have become as father and son in the Lord. When this point is passed, a greater grace is released.

To walk in such a father and son relationship is in itself the key to great blessing. It is as if inheritance is released, and the heavens opened. It seems that God is very pleased to bless relationships of the heart, for when we move from what was nevertheless a very good ministry association at the level of apostolic covering, to the more intimate and personal heart connectedness of father-son relationship, another whole level of profound blessing is discovered.

4. A father's blessing:

In such a father-son relationship, the apostle is now in a significant place of grace from which to command greater blessings over his sons. When an apostle has true sons, God will grant him great grace for them. When the pastor, prophet, apostle, evangelist, teacher, or any Christian leader becomes truly a son to an apostolic father, they have found grace by which a great generational blessing can be theirs.

The Apostolic Responsibility

Blessing is an apostolic duty, and the apostle has been given specific authority to bless. Apostolic blessing and life and power – there is nothing else quite like it in the church. This is the way God has designed it, and this is the way it has been from the beginning.

Even Abraham, our father in the faith, required the blessing of

Melchizedek before anything much happened in his life in accordance with the call he had been given. It is therefore a responsibility of apostles to bless. Apostles need to understand their purpose in commanding blessing, and to be constantly about the business of blessing the work and the people of God.

Apostolic authority is very personal. It does not come from institutional endowments, but from Christ. For example, in Matthew 16:13-20, Jesus holds a discussion with the 12, but in verses 17-19, Jesus speaks only to Peter, and this is personal for Peter. Consequently, Peter's shadow alone, amongst all the apostles, had great effect. (Acts 5:15) Each apostle will walk in an authority that is both personal and unique.

In general, I should say again, that every form of Christian ministry, including churches, schools, missions, outreaches, etc, and also every fivefold minister of the Lord Jesus, including every apostle and prophet, does need and should receive the blessing of Christ's apostles. This not only releases to God's people individually and to the church corporately a special provision of spiritual vitality and protection, but it is also the primary means by which, through the anointings of Christ, the body of Christ is made truly one, rather than remaining a motley collection of disparate believers and ministries.

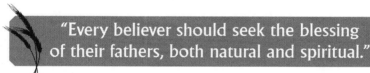

"Every believer should seek the blessing of their fathers, both natural and spiritual."

Every believer should seek the blessing of their fathers, both natural and spiritual. If you no longer have your natural father with you, then ask the pastor or apostle who is over you in the Lord to take the place of your father, lay hands upon you, and give you the blessing you never received.

Every ministry should seek to receive the ministry and the blessings of the apostles of Christ. Jesus said to His apostles, "He who receives you receives me." (Matthew 10:40)

Do you have a personal need?

Are you in a place where there is no one you can turn to at the moment for a prayer of protection and blessing? I can offer you my prayer, even if only as a temporary measure until you can establish proper relationships, or spend time with your fathers.

I will here ask the Lord to give you of heaven's dew and earth's richness. If you desire, believe with me as you pray the following prayer that the dew of heaven will settle on your soul. I have here poured out my heart in prayer for you. I will give you what I have. During this prayer, whatever you hear me name before God, whatever you hear me pray and release, you are to believe in your heart that it has been given to you.

A PRAYER

"Father, we still our hearts before the throne of grace. We humble ourselves and recognise, O Lord, that none of us can exist unto ourselves, but we belong to each other and to the Lord. I thank you there is a fount of blessing that has been opened to us. Your heart, O God, is toward us. The favour of God rests upon us. Lord, we honour you.

"I ask that your blessing would now rest upon this my brother or sister. I thank you for them. I ask, O Lord, that you would grant them now grace to succeed. I pray that the power of God would be multiplied in them and in their families. I ask that their children would really live before you. I ask that divine favour would rest upon them, and that you would watch over them, and protect them.

"I ask, O Lord, that you would now give my brother/sister every success. I pray that the hand of God would now be upon them, upon their marriage, upon their children, your hand of blessing upon their home, upon their heart, upon their finances, upon their future, upon their days and their nights. Lord, in all the years that are to come, protect them by your name, the name of the Lord Jesus Christ.

"In the name of the Lord Jesus, I cut off every accusation concerning them. I cut off the schemes of the devil. In Jesus' holy name I take authority over the spirit of death that has been assigned against them, and against the church, and I cut it off and cancel the assignment. Spirit of death, go back! In Jesus' name."

"Father, I speak your grace over them, and declare that the everlasting arms are about them, for surely they are. I ask that you would draw them near to the heart of the Father. I pray, Lord, that from this very hour they will know your blessing and your peace. So in the name of Jesus, I place your blessing upon them, and I release grace and peace to them.

"My brother/sister, I release grace to you in Jesus' name. I release peace to you in Jesus' name. The Spirit of the Lord and of peace rest upon you now in power.

"The goodness of God is present! Now Lord I ask that the Spirit of the fear of the Lord would come upon his/her heart, and I ask that the spirit of understanding, and the knowledge of the ways of God, would be given to him/her. Father, I cry out, and speak over him/her the very words of that ancient blessing given to the fathers,"

"May God give you of heaven's dew and of earth's richness – an abundance of grain and new wine!"

"Lord, I speak success concerning him/her, and fruit bearing. Let now the hand of God come upon him/her to protect, to keep, to hold him/her near to your own heart. Lord you have said that you would keep the man of peace from stumbling. I pray concerning this brother/sister that you will keep him/her, O God. He/she will not stumble over any rock of offence, or any stumbling stone, but you, O Lord, will keep them.

"Father, according to your holy command, I spread your protection over them in Jesus' name, and I say they are yours, O Lord!

"I place upon him/her your peace, in the mighty name of Jesus!"

"My brother/sister, I bless you, and I speak life to you, in Jesus' wonderful name."

Now Drink in His Peace

By faith, receive His peace right now. Believe to soak it in. The anointing of peace flows upon you in this moment. Say, "Lord, I receive your peace."

And Now, I Commission You

"You are blessed of God, and will be a blessing. Carry the grace of the Lord Jesus. Carry the peace of the Lord Jesus. I commission you to be a blessing wherever you go, a source of life and joy.

"May signs and wonders follow you, may the Lord place authority upon your lips, and blessing in your hands. May favour surround you all the days of your life, and the Lord make you very fruitful in the advancing Kingdom of Christ!"

Testimony

Michael Appleton
Executive Director, Peace Apostolic Missions
Principal, Central Queensland Christian College
Rockhampton, Qld, Australia.

I cannot think of what my life would have been like without the influence of my spiritual father. I hear some people talk about their life: the places they've lived, the many different churches that they have attended, and the benefit they feel they gained from a wide variety of experiences. My life has been the opposite. My family started attending *Peace* when I was three years old. I have been in the same church all this time. I was saved here, baptised here, married here, our eight children were dedicated here and for all I know I will die here. I have found being in the one place with a tremendous spiritual father, and a spiritual family that really loves me, central to my experience of Christ – and this is the main instigator of my growth in Him. My life in Christ would not be the same without the people I have around me.

Because I've been here so long, everybody knows me – the good and the bad – but they love me anyway. There is a very secure feeling knowing that I do not have to strive or compete to be recognised or given opportunity to serve.

I met John Alley when he came to be our pastor in 1988. As a 15-year-old I was immediately drawn by John's passion for revival. It was really exciting to see the Holy Spirit moving in our fellowship, to see people coming to Christ, to see healings and miracles – but we knew there was more. Our whole fellowship was on a journey together, and the only way we knew how to walk with God was to pray. With the encouragement of Debbie (who later became my wife) I started attending the early morning prayer meeting. Praying with John each day in that meeting was a powerful influence in my life.

John's messages each Sunday were like meat on a plate. He told us they were milk, and that we had to get our meat from the Word through the week, but it was teaching like we had never received before. This teaching helped all of us so much. But John was not just one to preach it – he lived it.

Perhaps the most powerful thing of all was John's example. I remember before Debbie and I were married, when we visited John and Hazel, we could see how they lived, how they raised their children, and how they prayed in their home. We knew the direction that we wanted to go when we got married, and when we had children.

Another remarkable influence has been John's loving correction. There have been plenty of times when John has had to call me aside for a "little chat". Discipline is never pleasant at the time, but I appreciate it so much. The errors I was making, the schemes of the devil I had not seen, the wrong directions I was taking at times, could have made shipwreck of my life. If it had not been for John's prayerful discernment and boldness in addressing the issues, I hate to think where I would be now. The thing I always appreciated about John's correction was his manner. I always knew he had my best interests at heart. And he was always quick to apologise if he thought he had been too harsh (though I can't remember a time when he was). His heart of love for Debbie and I has always shone through. Through this journey of becoming a spiritual son, I have learned so much about the love of God. I have learnt how to give my heart. The overflow of these discoveries in my marriage and in the relationship with my children has been transforming. I cannot overstate how important I believe these principles are, and how wonderful it is to walk with a spiritual father.

In this journey of sonship in the ministry I have learned a number of lessons, and still have many more to learn. But there were some obstacles I had to overcome.

First there was the obstacle of false expectations. I thought that having a spiritual father meant I would be given a certain amount of his time and attention for the purposes of personal discipleship. But I had to learn that it was all about the relationship, not a program. Having a spiritual father was not about receiving an hour's personal instruction every week, but the living of our lives together in the pursuit of God's purpose.

Then there was also the obstacle of a closed heart. Even though I had a good spiritual father and he was caring for me, there were times I was not walking in the benefit of that love because my heart was closed to it. At the time, I did not realise the way my heart was – I only came to see it afterwards. At the time, I thought everyone else was the problem. I became susceptible to lies and started to think that John didn't really care for me. I started interpreting everything through this preconception. On top of this, I had received many prophecies about the ministry the Lord was calling me to. I wanted to be obedient and fulfill the call. But in the pursuit I became focused on "my" ministry. And when I did not see John giving the opportunities to preach or minister, I started to think that the only way that I could fulfill "my" ministry would be to go somewhere else.

Of course, John could not promote someone in ministry who had not given their heart. But I could not see that at the time. I was under a deception. Eventually, Debbie was able to help me see the lies I was believing. The devil had gone too far, he told one lie too many, and things were not matching up. When I came to my senses, I decided that pursuing "my" ministry was not important right now. I didn't understand why God had given the prophecies, but I knew that the ministry John had been called to was an important one, and he needed help. I decided that it didn't matter what I was doing – cleaning, administration, whatever – I was going to do whatever I could to help John fulfill the vision the Lord had given him. I died to "my" ministry, and dedicated myself to serving the ministry of my spiritual father. I gave my heart and trusted him. When I turned my heart to him I discovered that his heart was already turned towards me.

And then a funny thing happened – John started to send me out with teams to preach and minister. When I gave my heart to serving his ministry, the Lord was finally able to start bringing about the fulfillment of the prophecies. When I stopped focusing on "my" ministry, he was able to use me. Now I enjoy the privilege of travelling all over the world carrying the message that our Lord Jesus gave to John.

So you can start to see the inheritance I am receiving. When I travel, I'm not ministering in "my" anointing – there is no power in that. John has prayed and imparted the grace and anointing the Lord gave him for me to minister. There have now been a number of times when I have spoken in places where John had ministered previously, and people said they saw visions of John speaking to them. Others said they heard John's voice when they closed their eyes while listening to me. These are just signs that I am flowing in the anointing of my spiritual father. What a wonderful grace – I am so happy – there is so much of the Lord Jesus' power in that. People's lives are changed – churches are turned around, and cities are touched with the power of God.

What a privilege we have in this day to see the Elijah/Elisha principle at work amongst us again. Just as the Lord said in Malachi, He is sending the spirit of Elijah to turn the hearts of the fathers to their children and the hearts of the children to their fathers.

Michael Appleton.

CHAPTER 10

PURSUING A
SPIRITUAL FATHER

*"But Elisha said, 'As surely as the Lord lives and as
you live, I will not leave you.'*
"...So the two of them walked on."

(2 Kings 2: 2, 6)

There are many who pray with a desire to receive what Elisha received –
a double-portion of the Spirit. I will show you what the Lord showed me,
which is, how to obtain it! In the purposes of God there is an available,
attested, and biblical way for us all to obtain such a grace.

What does it mean to pursue a spiritual father?

For myself, I have narrowed the answer to this question down to three
very important things. A son *imitates*, a son *honours*, and a son *pursues* a
father. Each of these words is a special term representing biblical concepts,
within the call to *love* and *serve* spiritual fathers.

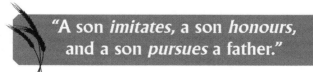

"A son *imitates*, a son *honours*,
and a son *pursues* a father."

A son pursues! Why does a son pursue a spiritual father? The heart of a
son, and the outcomes of this pursuit, are uniquely illustrated in the story
of Elisha.

Consider the Elisha Story

People tend to think that Elisha followed and served Elijah so as to receive the prophet's mantle, i.e. to obtain the position of the prophet. But 1 Kings 19:16, 19-21 tells us that when God spoke to Elijah on the mountain, He said, *"anoint Elisha... to succeed you as prophet."* So when Elijah found Elisha plowing, and threw his robe over him, the purpose of God was fully placed upon Elisha. He had been chosen. Elisha would be the next principal prophet for Israel. He was given the call, and both the ministry and the grace was available for him to walk in. He would indeed have the word of the Lord to proclaim.

But something in Elisha's heart knew to pursue the older man. He followed Elijah and became his servant. From that time he cooked his food, carried his water, and washed his hands. He waited upon him and served him. And the Scriptures do not tell any more of their shared story until the day Elijah was taken from this world.

Strangely, on this day Elijah seemed to be trying to leave Elisha behind, as if attempting to dissuade him from accompanying him, instructing him to take the day off and rest. He said to Elisha, *"Stay here, the Lord has sent me to Bethel."* (2 Kings 2:2) But Elisha replied, *"As surely as the Lord lives and as you live, I will not leave you."* So they walked on together.

Three times Elijah tried to leave him behind. *"Stay here, Elisha; the Lord has sent me to Jericho."* And then, *"Stay here; the Lord has sent me to the Jordan."* To which, on every occasion, Elisha replied again, *"As surely as the Lord lives and as you live, I will not leave you."*

Tests of the Heart

This was a test of Elisha's heart! And be very clear about the fact that various kinds of tests come to us all. Tests usually look innocuous, just like this one. They have to be, to be real tests of the heart. These show where the heart is really at. It is quite essential to pass them, if we are to qualify for greater authority and the advancement of God's purpose in us. Ponder these things carefully, for there is divine mystery here. And take warning also! Each of us is meant to be about the business of pursuing – of seeking the greater grace of God.

Over a long time, 40 years and more, I have heard many people pray for the very thing they thought Elisha asked for: "Father in Heaven, grant me a double portion of your Spirit" has been their passionate and heartfelt plea. Yet not once in all my life have I heard anyone later testify, "Praise God, I have been given the double portion I asked for." Why not?

The Available Greater Grace

Each of us in following Christ has been given a holy portion of His Spirit. I have grace from God, and you do also. But there is not one of us that does not want, and does not really need, *more*. And greater grace is available and offered to us in the Scriptures (Consider 1 Corinthians 9:8, for example). But how do we get this greater grace, and obtain great favour? How do we walk in greater understanding, greater wisdom, greater knowledge, and greater power? How do we come to the place where we have more to offer other people?

What I am about to show you is a powerful key to this greater grace – perhaps the principle key. As far as I am concerned, it *is* the principle key. If we would learn to walk in heart relationship with other people, and especially with those who have grace, as Elisha did with Elijah, then we have an opportunity to receive of the grace they have, and add this to the grace we have. That is double-portion!

There is a peculiar context in which this double-portion endowment takes place. The context to which I refer is that of a *father-son relationship*, in Christ, in the ministry. Elijah was a father to Elisha, and Elisha a son to Elijah, in public ministry. They walked together. And when Elisha finally found the opportunity to request a double-portion inheritance, his request was not a prayer to our Father in heaven, as in the many prayer meetings I referred to, but a personal request addressed to a spiritual father with whom he had walked in an accountable and submitted relationship.

If you would position yourself for greater inheritance, this relationship must also be the context of your own life of service to Christ. Then you will be able to enjoy, not only the grace that God has given you initially, but also the opportunity to walk in the grace that others have received, and which can become yours through inheritance and divine impartation.

Each one of us is quite free to seek the Lord in a personal way so as to develop spiritual giftedness. Through obedience and prayer we can and do grow in grace and faith. However, by walking with other people, i.e. spiritual fathers, we can effectively multiply what we have.

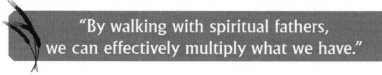

"By walking with spiritual fathers, we can effectively multiply what we have."

This is an important lesson. A great grace is available; God wants us to walk in it, but only when we choose to walk together.

The Lord wants us to add to one another – to make each other rich. But while ever we are independent, and it remains every man for himself – while ever churches and believers have a competitive spirit instead of a spirit of co-operation or community – we can never find a greater portion of grace and of the Holy Spirit. It is upon brothers who dwell in unity that God bestows the blessing! (Psalm 133)

If we cling to these old, institutional ways of doing things, instead of the personal and relational ways of God in Christ, we can never find this multiplied grace. Yet it remains readily available, if we will learn to walk in relationship with other people – to love and trust them, to serve and honour them. And we will find this lesson clearly revealed in the story of Elisha.

Elijah had made no advance offers to Elisha. Only when they arrived at the extreme end of the journey, and only to this one son, the one who had said, *"I will not leave you,"* does Elijah finally offer, *"Tell me, what can I do for you before I am taken from you?"* (2 Kings 2:9) Elisha at last is able to express the desire of his heart with this request, *"Let me inherit a double portion of your spirit,"* but to which he gets an unusual reply, *" 'You have asked a difficult thing,' Elijah said, 'yet if you see me when I am taken from you, it will be yours – otherwise not.'"* (2 Kings 2: 9-10)

"Tell me"

There are important ideas hidden in these words. Firstly, Elijah says, *"Tell me."* There has to be a clear communication between father and son. A son must make specific requests of a spiritual father, so as to indicate that he wants his father's blessing, and wants to inherit his grace. This somehow opens the way for gifts to be given, both in the hearts of the individuals and in the heart of God.

For me then, I must specifically request the endowment of my spiritual father's anointings, so that by the power of his prayers he may obtain favour for me, and by his spiritual authority he may impart grace to me.

However, this should not be in a demanding, negative sense. It is not to be a burden to him, but there is still a need to let him know the earnest desires of the heart. I must let him understand my hunger for grace, and my need of his help. A son does need a father's help. A father's approval is a key to great grace. So we need to present requests: "Pray for me, release to me the grace you have for me." When Elijah said, *"Tell me, what can I do for you?"* you know that Elijah wanted to give – he intended to be a blessing. A father always wants to give his best to his son.

"Let me"

When Elisha stated his request he said, *"Let me inherit..."* (2 Kings 2:9)
By using the words 'let me', Elisha was asking Elijah to give his consent.
Elijah's permission was an essential component for an endowment to take
place. Elisha's position was *"Allow me to receive a double portion of your
spirit."* From this we see that for you or I to receive this kind of inheritance
– a double-portion endowment of the Spirit – it will require the consent,
approval, and willingness of a spiritual father.

> "For you or I to receive this kind of inheritance,
> it will require the consent, approval,
> and willingness of a spiritual father."

Obviously God is Himself the giver, as we will see. But Elisha made
his request to the man who was over him in the Lord. This gives us to
understand that to successfully receive an impartation of the Spirit in
double-portion, we will need the agreement of *two* fathers – one in Heaven,
and the one who has walked with us on the earth. And this is, by the way,
an expression of *apostolic authority*, which the Lord ordains, and seems to
require, on earth.

"A Difficult Thing"

Even though Elisha addressed his request to Elijah, man does not have
the actual power to give the grace. Remember that even though Elijah
invited Elisha to make a request, when Elisha expressed his desire Elijah
responded with, *"You have asked a difficult thing."*

And it is indeed difficult, very difficult, for any of us to pass on the
fullness of our anointing to another. Here is what I have found: even though
a spiritual father might have great measures of grace, have God's favour
upon him, be carrying powerful anointings in keeping with his calling, and
even though the grace he has is available to you – despite all that, he can't
just give it to you!

It is available, but cannot be just given. So even though a spiritual
father's consent and agreement is required before it can be released, still,
even a father who longs to, cannot just give it to his son.

This is because a requirement exists that must be fulfilled in a son.
Here is the clue to understanding what this is: *"Elijah said, 'yet if you see
me when I am taken from you, it will be yours – otherwise not.'"*
(2 Kings 2: 9-10)

"If you see me"

Most of us have probably interpreted these words as meaning that if Elisha was allowed to see Elijah as he was being taken, this was a sign given to him that God had granted his request, and he could therefore believe. Let me tell you, it was not just a sign.

In early 2006, I had been asking the Lord to give me understanding of what it means to pursue a spiritual father. One night soon after, at around 2 a.m., the Lord woke me and spoke clearly, telling me many things about this. As I heard more and more I thought, "I'll never remember all of this; I have to get up and write it down." By the time I got to my desk it seemed like I had already forgotten much of what the Lord had said, and I couldn't quite recall it. But from what I did remember I began to write, and as I did it all came again.

What the Lord said that night was that if Elisha was to receive the anointing in double-portion, it was totally essential that he actually see with his own eyes Elijah to the very last, even as he was being taken away. In the story, no sooner had Elijah said this to Elisha than the chariot and horses of fire appeared, and separated the two of them, and Elijah was taken up in the whirlwind.

In the crisis of the moment, with Elijah being taken so suddenly, Elisha experienced a great rush of emotion – of affection, of longing, of desire, for his father in the faith – and he cried out, *"My father! My father! The chariots and horsemen of Israel!"* The text continues, *"And Elisha saw him no more. Then he took hold of his own clothes and tore them apart."* (2 Kings 2:12)

This was a deeply emotional experience for Elisha. In the same way that he tore his clothes, his heart had been rent too. And please understand, it was intended by God that it would be a wrenching emotional experience – of love and of longing – for a spiritual father. The heart of the true son had to be greatly enlarged, stretched by emotion, with a passionate longing out of genuine love, if the heart was to have the *capacity* to receive the anointing *in double-portion*.

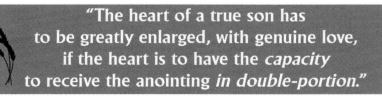

"The heart of a true son has to be greatly enlarged, with genuine love, if the heart is to have the *capacity* to receive the anointing *in double-portion.*"

That night I heard the Lord say that the emotions Elisha experienced were essential for him being able to receive the anointing – that without the greater capacity of the heart enlarged through longing, he would not have been capable of receiving the anointing.

Longing

The key word here is *longing*. The Lord said there *has* to be a longing in the heart. This is not a longing for the spiritual gift, rather it is the longing of a heart of love for the brother you walk with – your spiritual father. This heart of longing is for him! Your heart goes out to him! And this deep affection and heartfelt desire of love, being established in the heart of a son towards a father, means that the heart is being enlarged, and 'space' is being created, so that grace can be received. We will return to this point shortly.

"When I am Taken"

We notice that Elisha began to pursue Elijah from the very beginning, but the important lesson is that he was still pursuing at the end. When Elijah's mantle was first cast over him, this was like the casting of a vision, an opportunity being offered. And at the end, we find Elisha still relentless in devotion and faithfulness.

He did not slow down along the way, as if he thought he had now become mature enough as a man of God. And in the end, he was given the mantle that had first been cast in his direction.

But many of us stop short. In the 'middle' years there comes a time when it appears to many as if they have gone as far as the relationship will take them, and nothing much seems to be happening. It looks to them like they have already heard everything their leader has to say, or they have already received his blessing and think they already have the grace he can offer. They start to drift and look around, or they get interested in someone or something else. So they stop pursuing here, and they go pursuing there, for a while. Basically, they quit in the middle years. They turn away to other goals. And this is a mistake, a tragedy in the kingdom.

Or perhaps they do not pass the tests; or else they choose a selfish path; or even a deceptive one, as Elisha's servant Gehazi later did. (2 Kings 5: 20-27) There are tests of the heart that must come to us all, even in our mature years. The apostle Paul spoke openly of them: *"... we speak as men approved by God to be entrusted with the gospel. We are not trying to please men but God, who tests our hearts."* (1 Thess 2:4)

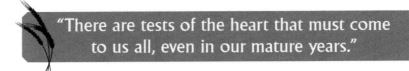

"There are tests of the heart that must come
to us all, even in our mature years."

Requirements for a Major Impartation

I believe there are several essential requirements that you and I will need to fulfill if we are to obtain a major impartation of grace through a spiritual father. Do you want to receive your spiritual father's anointing and walk in a double-portion endowment of the Spirit? Here's what I believe are those requirements.

1. Resolve

There are several things that need to be in the heart of a son in pursuing a spiritual father. The first of these is *resolve*. Elisha had said, *"...as you live, I will not leave you."* (2 Kings 2: 2, 4, 6)

Now a resolve is not a pledge. When Elisha said, *"I will not leave you,"* this was not a promise; it was not a vow or a covenant. It was simply the resolution of his heart. He had chosen what he wanted, and knew what he intended to do. He was stating his purpose.

That is what each of us has to do. There has to be resolve in the human heart with respect to our choosing to walk with our fathers. But this is not to be a pledge or a promise, and it is dangerous and contrary to the teaching of the New Testament to make them. Take my warning, and do not make vows or covenants. Simply make a choice in your heart that says, "I'm going to pursue."

The making of vows and pledges was the way of the old covenant, but not the new. We are not meant to live by the vows we make, but by the commands He has given us. When we make pledges and covenants, we are choosing to live by our own words, as if God's words are not enough to live by.

By this I do not mean to negate the value of setting goals, clarifying vision, and establishing priorities, all of which are very important. Nor am I against so-called 'pledges' in church giving programs, for these are only statements of intention, in fact, they are simply a form of resolve. But when we turn our words into vows, oaths, and pledges, we have turned them into a form of law that we must live by, and this is always destructive. This is the 'letter' that always kills and never produces life, even though it can look like 'life' to begin with. This is a far bigger subject than I can deal with here, but I remind you of the words of the Lord Jesus, who taught, *"Simply let your 'Yes' be 'Yes,' and your 'No,' 'No'; anything beyond this comes from the evil one."* (Matthew 5:37, and see also James 5:12)

Nevertheless, strong resolve will be a necessary attitude of heart, if as sons we are to obtain the benefit of pursuing our spiritual fathers.

2. Maturity of Relationship

Having the right *kind* of relationship is a critical factor if obtaining the greatest impartation of anointings is to be effected.

It is easy for any of us to obtain small amounts of the blessing or anointing of other people in ministry. We can all get something. I have been to many places in the world, and have received prayer from all kinds of good people; and from them all I get *something* of value.

I remember spending time with a very dear brother, George Stormont. George was an elderly Englishman, now gone to heaven, who was a personal friend of Smith Wigglesworth. They often ministered in each other's churches. George wrote and published a book about Wigglesworth, exploring the meaning of his life.[1] In his later years brother Stormont only ever preached about Christ, and as he did, people would often weep. He shared with me one of his personal wisdoms; every Sunday morning he would read Revelation chapter 1, and soak himself in John's vision of the Christ.

I asked brother Stormont to pray for me, and as he did, by faith I believed and received from him the anointing that was upon him. I hungered for that grace. As a result, I carried that sweet anointing home, and have the blessing he gave me to this day. But I only got some, a certain portion, of what that dear brother had. And I've been able to get a little from a lot of people. Every little bit helps.

But greater blessing, and greater favour, comes through *maturity of relationship*; depth of relationship increases the effectiveness of the flow of the anointing. If you want the 'mother lode', so to speak, the full impartation, a great download of the grace carried by another – if you want an inheritance experience like Elisha, you will need maturity of relationship with a spiritual father.

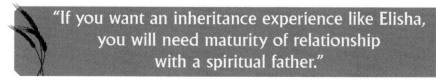

"If you want an inheritance experience like Elisha, you will need maturity of relationship with a spiritual father."

So what is maturity of relationship? This means you walk with them, and serve them. You will come to know them well, for you are committed to

1   *Wigglesworth, A Man Who Walked with God* published by Harrison House, 1989.

them from the heart, and you care about them deeply. Achieving 'maturity of relationship' is going to take time, both to develop and to maintain relationship. We are playing 'for keeps'. This is serious business. You are not going to do this in five minutes. You are going to walk with a father, and with other people, for a lifetime.

I've been walking with others in the church at *Peace Apostolic Community* for years. We leaders meet every Tuesday afternoon just to talk. We drink tea and coffee, and just talk. Why? We are building our lives together. After many years we have come to the place where we trust each other implicitly, love each other deeply, care much about each other, and feel we belong to one another from the heart.

This really does involve the heart! We are not to have just some intellectual approach to ministry; it should be an emotive experience also. Why, it's love! We must have real feeling for one another; there has to be passion. There should be no second rate attitudes here, no cold love, no stuffy formalism – which brings us to a third requirement.

3. Depth of Feeling – the Longing of the Heart for our Fathers

Of paramount importance in the heart of a son is this thing called *longing*. Elijah had said, *"If you see me,"* and there is this very important connection between Elisha actually seeing Elijah go, and the immediate release of the anointing to him. This separation triggered great emotion in Elisha, and the natural expression of his love and longing for Elijah was for him to cry out, *"My father! My father!"* This was the cry of a son out of the emotion of the heart.

There is a reason deep and personal relationships in the body of Christ are so important. Not only is it Godly, for this is how God conducts His own relationships, but these are the effective means by which the greatest impartations of ministry anointings, and the passing of inheritance from one spiritual generation to another, is to be achieved. Maturity of relationship, which brings us to a great love for one another, greatly increases the effectiveness of the flow of the anointing and power from father to son in the ministry.

The idea of longing in the heart, in association with the maturity of relationship we are meant to walk in, means having a significant *depth of feeling* toward your spiritual father. You are not going to win through unless you have holy emotions. Your emotions in Christ's service are very important. Do not let anyone convince you that Christianity is only intellectual, i.e. that faith is only expressed through what we say we believe. No, passion is crucial, and the love and faith attitudes of our hearts are to be as often expressed in emotions shared, as they are also to be in deeds. We must love, we must long, we must care, we must be willing to weep with those who weep, and rejoice with those who rejoice.

> "Passion is crucial.
> The love and faith attitudes of our hearts
> are to be as often expressed in emotions shared,
> as they are also to be in our deeds."

There has to be a depth of feeling in us with respect to our spiritual fathers. That depth of feeling means loving them, longing for them, and caring about them.

Some years ago I began to send teams to visit nations in Africa. The leader of the first team was Lloyd Gill, accompanied by Justin Morgan, to pioneer relationships and carry the apostolic message to places we had not been before. At the airport we prayed and said farewell, and when they disappeared from the gate, I left and went up a nearby hill, just to have a time of prayer over the city. But as I stood there praying, their aircraft took off from the Rockhampton City Airport below, and flew right past where I was standing on the hillside. Suddenly I felt such deep emotion, tears ran from my eyes, and deep feelings of care for those brothers filled my heart, as I watched that plane become smaller and smaller in the distant sky, until it disappeared. I'm weeping as I write now, just remembering this. I can tell you, my heart went with them. And the whole time they were in Africa, my heart was with them. There was a longing for them there; this was love. In my case, the love of a father for his sons, but in any case, this is the kind of love we have to learn. This is the kind of thing that has to happen in the ministry, or it is not real.

This brings us now to the climax of the matter. As well as *resolve*, *maturity of relationship*, and depth-of-feeling or *longing*, there is needed one more thing. There has to be a *'seeing'*.

SEEING Our Fathers

Remember that Elijah said, *"If you see me."* About this also the Lord spoke to me in the middle of that night. Each of us has to come to the place where we *see* our fathers, or else we cannot love them for who they are. We have to come to the place where we can *see* the grace in them, so that we may truly honour them, and appreciate them. The better and clearer we see what is in our fathers, the more hope we have of getting it. Therefore, we have to have eyes to see, as well as a heart that longs.

Here is my experience. Over the early years of the development of relationship between my spiritual father Chuck and myself, I went through three distinct stages, of which I have already spoken. In looking back, I realise now these were stages in which my eyes were progressively opened to what was in him.

Those who know him will know he has a great heart. With a huge capacity to love, he has the affections and deep feelings of a man who walks with God. But I did not see all that at first. It was over the years of getting to know him that I saw, more and more, the grace he has, and saw as well the integrity and intensity of the love of his heart.

But the interesting and important thing is this: the more I have seen in him, the more deeply I have loved him. And the great thing is, the more I have loved him, the more I can see. This seems to be a cyclical kind of thing that builds momentum after a while – as long as we keep our heart pure. And so this increasing love I feel for Chuck has enabled me to see even more, and to recognise there is a whole world of things in him I did not see before – good things that, in the early years, I could not understand or appreciate.

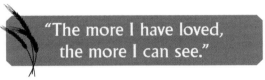

"The more I have loved,
the more I can see."

Therefore I have come to see Chuck and the grace of God in him more clearly. But my eyes were opened on each occasion by an _emotion_ – by increasing love and desire of the heart. Or to put it another way, increasing love *enabled* me to see!

You too need to see something in your fathers; you have to recognise the grace of God; you have to see the heart that God has given them; you have to see them for themselves.

And the wonderful truth is that what you *see*, you may *obtain*.

The GRACE Available

Over the course of a lifetime of walking with God, a father has developed giftedness, and has grown in grace. By definition, a father has grace with God! *"I write to you, fathers, because you have known him who is from the beginning."* (1 Jn 2:13) This is Abraham status, friendship with God.

So grace is available; it is in your fathers, though you might not be seeing it. You might think your pastor is just an ordinary man. Perhaps he doesn't preach that well, has a small church, and is small in your eyes – but I tell you, there's grace. If you have eyes to see, a heart of longing, and develop a depth of relationship, you'll find God makes great grace available through a father.

> "If you have eyes to see, a heart of longing, and develop a depth of relationship, you'll find God makes great grace available through a father."

I mentioned earlier the story about a young pastor who said to his friends, "I'm gonna get me a famous father." I'll tell you what that reminds me of. Israel in the desert craved meat, and God gave them the meat to eat, but sent leanness into their souls. (Psalm 106:15) Paul tells us not to take pride in one man over another. (1 Cor 4:6) These relationships I speak of are not fleshly, but God will give us someone to love and walk with. Even if you don't see much in that person at first, build depth of relationship and a heart of longing, and you will start to see Christ in them. It is God who will open the heavens.

The grace established in such a father is not received by us easily. We do not 'take it on board' and make it our own in five minutes. Obtaining it is not the work of a moment, and it is not given to us nor received by us on a whim!

We may have known a great father over many years, listened to his teaching on many occasions, and received his prayers and blessing, yet still not have caught the power of the grace that has been given to him.

Elisha had to pursue Elijah for many years before he came to the place where that grace was *fully* imparted, in a final, powerful, and significant impartation. Even then, Elisha had to *ask* for it, and Elijah had to be willing to give it – and even then, Elijah was not all that sure as to whether Elisha would receive it. Nevertheless, a powerful and complete impartation was available, and was given to the one who sought it by all means.

This makes me conscious of the fact that there is much in our fathers which we could obtain, but will not obtain, unless we recognise that such grace exists, and choose to truly walk with our fathers, seeking to obtain that grace before they pass from us. That we do desire to walk with them, choose to pursue them, and seek to know their heart, is also the honour that we should give our fathers.

Recognising My Father's Grace

In developing a good father/son relationship with apostle Chuck Clayton, the two of us have become friends. The blessing of this relationship has proven to be of immense benefit to me and our people.

But after the Lord spoke to me about Elisha, and the means by which we can obtain the double-portion, I began to realise that if anything was to happen to Chuck, I would have to start building such a relationship all over again. And there was so much in him that I could see we had not yet taken hold of for the cause of Christ.

Chuck has a big heart, a great love, and passion. In fact, he is a unique man, "a Noah to his generation" the Lord said to Hazel one day. I began to see that if he was taken from us to be with the Lord, then that rich grace he has been given would go with him. For none of his sons has yet taken hold of most of the grace that is in him.

When Elisha died, what he had went to the grave with him, even though he had himself received Elijah's anointing. And that is what would happen with most of our fathers right now, if they were to pass away. Most of the anointing they have would go with them, for the sons have not taken hold of their fathers.

It does not have to be like this. I have realised there is a great deposit of God's grace in my spiritual father which is available to me as a son. My feeling is that he has more grace within than any of us who are sons have ever recognised or taken hold of. When apostle Chuck comes to our conferences we appreciate his preaching, we receive impartation, we are better informed, we see more clearly, we are lifted to another level, and an enduring blessing afterwards remains. And it is a wonderful blessing. We receive good things from the Lord through him, and grace is deposited in us.

But this is just a part. There is yet in him a reservoir of giftedness and grace. He has, somehow, a holy attitude, a value system, a way of seeing things and feeling about things, a huge capacity for love and faith. If he were to go to be with the Lord, this vast resource would be lost to us, unless we can first apprehend it. None of us has yet taken hold of it or him; we have received only some of it. As for other fathers too, we must not allow him to pass from us without obtaining from him what he has been given.

How can I obtain from my spiritual father what he has, but is not able to just give me? Even Elijah said it was *"a difficult thing"*. The answer is, I must pursue him. I cannot take this all for granted. I cannot assume that this grace is already mine, or in easy reach. It must be prayed about; grace from God must be sought after. And I must ask Chuck for it, and spend time walking with him, loving him, and serving him.

This pursuing is not for the purpose of taking hold of just what he has, but trying to take hold of *him*. I must come to perceive his love, to know his heart, and to share his passion. It is the man I must love and apprehend, not so much the gift within.

> "It is the person I must love and apprehend, not so much the gift within."

I have said all this about myself and my spiritual father, not to give you instruction about us as such, but so as to demonstrate the principle. I am trying to give you a picture of how this works, to set before you a good model. What I have described pertains to how each of us must seek after grace in the matter of our own spiritual fathers.

And I have this assurance from the Spirit of God. What you *see,* you can *obtain*. If you can see grace in a spiritual father, be assured, God has opened your eyes to see it, so that you may seek to obtain it.

About My Sons

In the case of those who are my spiritual sons, they need to walk with me. But it is up to them to want to do it. They can, if they wish, seek to grow in and obtain the grace I have received, and seek to know me or apprehend me, by pursuing.

In doing so, they may well obtain not only whatever grace God has given me, but also the grace I may yet take hold of in the pursuit of my spiritual father. In other words, my faithfulness as a son to another man in the ministry of Christ will be the means of helping to advance the Kingdom of Christ in those sons who walk with me.

But I never ask anyone to pursue me. I will create the opportunity, as Elijah did, but give freedom. I tell everyone, if you want sonship 'lite', that's fine. If you just want a friendship – some love, and support, and encouragement, some accountability, pastoral care, apostolic covering and prayers of blessing, that's fine! But God will put it into the heart of some to want the greater grace, and to pursue.

A true father keeps us in freedom. What we are talking about is not enslavement. It is like Elijah saying to Elisha, *"Stay here, the Lord has sent me to the Jordan."* (2 Kings 2:6) No-one is compelled to follow. A father does not obligate or bind you to himself.

Nevertheless, there are sons who will want to 'apprehend' me, and as a father I must be willing to allow them to pursue. I must be willing to spend time with them. I must be like Elijah who said, *"What would you have me do for you?"* I must want for them their blessing and their good, and desire for them to find what they need. Others in the body of Christ must also become fathers like this, and sons must pursue them.

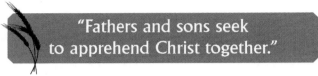

"Fathers and sons seek to apprehend Christ together."

Fathers and sons then seek to apprehend Christ together. That is what it is all about. Christ has ordained this as a means of grace. There are specific ways to obtain grace, and this relational way just happens to be a wonderful means by which we find the true grace of Jesus Christ. But it does have a distinctive measure to it – i.e. a way of measuring if the relationship is real, and therefore effective. And the measure, *"As I have loved you, so you must love one another"* (John 13:34), is the measure of Christ! That is not any small measure.

Don't tell me this does not require the whole of the heart – the giving of our hearts to one another. As the apostle John said, *"We proclaim to you what we have seen and heard, so that you also may have fellowship with us. And our fellowship is with the Father and with his son, Jesus Christ."* (1 John 1:3).

Therefore We Must Love

It is obvious that every Christian is to love other Christians, for this is Christ's major requirement of us, and proves whether we are obedient to Him, which in turn proves whether we love Him. You are, no doubt, surrounded by believers, and you will have leaders to relate to. These in particular are the ones you are to love. They have been given to you to love. They are 'yours,' in the same sense of which the gospel speaks of Jesus when it says, *"having loved His own... He loved them to the end."* (John 13:1 NASB)

A spiritual father, more than all, is one who has been given to you to love. Think how the Ephesian elders loved Paul: *"They all wept as they embraced him and kissed him."* (Acts 20:37)

And in case I happen to be falsely accused about the intent of this teaching, I hasten to say that from a biblical point of view, this is not idolatry – it is love! We are *not* talking about *worshipping* a spiritual father or leader, but of *loving* and *serving* our leaders.

In this we are doing the very thing we are commanded to do, and which Jesus Himself did during His ministry on earth, and still does. That is, He loves His own. And those He loved were mere men, just like us. If Jesus loves them, you should love them too!

Furthermore, Jesus came to serve, and so as to prove the point He took the towel and washed their feet, concerning which John wrote, *"Having loved His own who were in the world, He now showed them the full extent of His love."* (John 13:1, also vs. 12-17) He also said, *"I have not come to be served, but to serve."* (Matt 20:28) If Jesus serves men, in this case the ones He had chosen to be apostles, you should serve them too!

Jesus made these two particular things – our need to love and our need to serve – the object of His special instructions. His first great appeal is, *"...you must love one another. By this all men will know that you are my disciples..."* (John 13:34-35), and His other great directive was, *"...whoever wants to become great among you must be your servant... just as the Son of Man did not come to be served, but to serve."* (Matthew 20: 26-28)

Consider carefully: if Christ, the son of God, not only chooses to love and serve men but is righteous in doing so, don't you think we must also be following a righteous course when we do the same? If it is righteous for God in Christ to love and serve His apostles and the leaders of the church, then it cannot be idolatry for brothers and sisters, just like us, in whom Christ lives, to love and serve the same kinds of leaders Christ has appointed for the church today!

They are over us in the Lord. We make their lives easier, and their work a joy, as we should (Heb 13:16-17), and gain great advantage for ourselves in doing so, when we give them our hearts in the service of Christ.

Tests of the Heart in Relationships

I should briefly warn you. In relationships, from time to time, tests of your heart will come. But you will never know in advance when such a test is coming.

Please understand that when you choose to walk in relationships, anything could happen, and some of those things are going to test your love, or your faithfulness, or your trust, or your honour, or your submission, etc. What attitude are you going to take to those who lead you when difficult situations arise? How are you going to feel if your spiritual father appears to ask something unreasonable, or overlooks you, or is too busy some day? Will you take offence? Actually, you should continue to honour, because this opens the heavens. This is what sonship is: a steadfast loyalty in the bonds of love.

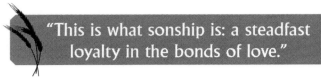

> "This is what sonship is: a steadfast loyalty in the bonds of love."

It will not necessarily be the fault of your spiritual father or ministry leader if something 'offensive' or very testing does occur – they probably had nothing to do with it, and didn't see it coming either. Be realistic! God Himself arranges many of these interactions and experiences, because only then do we learn, and grow. In fact, if a son has a weakness, the Lord will be looking sooner or later to expose the flesh, so as to deliver, heal, and mature.

This is the only way ahead – spiritual maturity through relational maturity! By choosing not to take offense, continuing to walk in humility, learning submission through the struggles, and never running away from confrontation or conflict when it should be faced and the issues resolved, we grow. We become mature sons, and we become fathers.

There is something about *pursuing*, about *loyalty*, about *faithful love*, that really does open the heavens.

Consider again the power and meaning of the biblical relationships. What of Ruth, who said to Naomi, *"Don't urge me to leave you. Where you go I will go..."* (Ruth 1:16-17) Think of the way that opened the heavens for her, and brought such blessing, such inheritance, such a wonderful posterity for her and her family, in the earth and in eternity.

But there are so many others:
Elisha said, *"I will not leave you."*
Joshua, night and day, *"remained at the tent of meeting."*
Of Timothy, Paul said, *"I have no-one else like him."*
About His Son, God said, *"With Him I am well pleased."*

Remember, *a son pursues!* If you are willing to understand such relationships, and choose to walk in them, you will find yourself enjoying a wonderful grace indeed.

Tony Ponicke, Senior Associate Pastor
Peace Christian Church,
Rockhampton, Queensland, Australia.

Authentic Christianity is based in love. And for me to submit to a spiritual Father is all about love.

Someone has said submission is a giving of the heart, and this is what I believe is truly Apostolic. I had spent many of my early years serving with an orphan spirit, and not giving my heart as a son to a father. Without love in submission, it is based in fear – fear of what will happen if you don't submit.

My heart was full of fear, until I received the revelation of the giving of my heart to my spiritual father. When I did that, my whole attitude of fear left, and I came into a great peace. John Alley, my spiritual father, has shown great patience and love for me to see me to this point. True love must be shown in authentic apostolic Christianity – caring for each other, being there for each other. I have a love now for John, as he has for me.

This is the only kind of relationship in the church in which we can find our full potential. If not for sonship, I would never have been able to mature into what God has called me to be. Without humbling myself in sonship, I would never have been able to receive the grace God has given me. Neither would I have found the satisfaction of the depth of relationship that I now have with apostle John.

Tony Ponicke.

CHAPTER 11

THE ORPHAN HEART

"The older brother became angry and refused to go in. So his father went out and pleaded with him. But he answered his father, 'Look! All these years I've been slaving for you...'"

(Luke 15: 28-29)

Tony Ponicke has been a pastor on my staff since 1998, having joined our church with his wife Carolyn in 1991. I tell the following story with his permission.

In 1998, I had been seeking the Lord about whether to appoint Tony to the full-time position of a pastor on our staff. He, with Carolyn, had been the youth leaders in our Church for some years, He seemed to have the calling and the gifting; he certainly had the heart for pastoral care, a love for the people, and a love for the Lord. As I was praying, knowing I would have to propose the thought to others for consideration, I heard the Lord say, "You will never raise a greater pastor than Tony Ponicke." That statement continued to impress itself upon me for years, and it was just as well, because of what we needed to walk through together.

I remember Tony saying to me in the first week or so of his employment, that he would never be able to receive correction from me. He would be able to receive it from someone else, such as David, but not from me, for he would find it too crushing. I did not realise what that really meant, but remained mindful of it. At the time, his brother-in-law, David Hood, was already serving as my senior associate in the leadership. David's role was to take whatever vision or purpose in ministry I had, and give leadership to it, so as to stand beside me in the effective building of the whole ministry. This meant that effectively David was Tony's direct supervisor anyway, and leader of the pastoral care of the church. Therefore I thought we had no problem. David would be responsible for training, and/or correcting Tony, working out what his responsibilities were, and how he should fulfil them. I would need to provide overall leadership, and love and pastoral care for them all. What we did not know at the time was that Tony had a huge orphan heart problem, but in those days we didn't know the term, let alone understand the condition. We were to carry a struggle for some years without even knowing what the issues were.

On the surface, Tony was a happy, relaxed, laid-back, caring, and very casual person. In fact he was so casual, it could drive you nuts. It seemed for a long time that he casually avoided carrying anything like the level of responsibility he should have, treated everything off-handedly, and often left the burden of organisation and practical leadership to others. He would invariably come late for prayer meetings, and sometimes leave early as well. Sometimes Tony would simply disappear and go home. As the years went by, it seemed there was a growing resentment in him.

I noticed that Tony would never be the one to come and greet me; I always had to go to him. This was more obvious if I had been away on an overseas ministry trip, for when I came home and walked in the door on Sunday morning, others would immediately look up and smile, greet me and welcome me home, but Tony always seemed to be looking the other way. I would approach him with a warm greeting, and get a warm response, but it was always me who had to make the approach.

I noticed too, that if we were discussing anything in leadership meetings, he would often remain quiet. If he had alternative views to mine, or didn't feel the same as the rest of us, he couldn't seem to just discuss it like we usually did. Instead he would eventually let out his feelings in a way that was inappropriate, often cynical, and just as often spoil the atmosphere of the meeting.

There was obviously something wrong, but none of us really understood it. We probably just put it down to personality, because these relational and personality struggles have always been common in the church. But Tony seemed to hold himself more and more distant from me, and seemed to be growing more resentful, especially in his fifth year on the staff.

I wondered if Tony was going to become the person he was called to be, yet the call of God remained upon him. He was meant to rise to leadership and responsibility.

Tony and I used to discuss this. I felt he had a great call to stand back-to-back with me in the ministry, and to work to win our city for Christ. I would have to travel, but he could concentrate on things at home. He felt the call and shared that vision too, but he himself wondered if he was ever going to become what he was meant to be. He used to say that he was not sure that I could rely on him.

At the same time, I hasten to say, Tony had a very great love for people, was really gifted with pastoral care, and was tireless in his willingness to talk with people, spend time with them, and visit them. But somehow, he was struggling more and more to walk with his leaders, both David and I.

What I never realised was that Tony struggled with such low self-esteem that he considered himself worthless and useless. Tony had been raised on a farm, with a good mum and dad who loved him. His family was stable, he was loved and cared for, but there was something repeatedly on the lips of his father that affected Tony profoundly in a very detrimental way. His father was always saying, in a kind of well-intended, half-joking fashion, "You're useless!" Tony says he must have heard this statement hundreds of times, and to this day, even though he has found healing, the words still ring in his ears, "You're useless!"

Tony grew up believing he was worthless, useless, of no value, a failure, could do no good, and could not be accepted or respected by anyone. One way or another, Tony ended up crushed through believing a lie, and by a father who, without realising it, had continually reinforced that lie in his heart. And this was in a case where Tony loves his father, and Tony's father loves him. Nevertheless, Tony became a man easily crushed by what others might say to him.

I was beginning to feel the burden of the growing resentment and distance Tony was keeping. Then one day, Tony came to me and said, "John, we have to talk." I knew this meant trouble.

In my office, Tony raised his complaint. I was, in his mind, too strong, unkind, crushing people. Tony spoke of several people in the church with whom we had had pastoral dealings over a number of years, some whom we had had to correct and discipline. His interpretation of these events was that I had beaten them up, so to speak. I allowed him to tell me what he was feeling, and then I gave this reply:

"Tony, you are either correct in your opinion of these things, or else it is your way of seeing things that is completely at fault. I am willing to ask David and Michael to join us, let them listen to everything you have to say, and let them decide what's right and wrong. But I have a feeling that if we do that, you are the one that is going to get hurt. The alternative," I said, "to protect you, is just for you and me to keep talking."

Tony said, "I think you're right. I think we had better keep talking, just you and me."

I knew I would have to get Tony to see the issues were in his own heart. I could see that Tony was misreading situations involving any exercise of authority. This is what I said to Tony:

"Tony, you have a really big heart, and your heart is full of good things. You love people, and you love the Lord. But there is one piece of your heart, one small sliver, in which there are not good things. In that sliver you have some things that need to be dealt with." I said, "In there, Tony, you have pride, independence, and cynicism. Further," I said, "you need to change the way you see me. You need to stop seeing me as the boss, and start seeing me as your father."

For a moment Tony struggled with what I said, but then he replied, "Yeah, you're right. But I don't know what to do about it." He then asked if he could have three days off work for prayer, so that he could seek the Lord.

Tony had some wonderful advantages for a person who needed to overcome an orphan spirit. To start with, he was a very honest man, and willing to be honest about spiritual things. If he saw a fault within himself, he would admit it. Secondly, Tony was a prayerful man. He didn't especially enjoy prayer meetings or the discipline of prayer, but he would genuinely seek the Lord, and he had often taken seasons for prayer and fasting. He was a genuine seeker after the Lord and the truth.

Then he had a third great advantage in life, which many Christians with an orphan spirit do not have. He was in a situation where his fault, or his problem, was being exposed on a regular basis by reason of the fact that he was on a pastoral ministry team and had to work closely with others in the leadership of the church. This is a huge magnifying glass. Unlike the average members of a congregation, who can turn up for the church service, and perhaps a cell meeting or a prayer meeting, and otherwise are not exposed too much in relationships, Tony was exposed to the pressure of personal and relational interaction in pressing spiritual matters every day.

Many Christians can cover up their struggle, their inadequacy, their lack, their self-hatred or low self-esteem, their resentment or pride or prejudice, by simply not being around much, or by leaving and joining another church. But to deal properly with an orphan heart, one has to remain in relationships and face the issues.

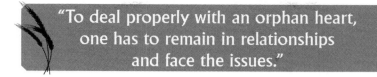

"To deal properly with an orphan heart, one has to remain in relationships and face the issues."

Tony took those days for prayer, and turned up the following weekend refreshed and renewed. In fact, that weekend was the autumn rain family camp we have spoken of earlier in this book, the weekend the Lord did amazing things amongst us. Tony and his family sat right near me in those meetings.

Before the opening meeting at the camp, Tony filled me in on what happened. During his three days of prayer, he had been given a wonderful revelation in a vision from the Lord. What had been revealed to him was the importance of the place and authority of apostles in the church – and that they were absolutely necessary to the purposes of Christ. Tony now held very clear and deep convictions – personal apostolic authority was essential for the work of God.

I wondered at the time why the Lord had given him that kind of revelation, when really what I thought he needed was a revelation concerning his own heart. He needed healing. But it is obvious now. Attitudes to authority and authority figures are amongst the biggest issues that anybody with an orphan heart has. The Lord was preparing the ground for a healing, by addressing Tony's belief system. Before Tony could be healed of an orphan heart, he had to have a heart that accepted authority and leadership with respect. Tony continued to pray, and over the following months continued to seek the Lord and to cry out concerning the state of his own heart.

Apostle Chuck came to teach his sonship message at our Summit in June 2002. Chuck preached for seven sessions i.e. seven hours of passionate, heartfelt, Bible teaching. On the Saturday night of the conference, he was preaching a message about Elijah and Elisha which he calls, "Pursue!" Somewhere in the middle of that message he preaches something like the following:

"Fathers don't follow sons, sons follow fathers. A son should pursue a father. It is not for fathers to go around following their sons. Jesus did not follow the 12. Paul did not follow Timothy. Elijah did not follow Elisha. If you want to progress, if you want to break through, you must pursue. You need to pursue a father."

In speaking of the need for a son to give his heart to a father, he then told this story. In his earlier years, he had a large church in which he had many fine people who would do anything he asked of them. They were prepared to work hard. They would clean the buildings and do the grounds. They would participate in meetings and work at all aspects of the ministry. But Chuck could not understand why he felt he could never really trust them. He had puzzled for years why this was so, but later came to realise why. They had never given him their hearts!

It is true that without the giving of our hearts to each other, trust is not established, and intimacy cannot grow. Without the giving of the heart, there is no sonship. Without the giving of the heart, we have not laid aside our own agendas. Without the giving of the heart there is always room for an Absalom to arise, who deceives the people, or steals away the ministry. You cannot build a work for God, you cannot build community, without the giving of the heart to each other in love, acceptance, and honour.

> "Without the giving of our hearts to each other, trust is not established, and intimacy cannot grow."

Tony was sitting under this preaching – "A son follows a father!" – "A son gives his heart to a father!" And as he was listening, sitting in the presence of God, the Holy Spirit moved upon Tony's heart in power – and Tony was healed, delivered, and radically changed.

The moment the meeting ended, Tony came looking for me. He was beaming, and I have never seen a more happy man. He hugged me, I think for the first time ever – Tony had given me his heart. He has been a different man, a new man, ever since.

Tony had been on our staff for over six years at that point, and no one in our congregation had ever seen Tony as a spiritual father. But the moment Tony became a son, he became a father. There was a new grace, a new anointing over his life. Within two weeks, a couple approached Tony and asked if he would be a spiritual father to them. The following Sunday morning I was speaking to the church before going overseas, when the Holy Spirit came upon the meeting, and told me that I was to lay my hands upon Tony, and give him my authority to bless the people. Then, in my absence, anyone would be able to go to Tony and receive from him the same blessing they might receive from me. This was another wonderful indication of the change of spiritual atmosphere over Tony's life. Authority was being added to him.

Since then Tony has made great progress. He became a man who grew in his ability to accept and walk in responsibility, and these days carries a great grace and fulfils such an important role in our lives. The change has been permanent, but Tony was always very humble about it. He would often say that work was still going on within him, and he was continuing to deal with attitudes.

A couple of years later, Tony stepped in the back door of the office, having just returned from his annual leave. I hadn't seen Tony in weeks, and I was standing in the hallway as he entered. I greeted him and said, "Tony, good morning, good to see you, how are you?" Tony replied, "I'm still in love." He meant, of course, in fellowship with me – he had given me his heart, and had not taken it back! We had walked together, and he was still enjoying the grace he had been given.

There is now another chapter to Tony's story. I sent Tony to Pakistan with another brother from the church about two years ago. While in Pakistan, Tony was going to preach father-son relationship, and authority in the body of Christ.

When Tony came home from that trip, I immediately began to notice something new. Tony's leadership of our Sunday morning meetings seemed to be at a new level. There was a greater understanding, a greater grace. In particular, I noticed a new wisdom evident in his speech, which was being spontaneously expressed in the meetings. Something was flourishing in him that had not been there before. I noticed it for two Sundays, and then a third, and still Tony had said nothing about what might have happened to him. In the end, I confronted him openly in front of others. I said, "Tony, tell me the truth. Where did you get all this wisdom? What happened to you?" Tony then told us this story.

In Pakistan, whilst preparing to preach, the Lord had gripped him with the story of the Centurion who had said to Jesus, *"Just speak the word, for I myself am a man under authority."* Tony said he read that Scripture over and over, for it had just gripped him. And right there he had another huge breakthrough, just like he did at the 2002 Summit. The Lord opened his eyes and he came to a place of inner rest, where he realised that he himself was a man under authority, and as such did not have to carry the burden and fear of all the responsibility. He could trust. In that moment, Tony became a freer man, again. All along he had told me the work in him was not finished, that he still had ongoing struggles, and had to keep dealing with his heart. I can tell you, the grace God gave Tony has been a gift to us all.

There are people everywhere who, like Tony, struggle with their feelings but don't know why. People who are suspicious, cynical, or resentful of leaders and of authority; and the trouble is that many of them think this is normal, the way it should be. So they operate out of resentment, or hurt, or pride, or cynicism, all their days; and all they do is harm the work of God, and keep themselves spiritually poor. There are too many that live in this kind of poverty, 'orphaned,' and often not even knowing that a restoration of their hearts is needed.

But Tony's story gives us all great hope.

Hurt from a natural father, or from any relationship involving trust, can result in difficulty approaching God or receiving God's love. On the other hand, dealing with hurts and relationships always opens up intimacy with God, and His people. This is not because God necessarily withholds Himself from relationships, but because people, even born-again believers, if carrying unhealed hurt, do not fully trust in relationships. Therefore they do not fully yield to the Spirit of God, or really draw near to Him– it is this kind of believer who struggles to find intimacy, even with God.

> "Dealing with hurts and relationships always opens up intimacy with God, and His people."

I wrote earlier, in Chapter 8, that we all need the voice of a father, but there are many that have only known cursing, disaffection, or disapproval from their father, and so their hearts have been wounded. As a result many struggle, often without knowing it, with what we are calling an orphan spirit, or an orphan heart.

I restate what I said earlier:

"This term does not refer to an evil spirit. It is rather a term used to help us describe and discuss the state of heart we find in many people who, through broken trust, or betrayal, or lack of parental care and affection, or other such experiences (but just as often through perceptions rather than actual fact), struggle with emotions such as fear, insecurity, and low self-worth, carry attitudes of mistrust concerning authority figures and others, and sometimes find difficulty maintaining relationships especially where intimacy or transparency is required.

"People who struggle like this often have perceptions of life that we equate with orphans – a sense of not belonging, not being loved, not approved, insecure, untrusting, wary of father figures, or just not knowing how to relate to a father figure, etc. These things are not usually on the surface, but hidden in the thoughts and feelings of the heart. They affect behaviour and attitudes, and warp the values out of which people live. Often people do not know why they act or feel as they do. Very often people like this do not remain in churches when confrontational issues arise, especially if they are challenged or under pressure concerning themselves. Instead of maintaining relationships, facing the issues within themselves, and becoming mature, they take offence, leave, and join another church. And the cycle will repeat itself."

Hurt caused by an abusive father is amongst those things that have the deepest, most long-lasting, and sometimes most debilitating effects on the lives and emotions of people – and sometimes the most difficult for some to find healing from. Not that healing is not available from Christ in the gospel, but the obtaining of this inner healing requires trust, submission, and forgiveness, and this is often what believers with these kinds of issues find most difficult to do.

Why would this be? It is because a father is the one person whom we should be able to trust more than all. He not only has the most powerful position of all in life to influence a child, but also has the God-given authority to do so. There is innocence in the heart of a child, and he or she is meant to be able to trust a father implicitly, and to feel safe in his care – provided for, loved, and protected. A child needs this sense of security that comes from dad, and will naturally trust a father's love. We are all made rich by these relationships.

So when a father betrays this trust, and systematically abuses a child, or neglects, or leaves a child to the emptiness and loss of desertion, this can and does cause the deepest possible harm to the human heart. Such abuse, or neglect, or desertion, or betrayal, or failure, has come from the single most important figure in a child's life. This father will have left deep impressions upon the heart of the child which make it difficult for them to trust others in relationships, and especially trust authority figures. They then struggle to trust pastors, or teachers, or the police, or community leaders, or God.

But please remember, there is also another cause. Often enough, when people feel like this, it is not because they did not have good parents (or a good pastor, or belong to a good church), but because these hurts are perceived! Satan, or circumstances, or their own inclinations, lie to them about life, and their parents, and authority, and the church, etc. Many will struggle with big orphan issues, even though the circumstances that might have caused them is small, and another person would simply have seen the circumstances differently, and thought no more about it.

The human heart is deceptive, and people can very easily deceive themselves. I know that many of the people who leave churches, claiming to have 'been hurt,' have actually hurt themselves by what they choose to believe. Pride, independence, unteachableness, taking offence, all take their toll. In other words, our sin and the weaknesses of the human heart account for a great deal of our so-called hurts.

And this is so with children as much as adults. Who is to know, when a sulking child having been correctly disciplined, is actually breeding resentment in their heart? It has been said that the powers of darkness actively seek to sow a spirit of rejection into the heart of every little boy and girl growing up. Parents must pray for discernment, and remain very active in the lives of their children with both discipline and affection.

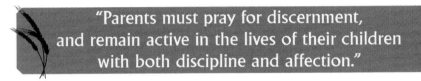

"Parents must pray for discernment, and remain active in the lives of their children with both discipline and affection."

I usually say that the person choosing to take offence, more often than not, is the greater sinner, rather than the one they claim caused the offence. Either way, the one offended is the one that must take responsibility for dealing with their own heart. They must choose forgiveness, clean out every root of bitterness, and address every lie that they believe.

There are times when someone new will come along to join a church, having moved from somewhere else. They will come in enthusiastic about the programme, or the preacher, or the love of evangelism, or in some other way claim to have come because they believe their 'needs' will be met in this new place. Then, a year or two later, they will walk out, unhappy, now claiming, "There is no love in this place." The problem is not that there was no love there –the problem was that this person could not receive love, or recognise love, or give love. It is the problem of the orphan heart.

And very often, a person with an orphan heart expects the leadership to do everything for them, but will do nothing for their leaders. Tony was like this too. He expected me to do everything perfectly, but he would do little – until he was set free – and then his heart functioned differently. When a person with that kind of heart leaves, they blame the leaders, usually the senior leader, for everything. Just like that day when Tony said to me, "John, we have to talk."

Tony teaches well on this subject now, and has depth of insight into heart struggles. He says:

"There are three big lies, or ungodly beliefs.

One, a sense of rejection. I don't belong; I'm not loved, wanted, or accepted.

Two, I am useless, and therefore worthless. I don't count; I have nothing to offer.

Three, I will never amount to anything. I can't cope with life; I can't do anything well if at all. I am incompetent. I can't do this. I have tried and failed, I am not failing again.

On the other hand, a healthy self-image will include a sense of belonging and of being loved, as well as a sense of being valuable and worthwhile, and a sense of being able to cope well with life.

People often ask me, "How can I solve my problem of an orphan heart?" How can anyone deal with orphan-type issues? What is to be done?

I have two basic pieces of advice I give to people, knowing that they themselves will have to pray consistently and see these issues through to healing.

1. Recognition of the problem is half the solution.

If a believer can and will look honestly at themselves, recognise their fault and their weakness, calling it for what it is, be open about it, and discuss it honestly with their leaders – then I believe they are halfway to addressing the problem. Recognition, honesty, being prepared to address the issues – these are the things that are necessary or healing can never begin.

2. Persistence in relationships.

Do not run away from issues, and do not allow offence to cause you to break relationship with anybody. Those with an orphan heart will feel the struggle of emotions, of offences, of insecurity, of low self-esteem, of anger, of being slighted, etc. There are many emotions, many feelings that a person with an orphan heart will experience during the course of their relationships with pastors, assistant pastors, youth leaders, worship leaders, or with any brother or sister in the church. A person can feel slighted, or overlooked, or offended, or vulnerable to exposure, and this could happen in a prayer meeting, the leadership meeting, or just fellowship after a Sunday service. A big lesson is to understand the need to not run, and not hide. Do not pull up stakes and shift camp. Healing only comes when we stay. Despite our feelings, keep working the issues through, and keep building relationships of trust. The people who stick it out are the ones most likely to reap the great rewards.

In the context of this advice, anyone with struggles of the heart should not blame other people but keep prayerfully seeking solutions from God, and believe and look for healing, growth in grace, progress in the faith, and the beauty of mature, trusting relationships. Healing does come.

Testimony

Justin Morgan
Member of Peace Christian Church,
Rockhampton, Queensland, Australia.

Sonship is very personal in its implications, but has many corporate out workings. For me the first steps along the path toward sonship were initially very difficult. I was at best an observer who was reluctant to jump in. Looking back, I can now see how the many years of self-sufficiency and independence with an associated self imposed isolation from any real relationship made it difficult for me to walk into sonship. I was close enough to know the basic theory of sonship, and knew that theory alone did not make me a son. I had this longing for more than what I had, but knew that it would require the giving of my heart, a whole new way of living.

I did, by the grace of God, become a son, and it did involve the giving of my heart to a father. I have found a sense of belonging that comes out of identity rather than simply out of what I might do or achieve. Even when I struggle and want to make myself alone, because of sin and shame, I know that I am not alone, I have a place of belonging where I can find love, acceptance and correction. I have a father. In addition I have found that as I have given my heart all the more to a spiritual father, I have been able to open my heart all the more to my Heavenly Father, and be a blessing rather than a burden to my spiritual father.

Sonship is many things, yet it is one thing out of which comes many things. What I mean is this: For me to walk in sonship, I let go of, and am still letting go of, the way I view myself and others in the household of God. I now don't just go to the same church as some people, I have a real affection for them. And the one who leads the church isn't just another pastor or preacher, he is my father from whom I have no need to hide. As I grow in sonship it is my attitudes that are continuing to be changed, the attitudes of my heart. So the one thing is the heart, and out of my heart, as I grow in sonship, comes an ability to grasp grace for relationships, for overcoming sin, for husbandry to my wife, for leadership, for fathering my children, and the list goes on. The spirit of sonship has and is truly saving me from myself.

Justin Morgan.

CHAPTER 12

TRUSTING AND IMITATING LEADERS

*"So then, men ought to regard us as servants of Christ and
as those entrusted with the secret things of God."*

(1 Corinthians 4:1)

Trusting Others

Many of us were brought up in churches and denominations where the corporate culture taught us, or we even heard people state outright, as I often have, that we were to not trust any man, only trust Christ.

We have to realise that while there is in that thought a truth – for our salvation we can only trust Christ and His finished work, for instance – it is also a very damaging false doctrine. For unless we learn to trust each other for the purpose of relationships and spiritual leadership, we will not be able to build anything worthwhile together. You cannot build churches, and you cannot build the Kingdom of God, if you do not build trusting relationships. There has to be trust, and besides which the Bible says, *"Love ...always trusts."* (1 Corinthians 13:6-7) If there is no trusting of one other in the church, then no real relational development has taken place, and there will be no mature love.

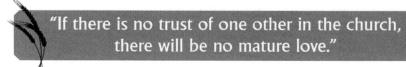

"If there is no trust of one other in the church,
there will be no mature love."

In 1 Corinthians 4:1, Paul writes, *"So then, men ought to regard us as servants of Christ and as those entrusted with the secret things of God."*

What is this telling us? Paul informs us quite clearly that God chooses to trust (some) men. I put the *some* in brackets because, quite obviously, not everyone can be trusted. But God has no choice, for He has given Himself no choice. God has chosen to work this way. He has always chosen to select, humble, mould, equip, appoint, and trust individual men and women to represent Him personally, and to carry out His purposes on earth.

The Lord moulds His chosen ones, correcting and training them, and somehow in the process breaks something in them that needs to be broken. Then, as they progressively mature, He step-by-step trusts them and establishes authority in them.

How else can you explain the apostle Peter, the apostle John, or the apostle Paul. How else can you explain Abraham, Moses, or King David? God takes hold of those He regards as His own, and chooses to put trust in them. Paul said that he was entrusted with the gospel! That is a huge claim. (1 Cor 9:17, 1 Thess 2:4, see also Titus 1:7) He further stated that the administration of God's grace was given to him for our sakes, a mystery made known to him by revelation, and he said the mystery of Christ was made known to other holy apostles and prophets as well. (Ephesians 3:2-5)

It follows that if God trusts some men, so as to appoint them as leaders, or deliverers, or apostles, or prophets, to the body of Christ, then His people are meant to trust them also. When God sent Moses to Egypt to bring about the deliverance of His people in answer to their prayers, not only did Moses represent God personally in doing so, but the Lord expected His people to receive him. And the record says, *"...the people feared the Lord and put their trust in him and in Moses his servant."* (Exodus 14:31) This is what they were meant to do, but when they rebelled and complained in the desert, God was angry with that generation.

There will be leaders appointed by God that everyone of us, including you and me, is meant to relate to. We must learn to trust. I am not saying that everyone is trustworthy – indeed we are warned to beware of false shepherds, and to guard against the dangers of false brethren. Some people are not trustworthy, and you should not trust them.

But this does not excuse you from developing relationships of trust. To do so, you should determine whom you are meant to walk with, who it is that loves you, and who has been appointed to lead you. You must come to love and trust these. If someone proves unworthy, that is very unfortunate, but we can still only build our lives, our families, and a greater work for Christ by developing relationships with leaders we can trust.

This does not mean that they will be perfect in your eyes. But if they love, if they are humble, if their heart is for Christ and for you, if Christ has entrusted them with a stewardship, and they are open and accountable, then you have in them the things that are needed in someone you can trust.

Remember that you are not perfect either, and you will want others to trust you. As we develop more intimate relationships of trust, people actually grow. But judgemental and critical attitudes destroy, and pull our leaders down.

> "As we develop intimate relationships of trust, people grow."

We must always be prepared to allow leaders to make honest mistakes. We learn from mistakes, and we all make them anyway. James said, *"We all stumble in many ways,"* so it seems there's no getting away from that. (James 3:2, also James 2:12-13) We have to have a supportive and understanding attitude to those who are over us, nonjudgemental and merciful, so that we can walk properly with them and help them achieve what they have been appointed to. It is those who persevere, especially those who persevere in relationships, who are the most likely to achieve the fulfilment of the vision they have been given.

> "It is those who persevere in relationships who are most likely to fulfil the vision they have been given."

To withdraw and cease from walking in trusting relationships because one has been hurt, or disappointed, or let down, is a defeat for you. You cannot live a fruitful life for the Lord Jesus from a position of cynicism and distrust of others because of previous hurt. God appoints leaders in whom He is putting trust, and we must trust also. Otherwise, our belief in the fellowship of the saints is meaningless.

Qualities of Apostolic Fathering

There is a certain kind of fathering that is called for in the church, and clearly described in Scripture. This is a tender-hearted, gentle, yet passionate fathering. This is fathering that is holy, has integrity, and designed to bless. This is what we are called to follow.

It is clearly seen in Paul's first letter to the Thessalonians, where interestingly Paul first describes himself and those with him, namely Silas and Timothy, as being like a mother, and then as a father. *"We were gentle among you, like a mother caring for her little children,"* he said.

Paul wrote the following declaration concerning the purity of true apostolic leadership:

"For the appeal we make does not spring from error or impure motives, nor are we trying to trick you. On the contrary, we speak as men approved by God to be entrusted with the gospel. We are not trying to please men but God, who tests our hearts. You know we never used flattery, nor did we put on a mask to cover up greed – God is our witness. We were not looking for praise from men, not from you or anyone else.

"As apostles of Christ we could have been a burden to you, but we were gentle among you, like a mother caring for her little children. We loved you so much that we were delighted to share with you not only the gospel of God but our lives as well, because you had become so dear to us. Surely you remember, brothers, our toil and hardship; we worked night and day in order not to be a burden to anyone while we preached the gospel of God to you.

"You are witnesses, and so is God, of how holy, righteous and blameless we were among you who believed. For you know that we dealt with each of you as a father deals with his own children, encouraging, comforting and urging you to live lives worthy of God, who calls you into his kingdom and glory." (1 Thessalonians 2:3-12)

This is the kind of fathering I am speaking about, and the kind of spiritual leadership provided by true and holy apostles. When we have leaders who love like this, we can have the confidence to trust, and we please God in doing so.

Paul could appeal to the record of the life he lived as proof of the apostolic grace he had received. *"You know how we lived among you for your sake,"* he wrote. (1 Thess 1:5) Neither spiritual fathering nor true apostolic leadership is a 'free ride' for someone who just wants leadership, or control, or for anyone who likes to be first. Jesus said that if anyone wants to be first (which is also a designation for the apostle's position, 1 Cor 12:28) he must become the servant of all. (Mark 9:35)

Furthermore, look again at Paul's description of his apostolic credentials: *"we were gentle among you... surely you remember, brothers, our toil and hardship... you are witnesses, and so is God, of how holy, righteous and blameless we were among you... you know that we dealt with each of you as a father deals with his own children, encouraging, comforting and urging you to live lives worthy of God..."* (1 Thess 2:7, 9, 10, 11)

It is no wonder we are called to imitate leaders such as this. And after Paul made the comment quoted above (*"You know how we lived among you for your sake"*), he went on to observe, *"You became imitators of us and of the Lord."* (1 Thess 1:5-6)

Imitation

It just so happens that the New Testament has a lot to say about imitation. It tells us to imitate the Lord, but also to imitate the apostles, imitate apostolic teams, to imitate the churches, to imitate those who were in the faith before us, to imitate those who because of their perseverance broke through and succeeded. And it tells us to imitate our leaders. That's a lot of imitation, isn't it? Here are the scriptural injunctions:

1. *"...for in Christ Jesus I became your father through the gospel. Therefore I urge you to imitate me."* (1 Cor 4:15-16)
2. *"Follow my example, as I follow the example of Christ."* (1 Corinthians 11:1)
3. *"You became imitators of us and of the Lord;"* (1 Thessalonians 1:6)
4. *"For you, brothers, became imitators of God's churches in Judea, which are in Christ Jesus."* (1 Thessalonians 2:14)
5. *"We... want you... to imitate those who through faith and patience inherit what has been promised."* (Hebrews 6:12)
6. *"Remember your leaders, who spoke the word of God to you. Consider the outcome of their way of life and imitate their faith."* (Hebrews 13:7)
7. *"Join with others in following my example, brothers, and take note of those who live according to the pattern we gave you."* (Phil 3:17)
8. *"For you yourselves know how you ought to follow our example... We did this... in order to make ourselves a model for you to follow."* (2 Thess 3:7,9)
9. *"...became followers of Paul, and believed."* (Acts 17:34)

The word *imitation* and the word *follow* are used alternatively, one in place of the other, in various translations of The New Testament. It refers to the concept of learning from another, of pursuing a leader, of walking with a teacher – but not just to learn facts or ideas, but so as to learn to be like them. This is what discipleship is.

But the simple question remains: Why all this imitation – of leaders, of churches, and of the faithful – when Christ is, after all, totally unique, and He is the only source of life, forgiveness, salvation, authority, power, and

glory, and He is the Lord whom we worship? Why do we say to follow a
spiritual leader? Why do we say to imitate a spiritual father?

Here is the reason. God understands the importance of putting good
models in place in our lives. There is always a need for good examples,
people that we can learn from. But these have to be living people, not only
the heroes of the past. We need someone who has 'skin on'; someone that
we can see, talk to, listen to, and watch. They've learned some things and
we must learn them too. They have made mistakes, and we don't have to
make the same mistakes. They have achieved things, and we can walk
with them. They have been through the school of experience and difficult
times, but we can go through the school of their instruction.

And there's more. They have attitudes and values they have learned from
Christ. There is something about them – grit, spirit, perseverance, faith,
wisdom, grace – there's an edge, an *attitude*, and it's holy. It's not really
taught with words, it has to be caught – like a holy infection – through
being with them, and through time, and touch, and laughter, and prayer,
and tears, and perseverance, i.e. the sharing of life and love.

The Bible indicates there are two ways a son can learn. A wise son
learns by listening to the voice of his father. But a foolish son learns by
stripes on his back, that is, by the rod of correction. What would you rather
be – a foolish or a wise son? You will need to listen to the voice of a father.
That is why in the church we must have all this *imitation*.

A Son Imitates a Father

The apostle Paul did not just say *"imitate me"* (or "follow me"). Rather,
in calling people to see themselves as sons to him as a father, his instruction
was, *"Be imitators of me, just as I also am of Christ,"* (NASB) or, *"Follow
my example, as I follow the example of Christ."* (1 Cor 11:1 NIV)

The whole purpose of imitation, or discipleship, is to follow Christ! And
to do so more effectively! The apostle, in his pursuit of God the Father and
the Son, was mature in Christ and a great model to follow. Paul was not
leading men after himself, but fulfilling the duty of his calling in Christ, to
present the church as a pure bride to Him. He wrote, *"I am jealous for you
with a godly jealousy. I promised you to one husband, to Christ, so that I
might present you as a pure virgin to him."* (2 Cor 11:2)

"The whole purpose of imitation is to follow Christ,
and to do so more effectively!"

A son following a spiritual father imitates all the good he sees in him, so as to perfect his own walk with Christ. Paul passionately exhorted the Corinthians, *"Even though you have 10,000 guardians in Christ, you do not have many fathers, for in Christ Jesus I became your father through the gospel. Therefore I urge you to imitate me."* (1 Corinthians 4:15-16) This was the greatest need. Even if they had 10,000 teachers in Corinth, this would not achieve for them what modelling themselves after a mature spiritual father would achieve. Paul urged them to follow the model of his own life, and for that very reason sent Timothy, whose purpose as a son to a father was to remind them of Paul's way of life in Christ. They would see Paul in Timothy. This is what a son in the ministry achieves.

One of the reasons for imitating those who have gone before us in the faith is so we can be more sure of walking in the truth, and of persevering to the end, and of not stumbling, but being found truly in Christ.

An Error to Avoid

The purpose of the apostle, as should be the purpose of every spiritual father and church leader, is never to 'draw' people after themselves. Paul's apostolic purpose meant he was showing them how to follow Christ – 'follow my pattern; I'm a good example, copy what I am showing you' – was Paul's position, and must be ours. That is the heart of the true leader, the true father, the true apostle, the true prophet, the true pastor.

The reason 'pure' Christian leaders do not draw people after themselves, so as to meet their own needs, is because it is not in their spirit. The true minister of Christ doesn't have a craving for a following, and isn't motivated by a lust for control or influence. Because their heart is so much for Christ, and so much for the good and freedom of their followers, there is a humility, and a servant-hood, that is not only safe, but healthy and life-giving to follow.

But there is a strange spiritual phenomenon I have seen in some people active in church leadership over the years. I have seen pastors who had something about the spirit of their lives whereby, instead of building all the people together, so that they would walk together, their spirit would draw people towards themselves. I find that kind of behaviour very disturbing. It never helps people, and always leaves problems even after those faulty leaders have gone.

We should never have that kind of spirit about us. We should all be prayerful to ensure our motivation is pure, and not a mixture. We are to have emptied and humbled ourselves, so that we might serve Christ. And when we do, suddenly we find the commission of God is upon us to lead people into the graces that we have discovered for Christ's sake.

Foundations

The church needs good foundations, and the Bible says that alongside Christ the lives of other people are being sown into that foundation.

Paul taught that the household of God, the church, is built on the foundation of the apostles and prophets. *"Consequently, you are no longer foreigners and aliens, but fellow citizens with God's people and members of God's household, built on the foundation of the apostles and prophets, with Christ Jesus himself as the chief cornerstone."* (Eph 2:20)

The term *household* means family. We are all members of one family, and belong together in that one family house. Properly understood, the foundation referred to is a *family* foundation, and these phrases, *"built upon the foundation of the apostles and prophets with Christ Jesus himself being the chief cornerstone"*, refer to *individuals*, who are themselves members of the family, and who are foundational to the family. We should note that it is their lives and their love, not just their position, authority, and teaching, which is important.

The chief cornerstone of this foundation is Christ. Again, it is His life and His love which is essential to this foundation, not only His teaching. At the same time, you cannot remove from the text of Holy Scripture the fact that it says that the apostles and prophets are the foundation upon which the house of God is built.

But what does it mean, and is there a conflict here? We need to understand the old building methods referred to so as to grasp the meaning of this picture. Today, a foundation stone is nothing more than a plaque fitted into the front wall of a building. But in the days when this Scripture was written, buildings were built differently.

The building project commenced with the chief cornerstone. A cornerstone had to be very carefully selected, then very carefully shaped or prepared for its purpose, and then it had to be very carefully positioned. Three important stages are seen here. For the eternal house of God, the right stone was chosen, then prepared, and then positioned – this was Christ, the chief cornerstone.

He was the one, amongst all men, who was chosen. Then, all the circumstances of His life on earth were a preparation for Him. Then He was positioned, by His earthly ministry, and then the cross, the resurrection, His ascension to the right hand of the Father, and by His being given all the authority, power and glory. Today, there is a man, the man Christ Jesus, son of God, son of Man, seated on the throne of His father. Praise God! He is the second Adam, and has been properly positioned as the cornerstone of all God's works.

In that old building method, once you had the right stone it had to be positioned very carefully, because the foundations of the building were to be aligned with that cornerstone. So its positioning was critical to the whole, for once it was in position, you could then lay out the rest of the foundation for the building. Once you had the whole of the foundation right, you could then raise the building.

This is a picture of how the house of God is built, using Christ as the cornerstone, and apostles and prophets as foundational stones aligned with Christ. The purpose of holy apostles and prophets in submission to Christ is to give a correct alignment for the whole house of God.

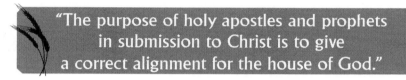

"The purpose of holy apostles and prophets in submission to Christ is to give a correct alignment for the house of God."

For apostles and prophets to be foundational to God's house, what do you think they have to do? Do they turn up on a Sunday morning to give a few nice words, and leave a blessing, and go on their way? No! What did Christ have to do to be the cornerstone positioned in the foundation? The answer is, He had to sow the whole of His life into this work for God's people. For Him it meant death, sacrifice, the giving up of His own will so as to be an apostle, and walking with the Father in submission as a son.

In the same way, the kinds of apostles and prophets who do actually become foundational for the family of God (not only in the past, but in the present also) are those who sow their whole lives sacrificially into the building of the house of God.

It is not those who are here just for themselves, who speak for themselves and represent their own interests. They are not apostles and prophets at all. Or if they had been called to be apostles and prophets, they have not become the holy apostles and prophets they were called to be. In this case, they are not the foundation stones of the house.

But those who are yielded to Christ and walk with God as mature fathers in the faith, are models for all the believers. These we must appreciate, and these we must follow. The house of God is a living and timeless house. He did not just prepare apostles and prophets in one generation as a 'one-off' or static foundation – no, there have to be apostles and prophets in every generation who are foundational to the building of Christ's eternal house.

And our fathers are not just those of past generations, but again, there must be fathers in every generation. Every age of the church must have fathers in the faith, and must have apostles and prophets.

Circumcision of the Heart

Paul wanted to take Timothy with him in the ministry, so (for cultural and social reasons) he circumcised him. (Acts 16:3) This is not the case of a son choosing a father, but of a father taking hold of a son.

Most of us have relationships with someone we regard as our spiritual father. Are we willing and prepared to allow a father to take hold of us? Are we willing for a father to lay his hands upon us, and circumcise our hearts? There is no such thing as a father's love without discipline, and all of us will require discipline.

Paul circumcised Timothy and then took him on a journey. This was painful. Not only is the circumcision painful at first, but the pain continues for many days. And the pain didn't end with the immediate circumcision, for much about the journey itself would have been painful. In all Paul's sufferings and trials, Timothy was standing by.

Timothy was also with him when Paul was sick. Paul had commented to one of the churches (Gal 4:13-14) that though his sickness could have been a trial to them, it was not. If Paul's sickness could have been a trial to the church in general, how much more of a trial might it have seemed to a son who was trying to follow a father. It may have seemed like the ministry was constantly being interrupted. Paul would be thrown into jail, or stoned and left for dead. These constant interruptions, not to mention the shipwrecks and other struggles, meant that there were times that even though Timothy was with Paul, it must not have seemed that they were busy about the actual work of the ministry.

Yet every interlude and interruption we face can be a critical part of the formation of spiritual character. And this was true both for Paul as well as for Timothy. Without the sufferings and trials, without the opposition of false apostles, and the infidelity, at times, of churches and believers, we would not have the Scriptures that we do have, nor would we have seen the formation of the great heart of the apostle Paul.

And neither would Timothy have been the Timothy we know – the faithful son, the one who stood by Paul no matter what, and who became another father to the churches both before and after Paul was taken from them.

> "We have too many who have grown up shallow
> because they have not known
> the discipline or circumcision of a father."

Without Godly fathering, and the discipline, correction, and pain that sometimes must come to us from the wisdom of a father, and without walking with a father through the difficult things fathers experience, we would have something in us less than a Timothy – we would be less than we could have been. As it is, we have too many who grow up shallow, take longer to mature, and who have walked in little that will give them the depth, the strength, and the wisdom to be of supreme value to the church, because they have not known the discipline or circumcision of a father.

"For this reason I am sending to you Timothy, my son whom I love, who is faithful in the Lord." (1 Cor 4:17) *"I have no one else like him... but you know that Timothy has proved himself, because as a son with his father he has served with me in the work of the gospel."* (Philippians 2: 20, 22)

Testimony

Lloyd Gill, Apostolic Ministry Team
Peace Christian Church,
Rockhampton, Queensland, Australia.

In my walk with the Lord there have been a number of things that have made a crucial difference in my growth and the grace that is on my life. Of these, the concept of father son relationships has possibly been the most important factor in bringing me to the place I am now.

In my mid teens, the Lord spoke to me about finding a man and serving his ministry. This was not just serving until my own ministry came along, or serving so that he could promote me. Rather, it was to serve as though another person's ministry was my ministry, and as if I had nothing better to do with the rest of my life but to help another succeed in his calling. And my dad had always taught me to serve, and to do so cheerfully without concern for reward or recognition.

I was not aware of the existence of modern day apostles, and I had no concept of the principles of father son relationships. All I knew was that the Lord made it clear to me that I was not to be concerned with finding a good bible college, instead I was to find a man that the Lord would show me, and walk with him, and that would be the training that I would need.

For me this has been a bountiful grace, for I realise now that in my life was a significant amount of pride and arrogance, and had this not been a deep conviction of the Spirit, there may have been times when I did not stay where God had placed me.

I started to walk in this instruction when in 1992 I felt the Lord direct me to begin to serve John. Over the years since then I have come to understand more about the concept of sonship, and that over the long term what it offers is far greater than other roads that might seem to appear better. A number of years ago I had a dream that indicated there will seem to be short cuts, but that I should stay on the course marked out, because those short cuts are distractions that will cost time and energy.

Proof of how effective walking in sonship is, is that I am writing this testimony from Africa, where I travel several times a year on John's behalf, carrying the apostolic message that he was given to take to the nations. I visit many nations and I am received with a lot of grace, because I carry the anointing and grace of my spiritual father.

Had I taken those other paths that seemed better, or taken a shortcut, I would certainly not be where I am now. Instead, I would have been spending years building a reputation and gaining acceptance. Instead I have grown as a son, and I have found an inheritance.

I have been given a depth of wisdom and understanding that has come from the guidance and correction that only a father can bring. Thinking about my attitudes today, and the changed ways in which I now conduct myself, I am so grateful for the principle of fathering that has built so much into my life. I give thanks to God for the spiritual father He placed in my life to be a blessing to me.

There is yet another benefit that comes with walking with a spiritual father, and that is the security and freedom experienced. I have a deep inner knowing that, regardless of what I do, I am loved and will be accepted. That is not to say that I won't be corrected or disciplined, but it does mean that I will be loved and accepted through the process. In fact the discipline adds significantly to the security I have.

Lloyd Gill.

On 16.4.2007, Lloyd wrote:

Hi John,

I appreciate you and the grace that is on your life, I feel so blessed that the Lord brought me to Rockhampton and to you. I know that this is where the Lord has Jenny and me, and that we experience a lot of blessing because of this. Thank you for being the man of God that you are. Jenny and I really appreciate you and Hazel and the love and friendship that we have experienced being in relationship with you. It is true that the Lord has done a wonderful work in all of our hearts, and just sitting here it really occurred to me that I really do not want to go back to the other form of church – what we have is incredibly precious, a pearl of great price.

Yours in Christ

Lloyd.

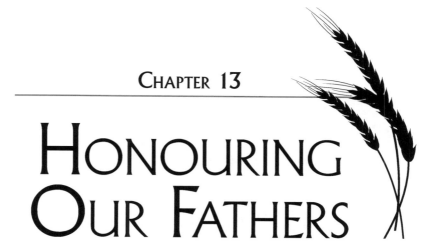

CHAPTER 13

HONOURING OUR FATHERS

"...respect those who work hard among you,
who are over you in the Lord and who admonish you.
Hold them in the highest regard in love because of their work."

(1 Thess 5:12-13)

"A son honours his father..."

(Malachi 1:6)

Honour is the lifeblood of community and relationships. Without honour there is no 'giving' in relationships, and the place of honour is instead filled with the dead weight of alternative attitudes and opinions which pull down and keep the church's common life at the low ebb of assumptions, pride, faint praise, cynicism, and independence.

This is what Paul warned against when he said, *"If you keep on biting and devouring each other, watch out or you will be destroyed by each other."* (Galatians 5:15) From the wisdom of Solomon we get this: *"The wise woman builds her house, but with her own hands the foolish one tears hers down."* (Proverbs 14:1) The women referred to can be taken as symbolic of churches everywhere. It is with the giving of honour that the believers of a church may build up their fellowship, or tear it down.

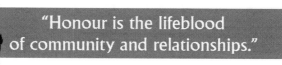

"Honour is the lifeblood
of community and relationships."

The Scriptures are clear enough: *"Honour one another above yourselves"* (Romans 12:10) and, *"The elders who direct the affairs of the church well are worthy of double honour, especially those whose work is preaching and teaching."* (1 Timothy 5:17) But the principle, I think, is not well understood, and churches the world over tend to operate more by the cultural norms and customs of the society in which they are placed than by understanding spiritual life in the body of Christ.

But we are here considering the need to honour spiritual fathers in particular.

Know Them

One of the most powerful texts that speak to the subject is printed at the head of this chapter, and is presented here in another version:

> *"And we beseech you, brethren, to know them which labour among you, and are over you in the Lord, and admonish you; And to esteem them very highly in love for their work's sake. And be at peace among yourselves."* (1 Thess 5:12-13 KJV)

Of immediate interest is the phrase from the King James version, "know them," which is common to a number of translations, but in others is variously rendered as, 'respect those', 'appreciate those', 'honour those', and the like. In the New Testament Greek used by the apostle Paul, the word he used was *'eido'*, which properly means to <u>see</u> (either literally or figuratively). By implication, this means to *know*, to *be aware*, to *behold*, to *consider*, to *have knowledge*, to *look on*, to *perceive*, to *be sure*, and to *understand*.

This takes us back to what we said earlier about pursuing a spiritual father. One of the requirements for us to apprehend the grace that is in a spiritual father is that we have eyes to see, to behold, to perceive or understand the grace that he has been given. We must <u>see</u> something in our fathers.

Paul, in urging us 'to know' those who are 'over' us and 'admonish' us, which is a perfect description of a spiritual father, is urging us to have a heart for them. We are to be fully involved in their lives. We must understand their vision, their loves, their motivation, and their hearts' desires. We must perceive their calling. But we must go further. We must be so fully involved in their work and their ministry for Christ that we share their passion.

> **"We cannot honour leaders over us if we do not know them, understand them, and willingly participate in their works."**

We cannot appreciate, respect, and honour leaders over us if we do not fully know them, understand them, and willingly share and participate in their works. The text said that we were to, *"...esteem them very highly in love for their work's sake."* The spirit of Christ calls for His appointed leaders to be loved, understood, accepted, supported, and appreciated above all. There must be honour in the house, and it must be given to our leaders.

Honour is not really honour unless it has a practical dimension. What are their needs? We must help to meet them. What are their struggles? We must carry the burden of prayer for them. What kinds of things do they like? We can seek to be a blessing to them. What kind of friendship and support would they appreciate? We must be there for them.

> **"Honour is not really honour unless it has a practical dimension."**

We are to be generous toward our spiritual fathers, for generosity is always, without exception, an expression of honour. The literal meaning of the giving of honour is to add wealth. The literal meaning of the Greek word Paul used for honour, when he said the elders who direct the affairs of the church well are *"worthy of double honour,"* is *'diplous'*, which refers to a value of money paid, and by analogy, to esteem of the highest degree. We should not be frightened to be personally very generous in our dealings with our spiritual fathers – and it is often the means of opening the heavens for our own financial blessing, as I have discovered.

But we should also be aware that by properly honouring those over us in our actions and speech, we are adding value to them in other ways. If we uphold their honour, giving due praise, encouragement, and appreciation, this builds them up spiritually to make them even greater. It is again the principle of blessing. Our words and our attitude can add value to them, making them richer than they were before, and making them to be of more value to the house of God. This is the principle of honour.

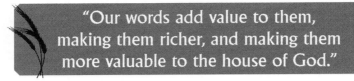

"Our words add value to them, making them richer, and making them more valuable to the house of God."

Contrariwise, when we fail to speak, or when our utterance is only what we call 'faint praise' (meaning feeble or weak praise), we do more harm than good. Faint praise is when we say something 'nice' about somebody, but understate their value. This is another form of character assassination, for to play down another's value or grace is to belittle them. This grudging approach to praise and appreciation is mean-spirited, and destructive of the work of God. It is never in keeping with the Spirit of Christ, for the unwillingness to honour another, or express appreciation, or give the esteem that is warranted, is always an expression of the flesh of man. It shows bad character, or perhaps unhealed hurt, or a despising, cynical, independent heart. Either way, it is bad grace. As the old saying informs us, "Faint praise destroys."

A Son Honours!

According to the prophet Malachi, he heard the Lord say, *"A son honours his father..."* (Mal 1:6). We need to consider the question, how does a son honour a father?

Consider the Life of Jesus

Firstly, let us consider the life of Jesus as a model. If you and I are to be transformed into the image of God's son, then the way in which Christ honoured His Father will be the way we too will honour God. But it will also be the model from which we learn how to honour our fathers in general.

Think about how Jesus lived and worked in unity with His Father. As a quick summary, we could say He represented His Father, spoke on behalf of His Father, repeatedly spent valuable time with His Father, sought intimacy of relationship with His Father, walked in a mature relationship with His Father, was never ashamed but proud of His Father, and remained teachable in relationship with His Father. He reverenced His Father, and upheld the honour of His Father.

The Time He Spent with His Father

Concerning the time Jesus spent with His Father, this was not occasional, but substantial time. He was always looking for a quiet place where He could be alone with His Father. He spent much time listening to His Father, conforming Himself to His Father's will, and learning His Father's ways. There had to be an intimacy between Father and Son that came from much time together, so that the relationship would not only be a mature relationship, but a true father-son relationship.

> "Intimacy between Father and Son came from much time together, so that the relationship would not only be mature, but a true father-son relationship."

Most of what I have just described, in its absolute sense, applies to our personal walk with the Lord Jesus. That is what you must do to walk with God. But we can and must draw lessons from it which will help us in respect to how we walk with our leaders in the faith. A son who wants to pursue and imitate a father will spend time with a father. He or she will want to sit and listen, and will seek to develop an appropriate and accountable relationship with his or her father. There has to be intimacy of relationship.

We simply have to spend time with each other, walk with each other, and care about each other, if we would obtain the grace that comes from a father-son relationship. So you will need to seek out your spiritual father. We all need to spend the time, sit and talk, share with them their thoughts and concerns, learn their heart, and learn their ways. This is the way in which you imitate, the way in which you honour, and the way in which you pursue.

Just How Does a Son Honour a Spiritual Father?

Ask yourself the following questions.

How did Timothy feel about Paul, and how did he serve him? How did Timothy 'see' Paul? What were Timothy's attitudes and values in serving him? How would he have spoken about him to others? How did Timothy treat Paul? (2 Tim 1:4, Phil 2:20-22) Answer these questions for yourself, and right there is all you will need to learn about how you should walk with a spiritual father.

Now ask, how did *Elisha* feel about *Elijah*? Deep in his heart, how did he feel about following, pursuing, and serving him? (2 Kings 2:6,12)

Think now about Joshua. How did he serve Moses? With what *fidelity*, what *extravagance*, what *submission* and what *yieldedness* – with what *wholehearted devotion* and *passion*? (Exodus 24:13, 33:11, Numb 11:28-29, 27:18) Do you think that you would be any poorer for such whole hearted devotion in the ministry? I know that I have been made rich by walking with another.

Finally, think about how the *disciples* followed *Jesus*? Would we find any less devotion in them than in Joshua or Elisha before them, or in Timothy who came after? (Matt 19:27) No, for except for the son of perdition, they all drank the cup of Christ's baptism. (Mark 10:38-39)

But the problem in modern, denominationalised, institutionalised Christianity is that people have not seen the need to be just as personally devoted to their spiritual leaders today – yet this is what the Scriptures call for in defining the apostolic faith of the cross of Jesus.

A Son is Not Ashamed

A son is not ashamed to be associated with a father, but feels blessed by the relationship, is proud of the association, and pleased to speak of his father's name. He knows the good that is in his father, is glad to represent him, and rejoices when speaking in honour of him. I am not ashamed of Chuck, but proud of the faith and grace in which he stands. But I think that often there are people who enter into a relationship for what they can get out of it, but are otherwise embarrassed by it. There is a principle, however, that we will reap whatever we sow. If you want to reap honour, you had better sow honour!

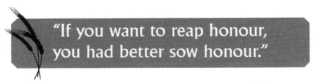

"If you want to reap honour, you had better sow honour."

Fathers are proud of sons, as we know. I am proud of the sons I have. I love them, I love to see them, they make me so glad. But as much as a father is proud of sons, an honouring son will be even more proud of his dad, his spiritual father. A son who is embarrassed about the relationship does not understand sonship, and is not spiritually mature.

A Son Honours a Father by Being Teachable

There are those who speak of being sons, but are not teachable. They want what they can get from the relationship – the blessing of a father, or the input of an apostle – but they really are not teachable in spirit; they just take what they want.

This is nothing other than independence, pride, and spiritual ignorance. Such a person is spiritually immature. Teachableness is an expression of humility, as is a submissive attitude.

A Father Holds a Unique Place in the Heart of a Son

A father's role is unique, and a son's love for a father is also unique. A spiritual son does not identify somebody as his spiritual father, only to treat them just like every other mature man in Christ. There is a special place of honour for a father in the affection and submission of a son, for a son has given his heart to a father.

Whilst in general we are all to honour the fathers of the church (1 Tim 5:17), and Scripture entreats us to respect every older man as if a father (1 Tim 5:1), there is nevertheless a special sense of affection and great respect toward the one we regard as our covering in Christ. And this is the way it ought to be.

In saying this, I do not mean that we don't have many fathers, or that there are not many other great men and women we should honour. But there are not many people from whom we get wisdom in an ongoing way, or who are as committed to us as we are to them. When you have determined that a certain person is really a father to you in the Lord, that is the one you should really love, serve, and honour.

A father-son relationship cannot really be prescribed by text. You cannot take a set of words and say, 'Here are the rules'. There is something that has to be established through the *grace* of sonship, through one's heart growing in spiritual maturity and wisdom, so that our love and faith come to a place of maturity.

It is a life to be explored, rather than a game simply played by the rules. But the substance of it is, a son must have a heart for his father.

A Son Honours His Father's Thought

What a father thinks should be important to a son, and when a father speaks, a son in his heart will honour what he says. Obviously, a father in the faith has much wisdom to offer sons, and this is a primary role of fathers. The calling for all spiritual leaders, especially fathers, is to teach, encourage, correct, discipline, and rebuke when necessary.

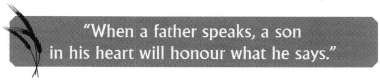

"When a father speaks, a son in his heart will honour what he says."

I do not need to say much about the positive nature of a father's wisdom and guidance for sons. This is a primary benefit for sons. But I want to comment on possible difficulties.

What about when a son does not agree with his spiritual father's opinions? What happens when a son is convinced of a certain course of action, but the father is not so sure? And sometimes, what a father says may seem to be quite wrong, or even inappropriate, to a son. But often the son will find out later, sometimes much later, that the father's opinion was right all along.

Recently this happened to me. There was something I was confident of, but of which Chuck had on various occasions expressed a different thought. However I assumed he was just sharing casual feelings, not really knowing the circumstances as I did. It turned out he was right, and I was wrong, and I have now addressed the matter.

Sometimes a son thinks his father is not in a place to know and understand what he, the son, does, and yet it is amazing how often God speaks through the voice of the father. A father may not always be correct, for he does not know all things, and can and will make mistakes too, but more often than not grace is at work, and God uses a father's words to instruct a son.

Even if not totally correct, often what a father says has in it the seed of truth the son needed at that time – but he didn't honour it enough to take it to heart and ponder it. That is what I mean when I say a son should honour a father's thought.

I am saying, be careful. Don't be hasty in judgement when you think a leader is wrong, or a spiritual father is mistaken, in giving advice. More often than not, they are likely to have been speaking the truth by the grace of God.

Therefore a father's thought and attitudes ought to be respected and heeded. Even if the thought expressed is only a personal feeling, it ought to be considered with respect; and in any case, the love and the heart of the father should be valued for itself.

If the father's words do express the heart of God toward us, we would be foolish and naive to discard the wisdom that has been given to us. So be thoughtful, be wise, be careful, don't be hasty in judgement, have respect, pay attention, and honour your father's thought.

Honour in the Household of God

In closing this chapter we need to ponder that most significant and prominent Scripture of all concerning honour, found in Deuteronomy 5:16, *"Honour your father and your mother, as the Lord your God has commanded you, so that you may live long and that it may go well with you in the land the Lord your God is giving you."*

This commandment is so important, and has such permanent and enduring principles, that Paul repeated it in the New Testament, and referred specifically to its promises, *"that it may go well with you and that you may enjoy long life on the earth."* (Ephesians 6:2-3) This means it was not only a commandment in the law of Moses, but has been refreshed and renewed as a promise and principle of life for the body of Christ.

It embodies a dynamic apostolic principle which is very powerful. On the one hand, to fail to honour our fathers and mothers, both natural and spiritual, is to effectively deny our blessings and cut ourselves off from the fountain of our supply. But to consistently give honour, firstly to our parents, but also in the household of God to our spiritual parents, is to activate the power of God on our behalf.

> "To fail to honour our fathers and mothers,
> both natural and spiritual,
> is to effectively deny our blessings and
> cut ourselves off from the fountain of our supply."

You are not only promised the possibility of a longer and presumably healthier life, but it will *"go well"* with you. This is not only the opening of that fountain of generational blessing we spoke of earlier, but implied here is that the great generosity of God will be extended to you with grace and favour to make you truly fruitful in the earth.

We must learn, then, to honour our fathers.

Testimony

Meng Aun Hour, Pastor
Followers of Jesus Ministries,
Phnom Penh, Cambodia.

Greeting from Cambodia.

I was born in Cambodia in 1968, and in the year 1989 I became Christian, and 1992 - 1995 I went to Bible school for training. We started a church called the Followers of Jesus Church in Phnom Penh in 1996. But we really pray to God to show how can we lead His church in to the way He want us to be? God is answer our pray by sending John Alley and Michael Appleton to met us.

Here is what we learn from Sonship. I fell that sonship is the right word to use and the right meaning to me as Cambodian, why? In Cambodia if we call someone father that mean we can feel his care, love, protections, covering to us. But if we call someone a teacher that mean we have to show respect to him by not looking to his face but looking to his foot when we meet him or talk with him. That is why I can say that fathering is the right word and the right meaning to be used for Cambodian people. This is also the word that the Bible uses too. I not found one place in the Bible that use the word mentor or mentoring.

So for me became a son to John Alley. I felt warm, I felt that I have protections and covering over me all the time and I felt loved and blessed, you can (tell the difference between those) who have the father and other son who (have) not the father.

And the relationship is very good. I feel John really is my father, why? Because I feel that he really love me, care for me, giving me advices and encouragement all the time. Whenever I have hard times, I know who I can talk to.

My heart as the son to John Alley is always want to honor him, love him, and protected him from the things that I can, and I all the time want see him bless by God, and success all the time. And I willing to pay any cost to served him.

I can tell you from my heart, I love John and honor him, and always want him to be a success in his life, and I believe 100 % that John Alley my spiritual father he want to see me growing in love in relation with God, and growing in leadership, and I believed strongly that he want me to be honored and successful in our ministries and in my life too.

We love John very much because we see the love of the living God in him.

I am sorry that my English are not good enough to tell you much. But if you let me tell you in Cambodian, for sure we can tell you more.

In Christ,

Meng Aun.

CHAPTER 14

THE EXPANSIVE BONDS OF LOVE

"Give everyone what you owe him:
If you owe taxes, pay taxes; if revenue, then revenue;
if respect, then respect; if honour, then honour.
Let no debt remain outstanding, except the continuing debt to love
one another, for he who loves his fellowman has fulfilled the law."

(Rom 13:7-8)

Some years ago, David Hood said to me one day, "John, I believe you are called to teach the five-fold ministry how to love each other." I had never thought of the idea in those terms, but it witnessed with me, and I have accepted that as a good word from the Lord.

This is one of the really worthwhile challenges before all of us in the body of Christ – a challenge central to everything we know about Christ's desire for the church. But it is not enough for the ministers of Christ to know how to love each other; we must teach the whole church how to love one another. We have to get down to the foundational issue of relationships. Relationship is what Christ has called us to.

Now it is Christ who has our whole heart; He is our passion. For 99% of our waking day, we think of nothing else. But we have to walk with His people, love them, esteem them, honour them, and hold affection toward them. So when it comes to preaching an apostolic message, we are going to spend much time talking about this. Why? Because this is what must be learned; this is what the whole church must walk in.

We should not be ashamed of talking about our affection for one another. We do so in the presence of Christ, and in the context of following Christ. Loving each other, and loving and honouring our leaders, is the way of Christ.

> "Loving each other, and therefore loving and honouring our leaders, is the way of Christ."

You know already that forgiving other people when they wrong you is the way of Christ. I do not have to convince anyone of that. Well, if built into your spiritual life and walk with Jesus are large amounts of time in which you must give attention to someone who may even hate you, so as to forgive them, love them, consider their needs, pray for them, and perhaps even cook them a meal and take it to them, then for significant parts of your life in Christ you will be thinking about other people. That's the way of Christ.

So we know that forgiving other people is the way of Christ. Well then, loving our brethren and loving our leaders, so that we have affection toward them, and esteem them, is also the way of Christ. When we walk in the way of Christ, our lives and our hearts are going to be filled with many other people.

"Love must be sincere"

The NIV translation of Romans 12:9 says, *"Love must be sincere,"* but the actual instruction given in the original writings of Paul was in fact telling us what love must *not* be, rather than what love is. This is better reflected in the King James Version which translated it as, *"Love must be without dissimulation"*. The apostle wrote that love is meant to be *without* something; and the closest we can get to that in modern English, since *'dissimulation'* is older English and not in common use today, is hypocrisy or falsehood or pretence.

Therefore, love must be 'sincere' in the sense that it cannot be shallow. It cannot just be an outward picture, i.e. just saying or thinking that you have love. There is something about the love we are meant to have for each other that has to go right to the depth of the heart. If it is not the fullness of the heart, if it is not the passion of our lives, if it is not the way we really feel about one another, then it is... dissimulation! That is, it is not the real thing.

"Be devoted to one another in brotherly love"

The next verse, Romans 12:10, continues, *"Be devoted to one another in brotherly love. Honor one another above yourselves."* This, *"be devoted to"* is an interesting phrase, because it means that we give the heart. This means there is a commitment, a longing after, a serving of someone. We have made a choice to walk in a certain way with other people. We love them, long for them, and choose to hold them in our affection.

This does not mean they are an object of our worship. That is a completely different thing. Consider this: God does not worship man, but He does love man – so that must be a holy thing to do. He commands us to love each other; He instructs us to love our enemy. There is something very important about love.

Now God can't help Himself; He loves to love, He wants to love, and He chooses to love. He made man in His own image. But unfortunately, you were born as much in the image of Adam. Adam's sin was in you, and by grace we have to learn again to walk in the image of Christ, which must be re-formed in us. It is this choice to love that is so critical.

In the text the Holy Spirit said, *"Be devoted to one another in brotherly love."* If you are going to be devoted to others, it means you make deep choices of the heart. This affects your time, attitudes, sacrifice, and service, if you're going to be devoted to it.

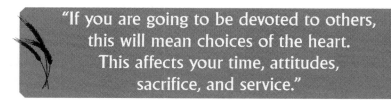

"If you are going to be devoted to others, this will mean choices of the heart. This affects your time, attitudes, sacrifice, and service."

Let us not take a shallow approach. We must not gloss over this kind of truth. Face it; if an apostolic message to the church is real, it is surely going to pick up at its heart the single most important message in the whole of the New Testament – the word of the Lord Jesus when He said, *"A new command I give you: Love one another. As I have loved you, so you must love one another."* (John 13:34) He has told us what the measure of our love should be – *"as I have loved you."* Jesus fully expected that we would learn the way of His love, and willingly choose to walk in it.

"Honor one another above yourselves."

This apostolic instruction, *"Honor one another above yourselves,"* also indicates a superior way of measuring what we are to do. You are going to have to take the time, you will have to go to some length, to fulfill this command – otherwise you are not doing what you are being asked to do.

You will have to make the effort and choose to give honour, not only to Christ, but to other believers. Can you now see that this emphasis on right relationships with one another is entirely biblical? We are on good ground here. This is safe ground. This is gospel ground. And we need to see this clearly, so as to have the freedom in our own hearts and minds to be able to go on and see some other very personal things concerning our relationships with one another.

"Give everyone what you owe him"

"Give everyone what you owe him. If you owe taxes, pay taxes. If revenue, then revenue. If respect, then respect. If honour, then honour." (Romans 13:7)

The command of God stated here is that we are to give specific things, including respect and honour, to other people. This is not a command about the way in which we are to treat every believer, for that command was given just a few verses earlier. Rather, this command is about the respect and honour we are to give people in authority.

The Scripture is, of course, referring to governing authorities, i.e. national governments, but this is not the only form of government we must relate to. These instructions apply in principle to all with whom we must relate or work, including church leadership. If you owe respect, give respect. If you owe honour, give honour.

I raised for discussion amongst my spiritual sons at our annual retreat the question of the place of public affection towards leaders and Christ's ministers, because we had held a few meetings in which people had said very kind things about me and honoured me in various ways.

I need to explain the context. The background is that I have ministered much in Australia and other nations, and shown Christian love to many people. I have been in the homes of many who are in the ministry, helping to solve problems for some and helping others see things more clearly. I have accepted and loved Christ's ministers, some of whom felt quite alone, and who were looking for fathering, support, and friendship. Consequently there are many, who because they were loved, accepted, and served by me, have in return a great love for me. There's a lot of affection around here. So when we get together in meetings, they talk about how much they feel loved, how much they love me, and how thankful they are to God. This kind of thing is spontaneously shared.

Now if this was to take place just 'one-on-one,' such as if I was visiting a couple in ministry somewhere, and they say something like, *"John, thank you so much. We appreciate you. Thank you for being a father to us. You've helped us; we're so blessed to have found such meaning in relationships, etc"* – well, that is all quite natural, and no-one would object to that expression of affection or appreciation. But if we were in a meeting, with people sharing their lives and testimonies in a large group, and four or five or more people speak like this openly, then I would start to feel really uncomfortable. And I experienced this two years running during our retreats.

I found myself asking this question: "Why is it that I feel so uncomfortable, when nothing that any individual has said is wrong or inappropriate. They have not said anything that they would not say to me, or someone else, privately. And if they did say these things in private conversation it would feel perfectly right. Not only that, but they have not said anything in appreciation of me, that I myself would not say in giving public honour to people that I myself love and appreciate. So why do I feel uncomfortable about it happening in a group setting amongst people who all know and love each other?"

Whenever I go to the United States and speak in various churches, most of whom relate to apostle Chuck Clayton, I make it my business in every place I go, and in every meeting, to honour Chuck. I speak of my love for him, the blessing he has been to me, and of the grace I find in him. I always include this place for giving honour to my spiritual father, whom I love and respect. So if that is good and right, which it is, why was I feeling so uncomfortable when in our own fellowship meetings a number of people spoke like this publicly of me?

All the people who were present in those meetings I knew personally, and love; I've been in the homes of each of them; virtually all of them are 'sons' to me in Christ. I have sat at their tables, eaten their meals, prayed for them, preached to their people, blessed their children, and left an apostolic impartation of gifts and grace. So if they want to express gratitude and give honour by speaking about how much they've been blessed by the relationship, that should be fine! Why then was I feeling uncomfortable? And why was I feeling even more uncomfortable if they included this appreciation, not just in testimony, but in prayers of thanksgiving in those meetings? Why was that?

I discussed this openly with them all in a subsequent meeting. I didn't want to hide anything. I asked them, "Is there somewhere an invisible line that we crossed? Did we perhaps go too far in some area we should not have gone?" Because, let me assure you, as much as anybody I know, I am careful to never put anyone in the place of Christ. I do not do this myself, and I will not allow anyone else to do it either. And I have walked with Christ. I love the Lord Jesus, and He has revealed Himself to me in many ways.

But still I was pondering this question, out loud, with all those associated with me, because I want to walk in a right place in the sight of God. And in answer to all this questioning, the Lord woke me in the middle of the night, and told me of some things that had been coming against us and affecting both our feelings and the meetings.

Here's what the Lord showed me. We had had amongst us the *previous* year a divisive brother, and he had come to the conference with an angry spirit. It became obvious that he had come to promote his own ministry, and showed evidence of being envious and jealous if some of my 'sons' shared any affection and honour toward me. He was critical and judgemental, even rude, but the odd thing was that if anything complimentary or honouring was said about him, he thought that was very fine.

By the end of the previous conference he was bitter and critical, and privately stirred up criticism and complaint amongst his few followers. In the months leading up to our next summit the following year, we began to feel oppression and spiritual resistance coming against us. In waiting upon the Lord we discovered what seemed to be a conspiracy of prayer amongst some false brethren, praying against the summit, cursing our finances, and praying, we felt, to separate my 'sons' from me. So for weeks we prayed earnestly to cut off those curses, and to bless the summit, our finances, and our relationships. This turned out to be a wonderful blessing in disguise, for we had the best summit in years, with a really good cash flow far exceeding our expectations, which included some great financial miracles.

I often hear the word of the Lord when I am fast asleep. It is a very useful gift. I went to bed burdened with the questions I have explained here about the public giving of honour; and in the middle of the night, the Spirit of God gave me these words: "The law of our enemies is present."

That explained a lot. Now I realised what the situation really was. There were people with critical and judgemental hearts towards us and our work who were 'laying down the law' in their own hearts towards our meetings. In a sense, the spirit of this man, and some others, was present in our meetings to condemn anything they didn't like. There may well be other factors, but the Lord was telling me very plainly that the main reason we were feeling uncomfortable was not because we were doing anything wrong at all, but because we had enemies who were accusing, and by their attitude their spirit was being projected against us. Thus, the condemnation we were feeling was from this – 'the law of our enemies' – being present. That is a form of control and witchcraft. Fortunately, it is very easy to break, once you know what it is.

There was something more the Lord said to me that night in answer to my enquiry. With great insistence, He said, ***"Don't lose affection! Don't lose honour!"*** He said this because of what we naturally tend to do when we think we have crossed a boundary. We become too cautious, and people pull back; people become inhibited. Once that happens, the expression of appreciation we ought to properly give to another person, or the expression of esteem we might have offered, we no longer offer. Instead, it becomes faint praise; it is now cold love.

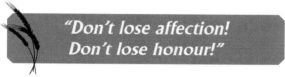

"Don't lose affection! Don't lose honour!"

The Bible teaches that one of the grave dangers for the church at the end of the age will be 'cold love'. Jesus Himself said, *"the love of most will grow cold."* (Matthew 24:12) But the apostolic movement sweeping the world today is meant to buttress the church with pure love. And those of us who are Christ's elect ***must learn the way of love!***

No matter what days may come, we must not let our love grow cold. Whatever you do, please hear the word of Christ. *"Don't lose affection! Don't lose love!"* Do not allow the law of your enemies to prevent you from giving honour and expressing affection toward another person.

I remember some very good times in the past – and many of those good times for me were in Salvation Army meetings. We had some truly great meetings in years long ago, with great old songs, and great preaching too. There were some wonderful old-style evangelists in those days. One thing I particularly remember about those Salvation Army meetings of years ago was that when anybody came to preach, they were spoken of publicly with great honour. As far as I know they still do this. It was one thing that was very well established in the leadership culture of the Salvation Army. It didn't seem to matter who the visitors were – whether local leaders, or some high-ranking officer visiting for special meetings, or a visiting missionary – they would always be introduced with the giving of honour and esteem. They would speak of what great work they had done, of how precious they were, and how valuable to the work of Christ. It seemed to me that the leaders of the Salvation Army always understood how to honour each other in public.

Amongst us all this should always be done. We should honour each other in public and in private. The Bible position is: we must honour one another above ourselves.

So cast off the law of your enemies. Remember and cling to the Law of Love. Don't let anyone, by despising us, make us fruitless; we have to love. Don't let anyone with cold love dictate the rules of the church; let us love one another, and so fulfill the law of Christ.

If you have heard the word of God that says "love one another," that does not necessarily mean that you have understood *how* we are to love. The message to love has been preached for generations in churches everywhere, but that does not mean people know how to love, or have chosen to love. So in a very practical way, we must come to the place where we understand what this love means, and choose to walk in it.

For me, the teaching of father-son relationship in the ministry is the greatest and most practical way of all of getting to the heart of the command to love one another. When we choose to walk in these kinds of relationships, and we choose to love and serve one another as we follow Christ, this opens the heavens. God brings those who choose the way of love into a far greater experience of His blessings – of His love, providence, and favour. In short, the heavens open.

> "Teaching father-son relationship is the greatest and most practical way of getting to the heart of the command to love one another."

There is a primary example in Scripture of this principle at work in the story of Ruth. Ruth was effectively a spiritual son to her mother-in-law.

Because of a drought, Naomi with her husband and their two sons had left Israel to live in Moab, where their two sons married Moabite women. Sadly, Naomi's husband died, and her two sons died as well. With all the men in the family deceased, this left the three women – a mother-in-law with two daughters-in-law – bereaved and burdened.

Then Naomi hears that good seasons have returned to Israel. She wants to go back, and her two daughters-in-law, Orpah and Ruth, begin the journey with her. But along the way Naomi begins to urge her daughters-in-law to return to their own people. She tells them she has nothing to offer them. She has no more sons they could marry. She is bereft of everything. "Call me bitter," she says to them, "because the Almighty has made my life very bitter." "Go back to your own people," she says, "and there find husbands for yourselves."

Orpah followed this kindly but despairing advice, and went back to Moab. And we hear no more of her. She kissed her mother-in-law goodbye, and by that gave up her place amongst the people of God forever. She went back to serve a foreign God.

But Ruth had a different heart, and took a different stand – *"Then Orpah kissed her mother-in-law goodbye, but Ruth clung to her."* (Ruth 1: 14) If you read the biblical account, you will discover that Naomi urged Ruth to go back to her own people three times. That is why Ruth was so emphatic in declaring her determination to stand with Naomi. *"Don't urge me to leave you or to turn back from you,"* she replied. *"Where you go I will go, and where you stay I will stay. Your people will be my people and your God my God. Where you die I will die, and there I will be buried. May the Lord deal with me, be it ever so severely, if anything but death separates you and me."* (Ruth 1:16-17)

Can you see what has happened here? Ruth has chosen the way of love. Her love is such that she will not remove her heart from Naomi. She has devoted herself to the service, and the honour, of this person who has a need. She loves her mother-in-law.

As a result of her love and devotion to another, the Lord brought Ruth into a great place in Israel. She was not aware of it, but her choice to follow her mother-in-law entitled her to a kinsman redeemer in Israel. For you and me, Christ is our kinsman redeemer!

I have found by personal discovery that, ever since I have chosen to walk closely with men and women in the faith – not only apostle Chuck as a spiritual father, but also many others that I have around me every day – the more I have come face-to-face with my kinsman redeemer, that is, the Lord Jesus Christ.

So Ruth, Naomi's daughter-in-law, was entitled under the inheritance laws of Israel to a kinsman redeemer – which meant a near relative could marry her, and give her children. This husband brought her into his house, thus providing security as well as comfort for her mother-in-law in her old age. Ruth gave birth to a son, whom they called Obed, and so her mother-in-law had a grandson to dandle upon her knees. Naomi, who thought she was barren and bitter for life, was made joyful again and satisfied with life.

The receiving of these good things is called *inheritance*. Ruth found great inheritance amongst the people of God – she found the fullness of life, a husband and children, was established in a good place, given the joy of life and the fullness of God's providence – all as a result of her choice to maintain faithfulness and love in personal relationships.

Ruth loved Naomi, who by her own admission had nothing to offer. Yet to this woman who had nothing to offer, the faithful daughter-in-law had said, *"Don't urge me to leave you or to turn back from you."* (Ruth 1:16) When you and I walk in the spirit of sonship, as Ruth did, we too find we are brought into a greater inheritance amongst the people of God.

But we find that it does not end there. Ruth has been given something else as well. She was not to know in her own lifetime what her faithfulness and love in relationships would produce in the earth. But because of her fidelity and loyalty to a mother who had nothing, something astounding has been given to her – and it is called *posterity*.

> "Because of her fidelity and loyalty to a mother who had nothing, something astounding has been given to her - it is called *posterity*."

Ruth's son Obed became the father of Jesse, and Jesse the father of King David. King David became the father of King Solomon. Thus the whole line of the kings of Judah, all the way down to both Mary and Joseph, and to Jesus our Saviour, all came from Ruth.

She was not to know that she would become the mother of David, the mother of Solomon, the mother of Mary, the mother of Joseph, the mother of Jesus – and ultimately, in some sense, the mother of us all; that's posterity!

Her inheritance and posterity came from just one thing – the fidelity, the loyalty, the deep love she gave to someone who did not appear to have great prospects in life. To the human eye at the time, she would have been better off going back to Moab rather than pursuing faithfulness in relationship with a mother in Israel. But an amazing posterity has been given to a Moabite woman, because she walked in the way of Christ.

For many of us there will be times when our spiritual fathers may also appear to have nothing, especially in the long, early years. They are ordinary people. They are small people. They are nothing in the eyes of the world. They are not much even in the eyes of the church. They might pastor a small church, they might not even seem to preach well, and might not be highly regarded. But whomever God has given us to love, serve, and walk with, then in loving them we will find more of the grace of Christ, and the heavens open. Don't be foolish like that young pastor reported to have said, "I'm gonna get me a famous father." God will give you those He wants you to love and serve.

At the end of the book of Ruth, a comment is made to Naomi by the women of Israel concerning Ruth. They said, *"...your daughter-in-law... loves you and... is better to you than seven sons..."* (Ruth 4: 15) If there is an apostolic message we all must hear, it is this message: we must choose again the way of love.

We are not here to promote ourselves. We are not here just to build our own ministries; rather, we are here to serve the ministries of other people, and in doing so we will find ourselves. Did not Jesus say, *"For whoever wants to save his life will lose it, but whoever loses his life for me will find it."* (Matt 16:25) He also said, *"whoever wants to become great among you must be your servant."* (Matthew 20:26)

We have to find the way of love, and we need to esteem our leaders. We need to choose the way of affection and the giving of honour toward the believers that surround us. We must choose the Law of Love, and not yield to the law of our enemies.

As I was praying with Hazel about this, suddenly one book stood out from among many on the shelves of my office. Down the spine was printed the title of the book: *Divine Alliance*. I knew immediately what the Spirit of God was saying. It is God who puts us together! It is not just that we are allied with Christ in our salvation, we are allied with each other as well, and this is a divine alliance! In other words, these relationships are God-appointed. It is Godly. It is a holy thing when we walk together with brothers.

The Heart of the Matter

Whilst we all strive for accuracy in what we teach, and seek competency in understanding and teaching the Scriptures, and soundness in biblical doctrine, nevertheless the crucial thing is to have a right heart. This whole subject is a heart issue – it is the *heart* that must be right before God. There has to be in us a right attitude, a right value system, a right outlook, and a right love. Our hearts must come to the place of spiritual maturity and the perfecting of love.

What kind of heart is this, then? If you are to have a right heart in the things of God, and in embracing His apostolic purpose for the restoration of the church, what kind of heart would that be?

In describing this kind of heart, we could say it would be a *full* heart, i.e. a *passionate* heart. We could describe it as a *loving* heart, an *earnest* heart, a *childlike* heart. We could say many things, but in the end, we would be describing a Christ-like heart, that is, the heart of a son.

If you want a right heart, then like every other believer, you also will need to have the heart of a son. What about church leaders? Every leader in the body of Christ, if he would have a right heart, must have the heart of a son – and the heart of a father also.

That is why we must use this terminology of fathering and sonship – it is because God is God in Father and Son. God has chosen for Himself to be a Father who loves a Son. God has chosen for Himself to be a Son who loves a Father. That is a very, very important revelation given to us. For *"The secret things belong to the Lord our God, but the things revealed belong to us and to our children forever, that we may follow all the words of this law."* (Deuteronomy 29:29)

Testimony

Rodney Samuels, Senior Pastor
Christian Life Church,
Ballarat, Australia.

Sonship is my opportunity to demonstrate obedience, honour, trust, gratitude, affection and co-operation toward God, by acting this way towards the man Christ gave us to provide covering for our ministry.

We have embraced John as a holy apostle of God, and as our covering and spiritual father. I have always been drawn by John's grace with people and the strong relational values which he holds. These qualities look and feel like Christ. To me, John is a father. There never has been any "lording over" type authority; but purely relational, which I believe is the hallmark of John's character. We want to imitate him. We have always counted it all joy walking with John as spiritual sons. We simply love John and Hazel, and seek to go the extra mile every time we are privileged to host them; and Daphne and I have found that this works both ways, for they love us. It is an honour.

I believe in that "ancient path" of honour and respect, and especially toward holy men of God, for the journey and cost that has brought them to this high calling we will never know. Since walking with John, we have experienced wonderful grace to build an apostolic community, and an awesome peace while doing it. We have found a new grace to love, accept, and forgive others. John's messages have greatly impacted my life, finding freedom in Christ.

Daphne and I love receiving his prayers and blessings. While we do not "live in John's pocket" so to speak, I believe that God has given us this man to love. Early in 2006, God spoke to me from Deuteronomy 1:6-8 and told me that I was to serve John's ministry and to help him possess all that our Heavenly Father has ordained for him to possess.

This has been a great joy to us and our offerings have increased. In November last year, John taught on tithing in our church, and I found there was so much on the subject that I never knew. I immediately obeyed God and begun sending our weekly church tithes to bless the great work of *Peace*. Our own income from tithes and offerings has been continually growing since then.

Not a day goes by that we do not uphold John in prayer before our Heavenly Father. Walking with John is helping us build apostolically and accurately. I am perfectly comfortable walking with an apostle who himself walks under the covering of another apostle.

Rodney Samuels.

CHAPTER 15

RELATIONAL BOUNDARIES

"I appeal to you, brothers, in the name of our Lord Jesus Christ, that all of you agree with one another so that there may be no divisions among you and that you may be perfectly united in mind and thought."

"One of you says, "I follow Paul"; another, "I follow Apollos"; another, "I follow Cephas"; still another, "I follow Christ." Is Christ divided? Was Paul crucified for you? Were you baptised into the name of Paul?"

(1 Corinthians 1:10, 12)

Over the years of walking in relationships, both as a father to sons in the ministry and as a leader concerned with the interaction of believers in daily relationships, I have had to ponder issues, solve problems, and seek answers for questions as they have arisen.

In fact, some questions have arisen simply because opponents, or sceptical people, or just hurting people, have jumped to wrong conclusions or made false accusations. There have been a few who have made wrong assumptions about what they thought we meant by teaching certain things, and turned these into criticisms. So there have been occasions when, in response, we have had to say, "No, that is not what we teach. Rather, what we say is..." So the following positions which I have called *boundaries,* have either arisen from experience, or are just the needed common sense on the subject.

Very often, when new understanding breaks upon the church, believers preach, teach, and organise themselves in line with that new understanding. But sometimes a movement goes too far, or grasps new ideas with incomplete understanding, and so there may be unintended consequences. People mean well, but find there are some unexpected outcomes which have to be corrected.

I am hoping that by setting out these guidelines, people who grasp the teaching of father-son relationships, and who pursue these relationships as a means of grace, which they are, will not make silly mistakes arising from inexperience or misunderstanding. These boundaries are those that will keep our feet on the ground, and as you read you will understand that this is, in the end, just good common sense.

In all probability there are many 'boundaries', or safety parameters, in addition to the ones we will discuss here. But the matters I raise are the ones I feel are most likely to help avoid or solve problems and will be especially helpful in building apostolic relationships.

Here, then, are seven boundaries that will provide safeguards for us, and help in the appropriate development of the biblical relationships we should walk in as an apostolic people.

1. The Place of Jesus

Christ's place – in the church, in history, and in the human race – is totally unique. He has first place, the central place, the highest place; there is no one like Him, and no one else can ever take or hold His place. He alone can save. From Him alone comes authority to the church and its leaders. He is the author and source of life. He is the one that has life within Himself. If anyone wants life, they must find it in Christ alone.

But we spoke in an earlier chapter about the need to follow and imitate spiritual leaders who are fathers in the faith. I think the point was clear, that following Jesus is the reason why we imitate others, who are good models of just how to make Christ and His purpose central to all.

In my own heart, Christ has the place that no one else can take. I spend most of my time thinking about Jesus, and the purposes of God, and not much else. My love for Chuck and other people is never far from my heart, but I'm busy listening to the Lord, considering the word of God, praying, and seeking to be a blessing to others. In the background of my heart is love for a lot of people – a love for people that is essential in service for Christ.

My Birthday Present

I still remember the day I turned 40. I had been looking forward to my

40th birthday for a long time, almost like I couldn't wait to get there. All of my life I had heard that life begins at 40. I was so excited about it, happy when I went to bed the night before, and when I woke the next morning, I fell on my knees and thanked God. Well, that's better than the usual attitude people have to getting older.

On my knees, I prayed to the Father and said, "Father, I would like you to give me a birthday present. The birthday present that I would like is to have a heart that loves Jesus more. I don't feel that I really have enough love for Christ. Would you give me a heart that really loves Jesus?"

I didn't notice the difference in just one or two days, but I can tell you that five years later I could look back and be overjoyed at the progress of my heart. I started to walk in a greater passion; something was deeper and purer. Anyway, I was given what I asked for. Since then I have asked for other things and received them too.

Not angels, Christ!

In 1996, I was wandering around the bottom paddock of the property where we live, in prayer. Our church had received the visit of a brother who had come to teach us about 'prophetic evangelism.' He said that in his experience angels help out with evangelism, and he had seen a lot of angels in his work for the gospel. As proof, he made the observation that in the Acts of the Apostles, every single story that has anything to do with evangelism has an angel in the story helping out. That astounded me. So I went home and checked my Bible. I read all those stories, and he was right. There was an angel in every one, in the whole of the book of the Acts of the Apostles – Philip, Peter and Cornelius, etc.

But I had never seen an angel in my life, so after he had gone home, I went down to the bottom paddock, where we have mango trees growing, and started praying. I said, "Lord, I've never seen an angel – how about some of the action?" He said, "No. This is not for you." He said, "For you, a revelation of Christ."

"Oh," I thought, "That is far better." And that is how it has been with me. He has made me rich in walking with Jesus. I can tell you, in every matter in this search for apostolic truth, I have come face to face with Jesus.

> "In every matter in the search for apostolic truth, we come face to face with Jesus."

It Must Be All of CHRIST!

In the messages I preach across this nation and others, I spend much time seeking to reveal Jesus. I mentioned our dear brother George Stormont, now home with the Lord, who laid hands on me and prayed for me. In his older years, he soaked himself every Sunday morning in John's vision of the glorified Christ seen on Patmos, and only ever spoke of Jesus – and when he spoke of Christ, people would weep. I know, for I was one of those weeping. He had prayed for me just a few months before I spent that time in our mango field, where the Lord had said, "For you, a revelation of Christ!" I believe something of what brother George had was given to me.

So let no-one misunderstand my purpose, or the heart of this subject, *'The Spirit of Sonship'*. It's all of Christ. And in everything we do in relationships, it must continue to be this way.

2. The Brotherhood Context

Even though we teach father-son relationships in the church, and encourage each believer to see themselves as a son who should walk with a spiritual father in the ministry, we must also be clear that the church is principally a brotherhood.

The one relationship that must pervade the whole Church is a brother-to-brother relationship. Anything we say about walking together as fathers and sons is meant to be fitted into a brotherhood context.

In Scripture Christ also calls Himself our brother. In Hebrews 2:11 it says Jesus is not ashamed to call us brothers – but two verses later He is quoted as calling us His children. So these concepts are not exclusive, and not incompatible. One does not push the other out.

So whether you have found meaning in relationship with a spiritual father, or come into an understanding of the spirit of sonship, or not, you are a brother in the house. You are beloved! You are accepted! You are honoured! You are equal, you are a peer; and you are no less in Christ or your salvation just because of a different use of vocabulary, or a different way of seeing things.

3. Careful Speech and Thoughtful Use of Terminology

Careful speech is a very important boundary. What I have written here should be considered in the light of what I wrote earlier, in Chapter Six, discussing Jesus' words in Matthew 23:8-10.

In my own personal conversation, I do not usually speak of myself as a father in relationship with someone as a son by the use of that vocabulary. When I meet with sons, if we are discussing relationship and therefore needing to use the terms of 'father' and 'son', I usually do not then use those terms when praying with them afterwards. The important thing is the nature of the relationship itself. The use of titles won't establish something that doesn't exist, nor the absence of the words diminish the effectiveness of the relationship. Jesus instructed us not to use these terms as titles anyway.

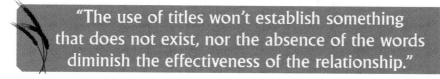

"The use of titles won't establish something that does not exist, nor the absence of the words diminish the effectiveness of the relationship."

If any of those who are spiritual sons come for prayer, when not referring to them by name in prayer, I almost always call them my brother or sister, rather than son or daughter. Yes, we have entered upon a father-son relationship and in that we walk together. But what does that mean? It means I will serve them as a father would serve a son, and they will serve me as a son would serve a father, but I would hardly ever *call* them a son, and I would hardly ever *call* myself their father. Why not? I think it is unnecessary, unrealistic, too theatrical, and can tend to assumptions, pride, and other wrong perceptions in the wrong hands. But basically, it is because the reality of the relationship does not call for it.

If there is a genuine relationship of trust being formed, with closeness and a sense of belonging, we just need to be ourselves. We are to fulfil the role of being a father or a son, without turning this into some religious title. To all my friends, and to all my sons and daughters, I am John.

There are times when we should make exceptions to this, and it becomes not only very appropriate to speak otherwise, but necessary. As, for example, when I am praying a fathering type prayer for someone, such as when someone needs a father's blessing. Or when someone has a certain amount of insecurity in them, and if to be called a son, or for me to say to them, "I will be your father," will produce in them a sense of acceptance, love, and belonging, I will use that language.

So I am not saying we should never use this vocabulary. I am just saying, please be wise. We should be measured in our speech, and careful in the way we use terminology.

4. Don't Make Claims over People

What I am about to say here is mainly intended for Christian leaders. Don't make claims. Do not claim to be somebody's father, or the right to be their father, and don't go around claiming sons. Just be a father, if you are one, and serve them, at least until your personal maturity, and the genuineness of the relationship, is established.

There is a lot more wisdom in this than might be immediately apparent. Suppose the pastor of a church hears this teaching on fathering and sonship for the first time. For him, the implications will be that he should be seen as a spiritual father by his people, and they need to walk more closely with him in relationship and love as sons to a father. But he should be cautious to not overreact, to not be over enthusiastic, so as to not try too hard to produce results too soon. A spiritual leader should never force change.

A basic principle of leadership is to not change church structure without first changing the values held by the people in the church. Therefore, a pastor should teach and instruct so as to establish understanding, and not be hurried by enthusiasm into making premature claims that are not understood. If a leader does make claims in the church, perhaps by declaring, "Well, I'm your spiritual father, you're my spiritual sons, you need to follow me", then, unless he has a very mature relationship with them, he's done something very foolish. He obviously believes in the concepts, and is using Christian terminology, but prematurely, unwisely, and inappropriately.

What we actually need to promote is the development of the meaningful relationships themselves, for the good of all, and this takes time. It cannot be hurried, and is not helped by hollow claims. So, until a leader is mature, established as trustworthy, and seen in the eyes of others as a father, don't claim to be a father – just *be* a father. And don't lay claims over people by saying they are your sons, unless the relationships are established, mutually appreciated, and you are trusted. Rather, just teach clearly the way of sonship, and let the Lord establish His graces in the lives of all.

> "Until a leader is mature, established as trustworthy, and seen in the eyes of others as a father, don't *claim* to be a father – just *be* a father."

5. The Principle of Freedom

The first principle for me in apostolic ministry is giving people freedom, and serving so as to bring people into spiritual freedom in Christ. Spiritual leadership cannot be controlling, nor driven.

As the leader of our Church, I used to say publicly from the platform, "You are free to come in, and you are also free to leave. Nobody is locked in. But if you choose to stay, then you are choosing to walk in relationship with other people. You are choosing to love, and you need to be willing to be taught what is required of stewards in the house of God, especially in relation to other people. This does require the giving of the heart, but we do not lock people into anything; we give freedom, and people are free to live their own lives."

You can ask any of the people in our fellowship today whether this has proven true. I don't make demands on people, but that doesn't mean I don't know how to invite people to walk in what we have, or to enlist co-operation. But I refrain from placing obligation on believers; they must willingly choose to walk with us in relationship and in the mission we have been given.

Years ago, the old phrase, 'live and let live', came to really mean something to me. I know this phrase can be confusing, and people attach all kinds of sentiment to it, but I gave it my own meaning. For me it came to symbolise a very important spiritual concept. It meant I was to allow other people to be themselves in Christ.

In other words, I was to walk with Christ as best I could, and try to be a good example to others, but without criticising, condemning, or judging others if they chose to walk in a different way from me in service to Christ. An attitude like this means we can enjoy life. We can freely enjoy what we are in Christ, without the dreadful burden of trying to demand the conformity of other people to our image. When we judge others, we lose our joy and freedom, because we are now under the law, and what is worse, a law of our own making.

This does not mean leaders are not to apply discipline if someone falls into sin, or if someone proves to be a divisive brother. The Scripture is very clear about what should be done in the matter of church discipline, and discipline is essential to the health and vitality of the house. But regarding everyday living in the service of Jesus Christ, we are not to be judgemental or critical of those who choose another way of fulfilling what they believe to be the call of God upon their lives. Freedom of conscience is still a very important and significant Christian doctrine.

6. Relationships Are Not Exclusive, but Inclusive

Father-son relationships, or any relationship in the body of Christ for that matter, should never be exclusive. What does *exclusive* mean? Shorten the word to another word that is easier to understand – the word *'exclude'*. When you have a good relationship with one person, this should not normally exclude another person from your heart or life. In healthy relationships we should find it easy to include other people in our love and fellowship.

> ## "In healthy relationships we find it easy to include other people in our love and fellowship."

There will be some circumstances that appear to make an exception to this rule, but actually they are not exceptions, they are requirements. Suppose your spiritual father is the pastor of your church, or if you are the pastor, then the apostle you walk with. Suppose your spiritual father is falsely accused by a divisive brother, or his teaching opposed by another Christian leader, perhaps a contentious pastor from another church, or a false prophet somewhere. Can you pursue relationship with both parties simultaneously, wanting to be friends to both? Can you be a son to your spiritual father, and also seek to promote the ministry of this other person?

No, you cannot afford to do that. In standing with your spiritual father, you are not breaking this principle. That situation is not the normal circumstance to which this 'rule' applies, and the Bible gives clear instruction that we are not to fellowship with divisive brethren, and are to beware the dangers of false brethren. To assert that you have the love of a son for a father, while at the same time uphold his 'enemies', shows a heart of infidelity and dishonour. More often it is selfish ambition at work in people who do these kinds of things.

But the normal relationships we enjoy in Christ should not be exclusive in the sense that we squeeze out some other good brother or sister. But you will at times find some who, because of jealousy and rivalry, or insecurity, if they don't get your undivided attention, struggle, feel rejected, take offence, and try to be controlling.

You will have heard the old saying, "two's company, three's a crowd." That is why God is a triune God – He had to be three, and not two. God could not be holy if He was only two, for that would be an exclusive relationship. He had to be three, and live in perfect harmony, with perfect unity, deep love, each one toward the other, in the Godhead. You know that the Father and Son do not get together and leave the Holy Spirit out, and it's the same with us.

So if you have become a son to a father, whilst that father will have a unique place in your heart, this does not stop you loving and serving other people, including other Christian leaders.

Neither are these relationships sectarian. They are not to produce a little group over here that follow one leader, whilst another group forms over there following another, in a way that divides the body of Christ.

To illustrate, a few years ago I was in Adelaide meeting with some pastors that relate to me. One of them asked an honest question, "What do we call ourselves now? Is this the John Alley ministry or what?" I said, "No! No! I am here to help you be a part of the church of Adelaide."

I went on to make it quite clear, "I do not come to Adelaide so as to form my own movement, or anything of the sort. This is not an apostolic network in the sense that you have joined an organisation and are separate from others. Your relationship with the whole church of Adelaide is as important as your relationship with me. I come as an apostle to serve you, and I can be a father to you, and you can love me and walk with me, but ultimately the goal is to build the church of the city, and to build you in as part of that church."

> **"Ultimately the goal is to build the church of the city, and to build you in as part of that church."**

That these relationships must not be sectarian is dealt with in 1 Corinthians chapters 1 & 3, which dealt strongly with some relational problems which were occurring in that church. Paul was quite straight with the Corinthians, saying basically, "What is wrong with you guys?" Because, he said, "You are now saying *'I follow Apollos'*, or *'I follow Paul'*." Yet in the following chapter 4, he also wrote, *"I became your father... Therefore I urge you to imitate me."*

This shows that his fathering, which he *urged* upon the Corinthians, was never intended in any sense to divide the church into separate camps. In conclusion he said, *"So then, no more boasting about men! All things are yours, whether Paul or Apollos or Cephas or the world or life or death or the present or the future – all are yours, and you are of Christ, and Christ is of God."* (1 Corinthians 3:21-23) This is why Luther, for example, belongs to every believer, not just to the Lutherans. And really, Luther belongs to the Catholics too. And John Wesley belongs to me and you, not just to Methodists, and so on. All things are yours, and the leadership gifts God gives to His body are not exclusive.

Like Paul, we are still going to urge every believer to walk with a spiritual father, because God gives us all leaders who are to be personally involved in our lives. With them we need to walk, submitting to them and learning from them.

(As an aside, I would comment that it is unfortunate that we find it necessary to refer to some Christians as Lutherans, and others as Baptists, and still others as Catholics or Wesleyans. This is precisely what Paul told us not to do, when he rebuked the Corinthians for saying *'I follow Apollos'*, or *'I follow Peter'*. Historically, the church not only went on to do this, but institutionalised the process as well – but this, I believe, is being dismantled in this day of the restoration of the apostolic life of the church.)

7. Sonship Is a Grace, Not a Duty

Sonship is not an obligation upon believers, but it is an opportunity. Whenever we teach the principles of sonship – i.e. that each of us should be a son in the ministry; that everyone should be walking with a leader as a spiritual father, learning how to love, serve, and honour them; and that this will help them in Christ – we must be especially careful to not make this a spiritual *demand* upon anyone. It is a means of grace, and should always be understood as an opportunity to grow in grace.

> "Sonship is a means of grace, and should always be understood as an opportunity to grow in grace."

If it is a grace, then it is a grace freely offered. It should never be seen as a demand – that would ruin the whole relational foundation of it, and be quite contrary to grace. It is not a duty, it is not an obligation, it is not a demand, it is not a regulation, and is not to be forced – please understand, sonship is an opportunity to grow in faith and find grace with God by walking in appropriate relationships. Yes, relationships are essential to Christianity itself, but grace must still be entered into by a heart made willing by the Spirit of the Lord, and not by any law.

I had to make this clear to my own pastoral team, because they always take their lead from what I say, and work to build it into the life of our congregation. Because of the teaching of fathering and sonship at home, we now have several generations of fathers and sons in our church. Our pastoral team has always been very committed to building everyone into relationships.

But I remember I had to temper their zeal by saying, "No-one *has* to do this. In the congregation, no-one has to be a son, no-one is required to think of themselves as a son. If they just want to come along, sit with us, enjoy the ministry, give their tithes and offerings, and see themselves as a brother to everybody, because they have no light on anything more, that's fine by me. We are not to force anyone into a mould, and we must not handle this in a way that would create a mindset of class A and class B Christians in the same congregation."

Finally, It's Love

In the end, this whole matter is all about love – and it is love in the context of a family, the family of God. This we consider more in the next chapter.

Testimony

Elaine Hans
Member of Peace Christian Church,
Rockhampton, Queensland, Australia.

I have been a member of *Peace* for over twenty years, and have known John and Hazel Alley for over twenty one years. When I first came to *Peace*, I joined in everything. I loved Hazel and John and dived in to support them in anyway I could. I was a real 'doer' so I easily fitted into the programs of the church. I was there cleaning, teaching Religious Education, helping with pastoral care, helping run our bookstore, wherever help was needed. I was an active part of home group life and whatever the leadership said they wanted to do, I tried to support.

But no matter what I did, the one thing that stayed with me all the time was the feeling that I never belonged. There was no reason for me to feel this way, and I can remember going to John quite a few times, in tears, because I'd feel so lonely and I would just feel as if I didn't belong in the church, or anywhere else really. But I continued to press into God. I have always loved God, since I was saved and knew I needed His guidance more than anything.

John started teaching about father-son relationships, about the need to be fathered and to father others, and I thought it all sounded logical and good. I felt sure that I had an understanding of what that meant and that I already really had that operating in my life, so I just continued the way I was going. Unfortunately, I still struggled with the feeling that I didn't belong and my spiritual life went on as though I were on a roller coaster.

I felt that my heart was already given to John and Hazel; after all I had loved them and worked hard to support them for a long time. It wasn't until I started hearing some of the testimonies from people who were finding this new freedom in these relationships, that I realized I didn't have that, and I felt even less like I belonged. I thought, "I've worked so hard, I've been part of everything, I have supported everything. Why can't I feel like I belong? Why can't I be recognized?"

Then God laid me low for a while, and I could no longer do the things I did before. I could no longer get to prayer meetings, so I came to a point in my own heart where I really felt I wasn't worth much at all. I couldn't 'perform' so I felt useless. But I continued to press into God, and John and Hazel continued to pray for me.

I was one of those people who had to really check everything out to see if it really was from God. I was one that always said, "I don't follow man, I follow God!" Even though I loved John, knew him and his walk with the Lord, I never wanted to be accused of following a man, so I was willing to follow John as long as I had checked it all out in my own mind and came to the same conclusions. But God rebuked me about that one day. He showed me that my heart was not with John, my heart was with *myself*, and *my* issues, and the things I wanted, and that my motives were not what I thought they were. I got to the point where I knew I had to trust God and give my heart to John and Hazel; really give it, and choose to follow them wherever they went; and that was not following a man, that was being obedient to God. I knew that this was what God wanted me to do.

I was not to give myself for what I could do; I was to give myself for who I was. So I went to John and Hazel and 'officially' gave my heart to them. I said, "Wherever you go I'm going to follow and nothing's going to change my mind." Now, my circumstances did not change, but I did. That heart commitment broke something in my life, and I can honestly testify that since that time I have never again felt like I don't belong. My heart was truly given and I now felt like I belonged. It was as if the enemy could no longer throw that lie at me, because I had given myself, for who I was, to the person God wanted me to follow, and so I felt very much loved, very much blessed, very much a part of what God was doing.

Along with that came a real freedom to just be me, and to share myself with John and Hazel, and I found that they actually liked me – me! Not what I could do for them, but actually me; and they desired to give into my life. So many times I would go to Hazel, as my spiritual Mum, and share things in my life that I would not share with anyone else, and I can testify that one word from Hazel, or one word from John, and it would break something in my life. It's like the father's blessing or the mother's blessing; it breaks something in my life and I walk away feeling victorious, because they have my heart and they are able to speak things into my life. I have given them permission to speak into my life; to bring rebuke, correction, challenge, whatever is necessary for me to grow. I really desire that.

This new freedom also released me to love in a new way. God was teaching us about community, and asking us to walk with each other in real love. I believed this and tried everything to achieve it, but even though I got on well with people, there were many who really niggled me. I have always had a bit of a critical spirit that I had to deal with, and this had hindered building community. I was taught that we can do nothing to achieve community ourselves, but it is a work of the Spirit. That was a real revelation to me, so I asked the Spirit of God to do a work in me so that I would come into community with those at *Peace*.

Not long after this John was speaking about the Moravians, and how in their meetings it was like the Spirit of God had made it so that their differences had disappeared. I can remember sitting in that meeting and looking around at my friends and church family, when all of a sudden I realized I could find no fault with anyone. I realized God had done a work in me, and I could see Him in everyone there, and I had a deep love for them all. This had been growing in me, and I had not realized it until that day. Even the people that had annoyed me before, no longer annoyed me. I know the Holy Spirit did that work, and I also know it has come from giving my heart, from becoming a daughter in the house. So I really thank God, and encourage everyone to find out who your father is, and give your heart to him/her because it brings a real freedom in Christ.

Elaine Hans.

CHAPTER 16

LOVE AND SPIRITUAL FATHERS

"If I have the gift of prophecy and can fathom all mysteries and all knowledge, and if I have a faith that can move mountains, but have not love, I am nothing."

(1 Corinthians 13:2)

In the end, this whole matter of fathers, sons, and meaningful, accountable relationships is all about love: it *is* love, and in the context of a wonderful family.

I feel great love for my spiritual father, Chuck Clayton, but I didn't feel that love to begin with. Love was something that grew as I went along, as I got to know him, and understand him and his purpose in Christ. I knew from the beginning that it was right and good to develop a relationship with him, as the Lord had told me to do, but it took time to feel at home with it. I am glad now that I did faithfully continue in what I was convinced of, and have now come to the place where I do feel a deep love for him, and for his people too.

From time to time we come across counterfeits to the apostolic message, both in Australia and other places. These are, often, all hung up over the teaching of father-son relationships, and over issues like the authority of apostles and spiritual fathers. This is because they can only see these things as a means of control, usually because they have had some bad experience in the past. Well, a wonderful thing is this: though some might criticise this teaching, according to the Bible there is no law against love!

"But the fruit of the Spirit is love, joy, peace, patience, kindness, goodness, faithfulness, gentleness, and self-control," wrote Paul. And the very next thing he recorded was, *"Against such things there is no law."* (Galatians 5:22) No one can say that you can't love a brother. So do not be hindered by what others might say.

The fact is that every Christian leader, such as apostle Chuck, needs to be loved and supported, and it is God who calls each of us to so love our leaders. It so happens that I am one of those appointed by the Lord to love him, and to esteem him highly for his work's sake. You have also been appointed by the Lord, to love *someone*. You do not and cannot know every Christian leader in the world, so you cannot love them all; but there will be someone that is appointed for you to love.

This kind of love, including the affection and honour of which we speak, is neither idolatry nor bondage. It is something else entirely. When we love like this, it is spiritual maturity. No one is spiritually mature, even if they are powerfully gifted, without walking in this kind of love.

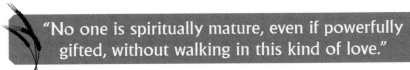

"No one is spiritually mature, even if powerfully gifted, without walking in this kind of love."

In our thinking we need to connect what Galatians 5:22 says about the fruit of the Spirit, against which there is no law, and 1 Corinthians 13, which tells us that without love, we are all noise and no substance, we are nothing, and we gain nothing. We must love, or we have nothing of eternal value and are still in bondage to the flesh.

We also have to trust. We have to build trust in relationships, or we have built nothing. If we do not have trusting relationships in the work of the ministry, we are building after the flesh and not the Spirit. Spiritual work is an inward work, and not measured in external things. The inward things, those of the heart, have to be in right order.

I have a great desire for people to feel strong love for their leaders, and for each other. I also feel a great yearning for the leaders of the body of Christ to have great love for each other, as well as for the believers. There is no other way in which we can truly be the church.

If Jesus told us to love one other, which He did, then obviously we are to love our leaders especially. There are all kinds of interesting instructions in the Scriptures about loving leaders, and when I travel to preach in churches,

I find that what I desire more than all is for the people I see before me to love their leaders.

A Father's Principal Task is to Love!

We have been talking much about a son's love, but a father's principle task is to love. There may be all kinds of things a father has to do in his work in Christ, and he may have to labour in various ways to help his sons. But his principal task is to love.

Take the father of the prodigal, for instance. The only thing he could do for a long time was to love and long for his son. And what about Jesus? In His recorded High Priestly prayer, He said that He had watched over and kept all those that the Father had given Him. (John 17:6,12) There is something about the love of a father that is designed to help 'keep safe' sons and daughters in the faith.

So by the grace of God, a father cares about his sons. The heart of a father wants to protect them, to bless, to inspire, to encourage, and so on. He wants to help his sons succeed. He wants to support them and stand behind them. A father loves to encourage sons, as Moses did Joshua, concerning whom the Lord had said to Moses, *"Encourage him, because he will lead Israel..."* (Deuteronomy 1:38, see also 3:21-22, 3:28)

The authority given to such leaders is not just a perk or easy privilege; it is not a free ride for anybody. These kinds of leaders carry a great responsibility, and will be judged more strictly. (James 3:1) Paul said that God, who had entrusted them with the gospel, tested their hearts. (1 Thessalonians 2:4)

Some years ago I was asked by a mature man, a man many years my senior who has been in the ministry for 50 years, a gifted man with sons, if I would become his spiritual father. As he asked this question, I remembered that one night in the Philippines many years before, the Lord said to me, "I am going to bring you into relationship with many great men and women of God all around the world, and you will serve them." I replied by telling him of that word I had received, and then said this: "You need a spiritual father. If that is what you would like me to do, then that is how I will serve you."

Leadership and fathering is always the great need of God's people. Leaders are sent to serve the people of God, and they serve by providing the love, fathering, and leadership that is needed.

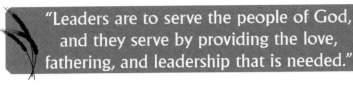

"Leaders are to serve the people of God, and they serve by providing the love, fathering, and leadership that is needed."

My little daughter, Susanna, when she was seven, gave me a birthday card she had made for me. On the front it said, "Happy Birthday," and she had drawn a picture of me wearing a crown, and there she had written: "I love you, I love you, I love you, I love you." I opened it, and on the inside she had written: "I love you, and I hope you have a good birthday. Happy birthday, I love you, and I think you are the best dad in the world."

She did not leave me in any doubt about the message. I get smothered with hugs and kisses everyday from all my kids, and there is one enduring message all through that experience of family life. I am loved, although I loved them long before they ever knew enough to really know me.

When someone in a good family expresses love like this, does anybody think they are doing the wrong thing? There is no law against this, is there?

We all know, too, that when a little child says, "I think you're the best dad in the whole world," this is a right, good, and healthy sentiment in the little one. That's what every little boy and girl is meant to think about their dad.

In the Lord's family there should be no difference. We are meant to have such a heart for our fathers too. In our hearts, as far as we are concerned, they are the greatest – and we want to offer them our best as we serve the Lord together.

You should not be reticent or ashamed to feel this kind of love, because, as the Scripture says – there is no law against love.

Testimony

A Pastor's wife:

Dear John and Hazel,

It is hard to find the exact words, but I want to say – Thank you!! for everything.

Having you both in our lives has made such a difference. Apostolic covering is a miracle and the most beautiful, enabling gift to the church. Over the years (my husband) and I have been blessed to be under some of the "best" teaching available. We have had resources and associations available to us and all of these things have added to our lives. None of this made the difference.

However, the last couple of years living under your covering and love has enabled us to really live in the stuff we knew. Having a "Dad and Mum" who love us makes such a difference. You allowing us such access to your lives has helped us do things differently, and we unashamedly imitate you with wonderful results.

I can't tell you how much has changed and how grateful I am.

Thank you, with much love,
(Name supplied, but withheld from publication).

CHAPTER 17

A FINAL WORD

"If anyone chooses to do God's will
he will find out whether my teaching comes from God,
or whether I speak on my own."

(John 7:17)

In John chapter 7, we read of Jesus being questioned about where He got His teaching and authority. *"How did this man get such learning...?"* they said. In answering the question, the Lord made some very interesting statements about Himself, and in doing so made clear a principle with respect to apostolic ministry. *"My teaching is not my own, it comes from him who sent me."* (John 7:16)

Christ is the Father's sent one, the apostle of the Father. Then Jesus said, *"If anyone chooses to do God's will he will find out whether my teaching comes from God, or whether I speak on my own."* He added, *"He who speaks on his own does so to gain honour for himself, but he who works for the honour of the one who sent him is a man of truth. There is nothing false about him."* (John 7:17-18) That is what an apostle is meant to be. As Christ was, one who works for the honour of the one who sent Him, we are all meant to be.

> **"A man of truth works for the honour of the one who sent him."**

An apostle does not represent himself, and does not speak for himself; like Christ, he has laid what was 'his own' aside. You remember that it is often said of Christ, "He laid aside his glory," a reference to the Scripture that says of the Lord, He *"made himself nothing, taking the very nature of a servant... he humbled himself, and became obedient to death."* (Phi 2:7-8)

In laying aside His glory, what does that mean? He laid aside His power, His ability to know everything, His ability to be everywhere at the same time, and He laid aside His own personal authority – in other words, all the attributes of God He laid aside. There is only one thing He did not lay aside, and that was His *identity* – He remained who He was. But everything else He gave up, so that He could come into this world solely as the representative of another.

He did not come in His own authority, but in the authority of the Father. There was no unilateral action with the son of God, no independence. He did not do His own thing, He was sent by the Father. An apostle always carries the authority of a higher authority. Whatever personal authority was His as God, He laid aside so as to be the apostle sent by the Father.

Not until He was baptised by John, at which time the Holy Spirit came upon Him bodily, did He begin to exercise authority and power.

He was then 30 years old, having grown in wisdom and knowledge. By the time He was 12 He could confound the Pharisees with wisdom and knowledge, so He had something. But He did not have power and authority until He went to the Jordan, and submitted Himself to a man who was "in Christ," as we would say – to a man who was in the ministry before He was. He went to the leader of the ministry of the day – John the Baptist – and submitted to him and his baptism. In reply to John, who did not want to baptise Him, Jesus said, *"...it is proper for us to do this to fulfill all righteousness."* (Matt 3:15)

It follows, then, that for Jesus to be able to enter upon His own ministry, and carry the authority of the Father, He had first to be a man submitted. He submitted himself to John's baptism, and as a result the power of the Spirit came upon Him.

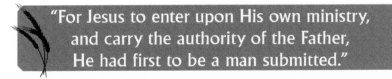

> "For Jesus to enter upon His own ministry, and carry the authority of the Father, He had first to be a man submitted."

He did not work for His own honour, but the honour of His Father. Because of that He carried the full authority of the Father, as even a Gentile centurion was able to recognise. (Matt 8:8-9)

Remember that He said, *"All authority in heaven and earth has been given to me."* (Matt 28:18) Notice the word *'given'* – the authority was not His own. This is what apostolic authority is. It is *always* a *given* authority, and always derived from being in submission to the will of another.

To be an apostolic people, we must learn to walk humbly in submission toward those who are over us and around us in the church. Our submission is not only to God, but to our leaders and our brethren as well. If we have a heart of submission, it will be an attitude that shows in all our relationships. This is why the Scriptures say, *"Submit yourselves to one another out of reverence for Christ."* (Eph 5:21)

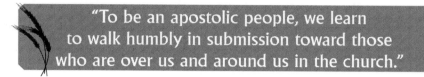

"To be an apostolic people, we learn to walk humbly in submission toward those who are over us and around us in the church."

We have no choice if we would truly learn the way of Christ. And if we do not learn this way, we might find in the end that we have believed in vain, since we may have been of another spirit, that of lawlessness, against which Christ warned us. After all, only those who do the will of God enter the Kingdom of God. (Matt 7: 21-23)

If we are to submit ourselves to one another, how much more should we submit to those who love us and lead us in Christ's name. This is a hard lesson for some to learn, because we are of such an independent spirit. We have been raised in such arrogant circumstances, and been taught, not only by the world in which we live, but often by our own family values and the religious systems in which we were raised as well, to be cynical. We were taught by the institutional atmosphere and personal attitudes around us to not trust people. This expression of cynicism, independence, and pride, is ingrained in our flesh. That is what we have to overcome.

We have to learn the way of Christ, who chose to do His Father's will in all things. So as to learn His way, if we are wise, we will not just walk away from the message of this book with an independent spirit. Independence is the very thing that must be cleaned out of all of us.

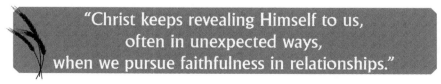

"Christ keeps revealing Himself to us, often in unexpected ways, when we pursue faithfulness in relationships."

For me, this whole journey of discovery of apostolic grace has been a constant experience of coming face-to-face with Jesus. I like to tell people this, because the emphasis on relationships and submission of heart to one another is not some tangent off from the main game – it *is* the main game. This is a pursuing of Christ, and He keeps revealing Himself to us, often in unexpected ways, when we pursue faithfulness in relationships.

In 1997 the Lord Jesus appeared to me. He instructed me to go to the nations with an apostolic message, and also to keep looking into the eyes of Jesus Christ. This book presents that message. May I say – as Christ and Paul also said – *this message is not my own.*

And according to Jesus in John 7:17, if you choose to do the will of God, you will prove the validity of the message.

Don Drayson, Pastor.
Mid-Coast Christian Fellowship,
Adelaide, Australia.

I have believed in the validity of Apostles for many years, and knew that if the Church was to ever reach maturity and oneness, Apostles and Prophets needed to be restored to their foundational position. On a personal basis, I also wanted a spiritual father to whom I could submit and be accountable, and who could speak into my life.

In 1999, my wife Heather and I began to pray seriously for God to bring us into relationship with an apostle. It was not until early 2003 that this eventuated after having read John Alley's book 'the Apostolic Revelation'. After spending time with John, we knew in our hearts that he was the spiritual father for whom we had been praying. Over many years we had had occasional mentors, but no true spiritual father.

We were greatly impacted by John's emphasis on relationship rather than power or control. To be truthful, initially we wanted this relationship because we were desperate for John's guidance, wisdom and input into our lives and church. However, during 2004 a shift occurred in my heart and God revealed to me that I, as a son to John, needed to get underneath his vision and lift it up. In doing so, I have been greatly blessed.

There is a great sense of security being in relationship with a spiritual father to whom you have given permission to speak into your life and to even bring correction where necessary. I must say it is so much easier to submit to someone who so obviously loves you as John does. John is concerned for me that I might realize my full potential in God. He has imparted grace into my life which has manifested in many ways, e.g. greater freedom and anointing in preaching, seeing more healings and financial breakthroughs, revelation and understanding of the true nature of the church. The revelation of sons receiving inheritance by being in relationship with a spiritual father is a much greater reality for me now.

Don Drayson.

PERSONAL OUTCOMES

"Remember me, O LORD, in Thy favor toward Thy people;
Visit me with Thy salvation,
That I may see the prosperity of Thy chosen ones,
That I may rejoice in the gladness of Thy nation,
That I may glory with Thine inheritance."

(Psalm 106:4-5 NASB)

Earlier in this book I related how the Lord woke me one night and explained why Elisha had to *see* Elijah in the moment he was taken from him, if he was to be able to receive a double-portion inheritance of the Spirit.

In response to this understanding of the need to pursue spiritual fathers, and in order to find the greater grace of a true double-portion as inheritance, I determined to go with my wife Hazel and visit Chuck and Karen in their home. I would like to tell you what happened as a result.

I received those insights from Christ in April 2006, and preached about it two months later at our annual Australian Apostolic Summit. By this time I had made plans to go to the USA in October, for the specific purpose of spending personal time with Chuck. I desired to pursue the relationship in a greater way, so that I might find the grace to obtain the greater inheritance. After all, that was the whole point of the 'revelation' that came in the middle of the night.

On the various occasions that I had preached this message in Australia between June and October 2006, I had made the remark to those audiences that I was not telling everybody else what they had to do. Rather, I was telling everybody what I was going to do. It would be up to my spiritual sons if they wanted to pursue me. In the meantime, I was going to pursue my spiritual father, in the hope of finding a greater grace through properly walking with him.

Thus it was that we arrived in America, and began the very pleasant and joyful task of spending time with people we dearly love. Chuck and Karen had cleared the week, especially so that we could relax and talk, shop and eat, and enjoy time together.

I began on the first day we were there to talk to Chuck about what I had learned, and told him what was on my heart. It was not new to him, as we had both for some time taught quite similar things, and in any case, he had been listening to the messages I had preached.

All week long we chatted about it, although he seemed a little bit quiet. I had been anticipating that we would get down to the business of praying for these outcomes right away, but no prayer was offered in relation to our discussion, then or during the week. Was I expecting to receive a full impartation, like Elisha did? No, my belief was that this was a process over time, and I was to walk in relationship with Chuck and continue to pursue a greater impartation over many years. But I had been expecting an initial response of making a good start to pray for the blessing.

The whole week went by, and though no impartation prayer was offered, we had wonderful fellowship. The Clayton's have a great grace for love and hospitality; they receive and care for many people. Hazel and I greatly enjoy the social interaction with them as much as anything that life holds for us.

The week was drawing to a close, and we would soon return home. I went to bed wondering what our last day would bring, and when I woke the next morning I sat alone with the Lord in quietness. I came to a realisation. I was not to place demands and obligations upon my spiritual father. I was here to serve him and be a blessing to him. It did not matter whether he had more to offer me or not, or whether he was even willing to pray for me.

I could see that I should put him under no obligation, have no expectations, but give myself completely to serving and being a blessing to him, no matter what. I prayed and released all expectation and obligation that I might have held in my attitudes toward Chuck, and chose the contentment of a son who knows he is loved, secure in a family relationship, and can trust God for outcomes in life.

At that moment, the phone rang. It was Chuck. He had been over at the office, and would I like to come over; he had some things to share with me.

We spent a delightful morning in discussion and prayer. It turned out that Chuck had been contemplating all week long just how to go about imparting a greater measure of anointing. All along he really wanted to do this, but was pondering how best to go about it.

He had lain awake all the last night, praying and thinking about it before the Lord. And the Lord had given him some really clear instruction and prophecy for me, and had also given him the specific anointings to release to me.

Chuck prayed with all his heart for me, and released to me what he believed was a great personal grace that he himself had walked in.

Upon returning home to Rockhampton, Australia, I rose early the next morning and sat with the Lord in listening and prayer. The Lord immediately directed me to Psalm 32, and spoke to me from verses 2 and 8.

"Blessed is the man whose sin the Lord does not count against him and in whose spirit is no deceit." (v.2)

"I will instruct you and teach you in the way you should go; I will counsel you and watch over you." (v.8)

The Lord said that as a result of my time with Chuck, He had given me some very specific things. He said I would have a new clarity of spirit, and that I had a new level of cleanness in His eyes. It is hard to explain what that means, but I could tell that a real grace had been released to me. The Lord also said that He had released to me a new level of His counsel, instruction, and guidance.

The results became immediately obvious, and continued over the weeks and months that followed. There seemed to be a permanent 'manifestation' of clarity of mind, spirit, purpose, self-discipline, motivation, and application to duty, of which I have been very glad. I felt a real advance in terms of the clarity of my mind, my sense of purpose, and my motivation to achieve. And all without striving.

I had been given a new level of grace! From that date to this, a closer sense of His counsel, and a more immediate sense of being guided every moment has remained with me, and it is wonderful.

That was not meant to be a one-off experience. I intend to make it my business to take the time for personal relationship development, the deepening of love and affection, and the spending of personal time with Chuck and Karen, every year if possible. And of course, it is my ongoing business every day to continue to love, honour, serve, and be generous with the spiritual father God appointed to be a blessing to me.

It is an ongoing part of the ministry of Christ to really walk with our brethren, and I expect to do this for the rest of my life in following Christ.

ADDITION TO THE POSTCRIPT –
Revised Edition, August, 2015.

On Friday, 2nd December, 2011, my spiritual father Apostle Chuck Clayton, to whom much in this book refers, passed away. I wept for him, and continued to weep over the following days, and found that other Christian leaders who loved him had been weeping too.

This is very significant. We do not usually see weeping when church people hear of leaders passing. But we do see that Jesus wept for Lazarus, and did so just prior to raising him - I never understood that. The Ephesians wept over Paul, though he was just farewelling them; Elisha cried out after Elijah, yet he went alive into heaven; Paul wept for Timothy, missing him so much in his absence. This weeping is holy, and it occurs wherever Christian leaders love each other deeply from the heart.

I always thought of Chuck Clayton as 'the great apostle,' and whenever he answered the phone I would often cheerily, if hyperbolically, quip, "How's the great apostle?" – sometimes "How's the *truly* great apostle?" But I had genuinely come to regard him highly, and I loved him.

Some years ago, I was in prayer with my wife Hazel when she heard the Lord say that Chuck Clayton was a totally unique man, a Noah to his generation. And truly, there was no-one else like him.

Long years before, just prior to meeting him, I was praying about spiritual covering when the Lord said, "I myself will provide your covering." That seemed curious, but by that He meant that He would provide an apostle for me. And sure enough, soon afterwards He brought Chuck to Australia, in 1994, and the Lord made it plain, along with various dreams and visions, that I was to join myself to him. Thus I began to visit, and found apostolic covering and what was to become a rich, ongoing relationship.

But it took me a while to really get it. Years later, in 2002, I was spending a night in the prayer room with one of my key leaders, when at 5.30am, after we had prayed at length, this brother said to me, "John, while you were praying, the photo of Chuck and Karen Clayton just stood out on the wall, and I heard the Lord saying that this man is meant to mean a great deal more to us than we understand, that he has a great deal more to give us, and that our future is closely connected to him." At the time, I could not see how any of that could have possibly been true. But five months later, Apostle Chuck was preaching about Sonship in my church when the Holy Spirit moved powerfully amongst us. Grace was released, lives were transformed, and we came into the great revelation of love and relationships I have spoken of in this book, and which was also a big part of the apostolic message we were to carry. There was from that time a deep sense of us all belonging to one another - of Chuck and Karen belonging to us, and us to them. For the first time, I felt that he really was my father.

Up until then it had all been nice, but more a theory, a doctrine of church structure – but now it became a heartfelt reality. He taught us of the Spirit of Sonship, and in that we caught the spirit of fathering too.

I liked nothing better than what might be called 'tag-team' preaching with Apostle Chuck. For me, it was always a good day in a conference when he would speak and I would follow, then he and then I again. We did this in India, Australia, Canada, and the US. They seemed to me amongst the sweetest and most wonderful of times, and always seemed to be times of great impact on people's hearts.

On the morning of the Friday he passed away, I was in my office in Australia praying with my staff. It was only Thursday evening in the US, and he was still with us, and I was not expecting him to pass away. Yet I was somehow deeply grieving for him. I took my ukulele to the office prayers, because I felt I wanted to sing with God's faithfulness and Apostle Chuck in mind. There I sang,

"The love of God, how rich and pure, how measureless and strong,
it shall forevermore endure the saints' and angels' song."

As I followed on from the song with prayer, something very revealing unfolded. The Lord opened my eyes and gave me visions and illustrations of what God had done for me by joining me in a relationship of the heart with a spiritual father. I saw clearly what being one with Chuck had meant for me in the economy of God's grace.

There were two principle illustrations in these visions. The first was of the nature of electricity, ie AC power. Alternating current operates through two wires, the red and the black. BOTH of these wires have to be connected for the current to flow. In the same way, when we are connected to TWO FATHERS – when we walk with God as our father AND walk with a spiritual leader as a fathering gift from God – a great circuit of spiritual power flowing to us is joined. Thus it was in my life; the Holy Spirit teaching, and Chuck teaching, in one accord.

The second illustration was of the double helix structure of DNA. And thus it was that with both the Holy Spirit at work in me, and God using Chuck as a father to walk with me, a more effective spiritual DNA, something more like the life of Christ, was established in me, along with better understanding.

Here is how that worked in practice. Looking back, the following dynamic became obvious:

The Holy Spirit guiding, and Chuck sharing.

One instructing, the other teaching.

One anointing, the other imparting.

One leading, the other bearing witness.

One assuring, the other confirming.

One encouraging, the other supporting.

A few days before his death, feeling he was dying but still looking for a miracle for him to be restored and live much longer, we held a Solemn Assembly of our church in Rockhampton to cry out for him. But led by the Holy Spirit, we spent much time giving thanks to the Lord for Apostle Chuck, for all he had done for us, all he taught us, all he meant to us - I have to say he was much loved by our people young and old. It was plain, it has always been plain, he was cherished. And he was clearly seen by our people as having integrity, humility, and courage. He was not afraid to stand.

One of our number was Wendy, a young mum whose own life had been saved from cancer through a Solemn Assembly of the church a few years before. She gave me this note: *"We have been guilty of taking the lives of our fathers for granted. This is not to be so. We are not to assume they will continue to be with us, but are to protect them with our prayers and consciously honour the men that God has given us."*

Brother Chuck had great grace! A huge heart, filled with a great, unique love. But if we do not love our fathers, our eyes are never opened to see what's in them. Yet the more we love them, the more we will see the grace that has been given them - and if we can see it, the way is open for us to inherit it.

Apostle Chuck pioneered the idea that relationships are the true apostolic structure of the body of Christ. In this, he was God's man, not only ahead of the game in the church worldwide, but moreso in his own culture. I remember him telling me in 1995 that he was rebuilding the ministry after making mistakes. He developed and stuck by the principle, "Relationships that build people," which we came to discover was the truly enduring principle of any church that would have an apostolic life, and the key to the very grace we are being led into by the Lord for the real maturing of the Body.

Like Noah, Chuck Clayton was building an ark that will save this generation, and every generation. Although not everyone was listening so as to enter the ark, the ark continues to be built, for, as the scripture says, God is the builder of all things.

For me, he lives yet. Not that he is here in person, but what he taught, and how he loved, and what he imparted, and that sense of being one with him, remains. Jesus prayed for us, ***"...that all of them may be one, Father, just as you are in me and I am in you. I have given them the glory that you gave me, that they may be one as we are one."*** With Chuck I came to feel that oneness as a reality, as part of the fabric of life in Christ. He was my father, and my brother, and the great love of my heart.

Over 23 years ago I turned 40, and on that day I asked the Lord for a birthday present. I told Him that I felt I did not love Christ enough, and asked if He would give to me as a gift a greater love for Christ. Soon after, the Lord sent Apostle Chuck into my life, and he became a very big part of the growth of my heart in love. I say this to reveal the nature of the great apostle's work, of which I am just one example.

God's people always need fathers, and the Lord raises them. Sons arise and take the place of their fathers, as did Joshua, Elisha, and Timothy. I did not know at that time whether I would ever find again, in this life, the kind of relationship I had with Chuck with another spiritual father, but I was certain of one thing – what I had found with Chuck, I could offer to others who were as sons to me.

I am pleased to report also, that since then, the Lord has been pleased to grant me the ongoing development of a sincere and mutually beneficial relationship with another mature spiritual father. I believe that, no matter our age or maturity or how well-established in the ministry, each of us should always love, serve, and honour a spiritual father.

Other great resources
are available free
www.peace.org.au

Listen/Download recent messages
Watch video messages

Peace Apostolic Ministries

POSTAL ADDRESS:
PO Box 10187, Frenchville QLD 4701, Australia

OFFICE ADDRESS:
8 Thozet Rd, Koongal QLD 4701, Australia

PHONE: +61 (07) 4926-9911
FAX: +61 (07) 4926-9944

EMAIL: mail@peace.org.au
WEB: peace.org.au

Manufactured by Amazon.ca
Bolton, ON